The Life and Times of

SULṬĀN

MAḤMŪD OF G͟HAZNA

The Life and Times of
SULṬĀN MAḤMŪD OF GHAZNA

BY

MUḤAMMAD NĀẒIM
M.A., PH.D. (CANTAB.)

With a Foreword

BY

THE LATE
SIR THOMAS ARNOLD

والله هو المحمود

God alone is the Glorified (*al-Maḥmūd*)
Signature of Sulṭān Maḥmūd
Mujmalu't-Tawārīkh, f. 279 b

CAMBRIDGE
AT THE UNIVERSITY PRESS
1931

CAMBRIDGE
UNIVERSITY PRESS

University Printing House, Cambridge CB2 8BS, United Kingdom

Cambridge University Press is part of the University of Cambridge.

It furthers the University's mission by disseminating knowledge in the pursuit of education, learning and research at the highest international levels of excellence.

www.cambridge.org
Information on this title: www.cambridge.org/9781107456594

© Cambridge University Press 1931

This publication is in copyright. Subject to statutory exception and to the provisions of relevant collective licensing agreements, no reproduction of any part may take place without the written permission of Cambridge University Press.

First published 1931
First paperback edition 2014

A catalogue record for this publication is available from the British Library

ISBN 978-1-107-45659-4 Paperback

Cambridge University Press has no responsibility for the persistence or accuracy of URLs for external or third-party internet websites referred to in this publication, and does not guarantee that any content on such websites is, or will remain, accurate or appropriate.

To

My Esteemed Teacher & Friend

PROFESSOR REYNOLD A. NICHOLSON

CONTENTS

PART THREE

Map   Available for download from www.cambridge.org/9781107456594

FOREWORD

AMONG the finest products of the literary activity of the Indian Muhammadans has been their historical literature. It includes such noteworthy contributions to autobiographical self-revelation as the *Futūḥāt-i-Fīrūz Shāhī*, and the *Tūzuk-i-Jahāngīrī*, the numerous contemporary chronicles by court historians, as well as the comprehensive works compiled in a more critical spirit by later writers. This literary tradition has been revived in recent years by a new school of historians—men acquainted with modern methods of research, trained to weigh evidence and arbitrate between conflicting points of view. A number of valuable contributions to historical science have been published by this younger group of Indian historians, and the present work will give to its author an honourable place among them. None of his predecessors has ventured to write the separate memoir of Sulṭān Maḥmūd of Ghazna. The difficulties that have hitherto faced the student of the reign of this great conqueror may be illustrated by the bewildering account of his expeditions into India which Sir Henry M. Elliot appended to the second volume of *The History of India as told by its own Historians*. Considerable courage was needed to undertake such a task, and the competent reader will at once recognise the excellent character of the achievement, for no such extensive survey has hitherto been attempted and the sources drawn upon have included a large number of hitherto unpublished manuscripts. As practically the whole of Sulṭān Maḥmūd's life was taken up with fighting, a recital of his various campaigns must necessarily constitute a large part of the task of his biographer, and Dr Muḥammad Nāẓim, in order to give a clear and intelligible account of these campaigns, has adopted the admirable device of putting them in their geographical setting, thus enabling the reader to follow the progress of the contending armies free from the confusion which a rigidly chronological sequence of events would have implied, while the demands of such a purely temporal order of events are satisfied by the detailed summary which he has provided in his Appendix N.

For the student of Indian history, Dr Muḥammad Nāẓim's book will not only shed light upon a hitherto obscure period in the annals of that country, but will clear up many confusions and misunderstandings, to the discussion of which his Appendices and many of his notes are devoted. To a wider circle of readers the work should prove of interest as coming from the pen of a modern enlightened Muhammadan scholar who defends the subject of his memoir from the accusation of fanaticism, so commonly connected with his name.

T. W. ARNOLD

PREFACE

In these days sober students of history busy themselves with the problems of social, economic and political evolution of nations rather than with tiresome stories of wars and battles; but there are some wars which will always command an absorbing interest because of their far-reaching consequences, and some of the wars of Sulṭān Maḥmūd of Ghazna, particularly his expeditions to India, are assuredly deserving of such interest. He was the first sovereign to give practical shape to the idea of a Muslim empire in India. The flood-gates of the north-western passes, which were opened by his victorious armies, continued for centuries to pour down streams of Muslim invaders into the plains of India, till the tide of their conquest was stemmed by the advent of the English.

Notwithstanding the numerous scattered notices of Sulṭān Maḥmūd in modern historical works, he has not so far received due attention from Oriental scholars. This book, which was originally presented as a thesis for the Degree of Ph.D. at the University of Cambridge, is intended to supply the desideratum to some extent; and though it does not profess to be exhaustive, an attempt has been made in it to sift and arrange the huge mass of material relating to the period of the Sulṭān, to give an accurate and impartial study of his life and work, to determine the exact chronology of his reign, to identify localities captured by him, to construct an outline of his system of administration, to exonerate him from the charge of fanaticism so often levelled against him, and to show that his wars in India were not the haphazard movements of a predatory warrior but were the result of a well-considered programme of conquest and annexation. I have based the account on trustworthy authorities, and have scrupulously excluded from it anything that could not be authenticated. Consequently numerous details that have been passed off as established facts have been omitted. As I believe that most of the modern historians and critics of Sulṭān Maḥmūd possessed only a superficial knowledge of his career, I have not considered it worth while to enter into lengthy discussions of their arguments, and have contented myself with drawing attention in the footnotes to some of their most obvious mistakes.

I have not dealt with the literary history of the period of the Sulṭān, partly because the subject is so vast that it requires detailed and exclusive study, and partly because much has already been done in this direction by eminent scholars like the late Professor E. G. Browne, Shamsu'l-'Ulamā Mawlavī Muḥammad Shiblī Nu'mānī, and Professor Maḥmūd Khān Shīrānī.

In the transliteration of Arabic and Persian words, I have adopted the system approved by the Oriental Congress of 1894 and recommended by the Council of the Royal Asiatic Society of London. I have followed the same system in writing place-names, but I have retained the familiar spellings of such well-known places as Delhi, Lahore, Jhelum, Muttra, Kanauj, etc. Certain inconsistencies will, however, be observed in the transliteration of Sanskrit and Hindī names but I hope they are not such as to mislead the reader. In converting Ḥijra dates, I have followed the extremely useful tables entitled *An Indian Ephemeris* by L. D. Swamikannu, Dīwān Bahādur (Government Press, Madras, 1922).

In the preparation of the Map which is intended to give roughly the extent of the empire of Sulṭān Maḥmūd, I have largely drawn upon the material collected in the *Lands of the Eastern Caliphate* by Guy Le Strange, but I have omitted the names of places which could not be identified, or for the position of which sufficient indication was not given by Oriental geographers.

I take this opportunity to acknowledge my gratitude to Professor Reynold A. Nicholson for kindly looking through the book and suggesting numerous improvements. To his profound scholarship and extensive reading I am indebted for much information that would otherwise have remained unknown to me. My sincere thanks are also due to Dr U. M. Daudpota, Principal of the Sind Madrasah, Karachi, and Mawlavī Badru'd-Dīn, Lecturer in the Muslim University, 'Alīgarh, for valuable help in elucidating abstruse Arabic passages, to the Syndics of the Cambridge University Press for undertaking the publication of the work, and to the Secretary of the Press for the courtesy with which he received and carried out my frequent suggestions and alterations.

M. NĀẒIM

10*th March*, 1930

Part One

CHAPTER I

AUTHORITIES

BEFORE proceeding to the extant authorities on the period of Sulṭān Maḥmūd of Ghazna, it is necessary to state the works that have perished. Of these, the contemporary or nearly contemporary works were, firstly, an official chronicle, most probably named *Dawlat Nāmah*;[1] secondly, the metrical *Tāju'l-Futūḥ*,[2] dealing with the exploits of Sulṭān Maḥmūd; thirdly, *Kitāb fī Ghurar-i-Akhbār-i-Mulūki'l-Furs* by 'Abdu'l-Malik b. Muḥammad b. Ismā'īl ath-Tha'ālibī, dealing with the history of the kings of Īrān, from the earliest times to the reign of Sulṭān Maḥmūd;[3] fourthly, three works composed by Abu'l-Faḍl Muḥammad b. Ḥusain al-Baihaqī,[4] namely the *Maqāmāt-i-Abū Naṣr-i-Mushkānī*[5]

1 Farrukhī, f. 23 b. No reference has hitherto been made to this work.

2 'Unṣurī, pp. 79, 85, refers to this work in glowing terms which shows that it was most probably composed by himself. It is incorrectly stated in E. and D. ii, 53, that *Tāju'l-Futūḥ* was the title of that portion of Baihaqī's *Mujalladāt* which dealt with the history of Sulṭān Maḥmūd. Cf. *infra*, p. 2.

3 This work was written in four volumes for Abu'l-Muẓaffar Naṣr, brother of Sulṭān Maḥmūd and commander of the troops of Khurāsān. Only the first two volumes dealing with the history of the Pre-Islamic period and the history of Muḥammad have come down to us, and have been edited and translated into French by H. Zotenberg (Paris, 1900).

4 For an account of his life see Ibn Funduq, ff. 101 b–103 a; and *Ency. of Islam*, i, 592. In Bākharzī, f. 104 a, his name is mentioned among the poets.

5 *Āthāru'l-Wuzarā*, f. 106 a, and Baihaqī, p. 749. His full name was Abū Naṣr b. Mushkān (?) Aḥmad b. 'Abdu'ṣ-Ṣamad. He was the head of the Correspondence Department of Sulṭān Maḥmūd. Extracts cited from this work in the *Āthāru'l-Wuzarā* show that it contained valuable information. Cf. Baihaqī, p. 461.

containing, among other things, useful details about the history and court life of the Sulṭān, the *Mujalladāt*,[1] or a history of Sulṭān Maḥmūd and his successors in thirty volumes,[2] from the year 409 to about 460[3] (1018–68), and a collection of important diplomatic correspondence of Sulṭān Mas'ūd,[4] and most probably that of Sulṭān Maḥmūd, named *Zīnatu'l-Kuttāb*.[5]

It is evident from the extracts preserved in the *Jawāmi'u'l-Ḥikāyāt* and *Āthāru'l-Wuzarā* that the *Maqāmāt* contained much useful material for the history of Sulṭān Maḥmūd, while the *Mujalladāt*, of which only the second half of the sixth volume, volumes seven, eight, nine and the part of the tenth dealing with the period of Sulṭān Mas'ūd are preserved, was a comprehensive work several parts of which were known by special names derived from the titles of the sovereigns to whom they related. Thus the history of Sulṭān Maḥmūd was named *Ta'rīkh-i-Yamīnī*,[6] that of Sulṭān Mas'ūd, *Ta'rīkh-i-Mas'ūdī*, and so on. The importance of Baihaqī's *Ta'rīkh-i-Yamīnī* appears from the fact that

1 This title was given to Baihaqī's history in later times on account of its voluminousness. It has been named *Ta'rīkh-i-Nāṣirī*, *Jāmi' fi't-Tawārīkh banū Subuktigīn*, and *Jāmi'u't-Tawārīkh*, by Ibn Funduq, f. 101 b, and Ḥājjī Khalīfa, ii, 508, 580. These titles have misled some writers like Major Raverty (*Ṭab. Nāṣ.* p. 105), and Elliot and Dowson (ii, 53), to attribute to Baihaqī a history of the predecessors of Subuktigīn as well.

2 Ibn Funduq, ff. 12 b, 101 b; and *Rawḍah*, p. 7. Raverty, *Ṭab. Nāṣ.* p. 105, note, however, limits their number to twelve without specifying his authority.

3 Baihaqī, pp. 233, 317. Ibn Funduq, f. 12 b, says that it was a history of Sulṭān Maḥmūd and his descendants but he contradicts himself on f. 101 b by saying that it included the history of Subuktigīn as well.

4 Baihaqī, p. 528.

5 Ibn Funduq, f. 101 b. Probably Baihaqī refers to this work on p. 528.

6 Baihaqī, pp. 10, 26, 66, 158. This work has sometimes been confused with 'Utbī's *Kitābu'l-Yamīnī*.

it was based on original state documents[1] and a diary which the author used to keep.[2]

Fifthly, the universal history of Maḥmūd-i-Warrāq ending with the year 409[3] (1018); sixthly, the *Dhail Tajāribu'l-Umam* by Hilāl b. Muḥassin b. Ibrāhīm aṣ-Ṣābī which contained *in extenso* the letters of victory despatched by Sulṭān Maḥmūd to al-Qādir Bi'llāh, the 'Abbāsid Caliph;[4] and finally, the *Farīdu't-Tawārīkh*, dealing with the history of Khurāsān, by Abu'l-Ḥasan Muḥammad b. Sulaimān.[5]

Besides these contemporary works, at least five later works have also been lost. Firstly, *Ta'rīkh-i-Mujadwal* by Imām Muḥammad b. 'Alī Abu'l-Qāsim 'Imādī;[6] secondly, the *Mashāribu't-Tajārib* in four volumes by Abu'l-Ḥasan 'Alī b. Zaid b. Amīrak Muḥammad b. Ḥusain b. Funduq, known as Ibn Funduq;[7] thirdly, a history by Abu'l-Ḥasan al-Haitham b. Muḥammad-i-Nājī;[8] fourthly, a history of Khurāsān by Abū Muḥammad Hārūn b. 'Abbās al-Ma'mūnī who traced his genealogy from the Caliph al-Ma'mūn;[9]

1 Baihaqī, pp. 120, 354, 528.

2 *Ibid.* pp. 177, 268, 693.

3 *Ibid.* p. 317.

4 Only a small fragment of this chronicle, embracing three years (A.H. 390–2) has been preserved, and published by Professor D. S. Margoliouth as a part of the third volume of the *Tajāribu'l-Umam* of Abū 'Alī Aḥmad b. Muḥammad Miskawaih and its Continuation by Abū Shujā' ar-Rūdhrāwarī.

5 Ibn Funduq, ff. 12 a, 53 a, 76 b, 77 a; and Yāqūt, *Irshād*, ii, 60.

6 *Ṭab. Nāṣ.* p. 69. It is probably the same work to which reference is made in *Mujmal*, f. 263 b, as *Ta'rīkh-i-Amīr 'Imādī Maḥmūd b. al-Imām as-Sinjarī al-Ghaznawī*. See also Barthold, p. 24.

7 Ibn Funduq, ff. 12 a, 40 a; Ibnu'l-Athīr, ix, 249; and *Guzīda*, p. 8. Ibn Funduq (f. 12 a) himself speaks of this work being a continuation of 'Utbī's *Kitābu'l-Yamīnī*; but Juwainī, *Ta'rīkh-i-Jahān-Gushā*, p. 1, says that it was a continuation of *Dhail Tajāribu'l-Umam* of Hilāl aṣ-Ṣābī. See also Yāqūt, *Irshād*, v, 212.

8 *Ṭab. Nāṣ.* pp. 11, 19, 26, 31, 56, 60, 116, 317, 320. It was written before the seventh century A.H.

9 Ibn Khallikān, ii, 334. Al-Ma'mūnī died in 573 (1177–8).

and fifthly, *Ta'rīkh Maḥmūd bin Subuktigīn wa Banīhi* by Jamālu'd-Dīn Abu'l-Ḥasan 'Alī b. Yūsuf al-Qifṭī.[1]

The extant authorities may be divided into four classes:[2] (1) contemporary, (2) early non-contemporary, that is those composed roughly from the middle of the fifth century to the middle of the ninth century A.H., (3) later works, and (4) archaeological records.

I. CONTEMPORARY AUTHORITIES

The first among the contemporary authorities is the *Kitābu'l-Yamīnī* of Abū Naṣr Muḥammad b. Muḥammad al-Jabbār al-'Utbī.[3] It covers the full period of Subuktigīn and of Sulṭān Maḥmūd up to 411 (1020).[4] The style of *Kitābu'l-Yamīnī* is very ornate and verbose, and the author has concentrated on beauty of diction rather than historical precision. His descriptions are singularly lacking in detail. In his account of the expeditions beyond the river Indus, 'Utbī usually makes the Sulṭān penetrate "the interior of Hind", defeat the "infidels", and "return laden with plunder".[5] He rarely mentions the route followed by the Sulṭān, and does not give any indication of the locality of the forts that he cap-

1 Yāqūt, *Irshād*, v, 484. Barthold, p. 27, mentions another work named *Lama'u't-Tawārīkh* by Abu'l-Futūḥ Barakāt b. Mubārak b. Ismā'īl. The author was born at Ghazna after 460 (1067–8), and his chronicle was brought down to 500 (1106–7).

2 It is necessary to point out here that since there is no work dealing exclusively with Sulṭān Maḥmūd, the criticism of the different authorities given in the following chapter is not general but specific, that is, it is applicable only to those portions of the works which deal with Sulṭān Maḥmūd.

3 For an account of 'Utbī's life, see my article "al-'Utbī" in *Ency. of Islam* (in preparation).

4 And not 422 (1031) as stated by Reynolds, p. 474.

5 For example, the expedition to Nārāyan as translated in E. and D. ii, 36.

tured. The expeditions to Central Asia and Sīstān are also treated in the same superficial manner as those against India; while other matters of interest to a modern historian, viz. the early life of the Sulṭān, his system of administration, his method of warfare, and the condition of "the dumb million" under him, receive scarcely a mention. *Kitābu'l-Yamīnī* is deficient in dates, and even as a record of the military exploits of Sulṭān Maḥmūd it is neither comprehensive nor exhaustive. Nevertheless, being the only history of Sulṭān Maḥmūd written during his lifetime, its value as an authority cannot be overrated.[1]

The second in point of importance is the *Zainu'l-Akhbār* of Abū Sa'īd 'Abdu'l-Ḥayy b. aḍ-Ḍaḥḥāk b. Maḥmūd al-Gardīzī. It deals with the history of Īrān from the earliest times to the middle of the fifth century A.H.[2] It was named after the reigning sovereign Sulṭān Zainu'l-Millah Abū Manṣūr 'Abdu'r-Rashīd, son of Sulṭān Maḥmūd (441–4/1049–52). In his introduction to the account of the Ghaznawids, the author proposes to narrate briefly only the most conspicuous events of the reign of Sulṭān Maḥmūd, and offers very little criticism or reflection on them, not even enough to break

1 There are several Persian translations of *Kitābu'l-Yamīnī*. The best known of them is the one by Abu'sh-Sharaf Nāṣir al-Jurbādhqānī which was completed about 603 (1206). It was printed in Ṭeherān in 1272 (1855). It is a free translation and some portions of the text have been altogether omitted. A literal Persian translation of *Kitābu'l-Yamīnī*, entitled *Ta'rīkh-i-Amīnī*, was made in the beginning of the nineteenth century A.D. by Karāmat 'Alī. A copy of it is preserved in the British Museum (Or. 1888). The translation of Jurbādhqānī into English by the Rev. J. Reynolds is hopelessly incorrect.

The most valuable of the several commentaries on *Kitābu'l-Yamīnī* is the *Fatḥu'l-Wahbī*, written about 1150 (1737) by Aḥmad b. 'Alī b. 'Umar aṭ-Ṭarābulusī al-Manīnī. Cf. also E. and D. ii, 14–18; Barthold, pp. 19–20; and Browne, ii, 471.

2 The manuscript however breaks off abruptly in the beginning of the account of the reign of Sulṭān Mawdūd, son of Sulṭān Mas'ūd (432–41/1041–9).

the monotony of the narrative. He has consequently omitted some expeditions and described others in such a sketchy manner as to excite rather than satisfy the curiosity of the reader. Although a brief and colourless chronicle of dry facts, the *Zainu'l-Akhbār* is a work of considerable importance, as it is the only extant contemporary history which covers the full period of the reign of Sulṭān Maḥmūd, and, unlike *Kitābu'l-Yamīnī*, it is precise in assigning dates to the events recorded.[1]

About the time of the death of Sulṭān Maḥmūd, Abū Raiḥān Muḥammad b. Aḥmad al-Bīrūnī finished his famous work on India,[2] dealing with the religion, philosophy, literature, geography, astronomy and customs of the Hindūs in the fifth century A.H. Though not a historical work, it contains some valuable references to the Hindūshāhiyya Dynasty of Waihand and the origin of the idol of Somnāth.

Another work of importance is the *Ta'rīkh-i-Mas'ūdī* by Abu'l-Faḍl Muḥammad b. Ḥusain al-Baihaqī which deals primarily with the reign of Sulṭān Mas'ūd, but contains numerous digressions on the history of Sulṭān Maḥmūd and his predecessors, and gives a close insight into the working of the different departments of the Ghaznawid state. Baihaqī gives a vivid description

1 Only two manuscripts of this work are known to exist, one in King's College Library, Cambridge (MS No. 213), and the other, in the Bodleian Library, Oxford (Ouseley, No. 240). The text is confused at many places, but as the Bodleian manuscript is a copy of the King's College manuscript, it is difficult to remove the confusion by collation. For a detailed account of the contents, see Ethé and Sachau's *Cat. of Pers. MSS in Bodl. Library*, coll. 10–12. A portion of it from f. 81 b to f. 141 a, King's College MS, dealing with the history of Khurāsān from the Ṭāhirids to the beginning of the reign of Sulṭān Mawdūd, son of Sulṭān Mas'ūd the Ghaznawid, has been edited by me for the Managers of the Browne Memorial Fund, Cambridge, as the first volume of the Browne Memorial Series. See also Barthold, p. 21.

2 The title of this work is *Taḥqīq mā li'l-Hind...*, and not *Tārīkhu'l-Hind* or *Tārīkh-i-Hind*, as incorrectly given in Brockelmann, i, 475; Huart, p. 302; *Ency. of Islam*, i, 726; and E. and D. p. 1.

of the court life, the intrigues of officials and rivalry of persons who sought to influence the sovereign one way or the other. Appended to *Ta'rīkh-i-Mas'ūdī* is a portion of the lost history of Khwārizm by al-Bīrūnī which, besides containing interesting details about the conquest of that country, makes numerous allusions to the political relations of Sulṭān Maḥmūd with the rulers of Central Asia.[1]

The last, though not the least in importance, are the *Dīwāns* of the poets 'Unṣurī and Farrukhī. Their *qaṣīdas* in praise of Sulṭān Maḥmūd contain many historical facts which are useful in correcting and supplementing the accounts of the contemporary historians. These poets usually accompanied the Sulṭān on his expeditions[2], and their descriptions of some of the journeys help to fix the routes which he followed.

2. EARLY NON-CONTEMPORARY WRITERS

These are all the contemporary works which give an account of the reign of Sulṭān Maḥmūd. Among non-contemporary works, the earliest is the *Siyāsat Nāmah*, composed in 484 (1091–2) by Abū 'Alī Ḥasan b. 'Alī, commonly known as Niẓāmu'l-Mulk, wazīr of the Seljuk[3] Sulṭān Malik Shāh. It contains numerous anecdotes about Sulṭān Maḥmūd and his predecessors but from an historical point of view, they are not trustworthy and defeat the expectations aroused by the high reputation of the author. The *Siyāsat Nāmah*, however, is a mine of information regarding the Ghaznawid system of administration.[4]

1 See also Barthold, pp. 22–4.
2 Farrukhī, ff. 8 b, 48 a.
3 For the correct form of this word, see Barthold, p. 257, note 1.
4 Cf. also Barthold, p. 25.

The *Mujmalu't-Tawārīkh*, of unknown authorship, was written about 530 (1135) in the time of the Seljuk Sulṭān Sinjar, son of Sulṭān Malik Shāh. It dismisses Sulṭān Maḥmūd with a brief and unsuggestive paragraph, but, in the chapters on the Sāmānids and the Buwaihids, it contains some useful references to him.

The *Rājataranginī*, a metrical chronicle of the kings of Kashmīr, was composed by Kalhana about 545 (1150). It is the only Sanskrit work that contains even a brief reference to Sulṭān Maḥmūd in the account of a battle between *Hammīra*,[1] as the Sulṭān is called, and Rājā Trilochanpāl of the Hindūshāhiyya Dynasty.

The *Chahār Maqāla* of Abu'l-Ḥasan Niẓāmu'd-Dīn Aḥmad b. 'Umar b. 'Alī an-Niẓāmī al-'Arūḍī as-Samarqandī was written about 552 (1157). It is the earliest extant work to give in the form of a story the relations of Sulṭān Maḥmūd with Firdawsī and al-Bīrūnī and the ungenerous treatment which they are supposed to have received at his hands.

Al-Muntaẓam fī Tawārīkhi'l-Mulūk wa'l-Umam is a universal history composed about the end of the sixth century A.H. by Abu'l-Faraj 'Abdu'r-Raḥmān b. 'Alī Ibnu'l-Jawzī al-Bakrī. It contains numerous quotations from some earlier work, probably aṣ-Ṣābī's *Dhail*, and large extracts from the Sulṭān's letters of victory to the Caliph.

Akhbāru'd-Duwali'l-Munqaṭi'a, which is a general history arranged according to dynasties, was composed about the beginning of the seventh century A.H. by Jamālu'd-Dīn Abu'l-Ḥasan 'Alī b. Abi'l-Manṣūr Ẓāfir b. al-Ḥusain b. Ghāzī al-Ḥalabī al-Azdī. The Ghaznawids are not treated in a separate chapter but are mentioned under the account of the 'Abbāsids. The author gives a valuable quotation from the Sulṭān's letter of victory to the Caliph concerning the expedition to Somnāth.

1 See *infra*, p. 92, note 4.

About the year 625 (1228) three important works were composed, namely, the *Jawāmi'u'l-Ḥikāyāt* and *Lubābu'l-Albāb* by Nūru'd-Dīn Muḥammad 'Awfī, and *Ādābu'l-Mulūk wa Kifāyatu'l-Mamlūk* by Muḥammad b. Manṣūr b. Sa'īd b. Abu'l-Faraj al-Quraishī, known as Fakhr-i-Mudīr, one of whose ancestors was connected by marriage with the Ghaznawid house. The *Jawāmi'u'l-Ḥikāyāt* is a collection of anecdotes some of which relating to Sulṭān Maḥmūd are taken from the works of Baihaqī, but they furnish very little information, because, the main object of the author being usually ethical rather than historical, he has occasionally distorted facts in order to illustrate some vice or virtue.

The *Lubābu'l-Albāb* is a poetical anthology with brief biographical sketches of poets prefixed to selections from their works. It gives an idea of the large number of poets who thronged the court of Sulṭān Maḥmūd.

The *Ādābu'l-Mulūk wa Kifāyatu'l-Mamlūk* is a treatise on the art of war and bravery and contains numerous historical anecdotes relating to Sulṭān Maḥmūd which, from their language and style, appear to have been taken from Baihaqī's *Mujalladāt* or some other work of that period.

Al-Kāmil fi't-Ta'rīkh of Abu'l-Ḥasan 'Alī b. 'Abdu'l-Karam Muḥammad b. Muḥammad b. 'Abdu'l-Karīm b. 'Abdu'l-Wahhāb ash-Shaibānī, known as Ibnu'l-Athīr, is a voluminous chronicle of events up to the year 628 (1230). It has been deservedly called by Ibn Khallikān "one of the best productions of its kind".[1] Ibnu'l-Athīr does not mention his sources, but he seems to have drawn upon aṣ-Ṣābī's *Dhail*, 'Utbī's *Kitābu'l-Yamīnī* and Ibn Funduq's *Mashāribu't-Tajārib*. With the exception of a few confused and inaccurate statements, Ibnu'l-Athīr's account of Sulṭān Maḥmūd is generally very authentic and trustworthy.

Mir'ātu'z-Zamān fī Tawārīkhi'l-A'yān is a universal

1 Ibn Khallikān, ii, 289.

history composed about the middle of the seventh century A.H. by Abu'l-Muẓaffar Yūsuf b. Qizughlī, known as Sibṭ Ibnu'l-Jawzī (that is, daughter's son of Ibnu'l-Jawzī, author of *al-Muntaẓam*). In this work large quotations are given, on the authority of aṣ-Ṣābī's *Dhail*, from the Sulṭān's letters of victory to the Caliph.

Ṭabaqāt-i-Nāṣirī was written by Abū 'Umar Minhāju'd-Dīn 'Uthmān b. Sirāju'd-Dīn Jūzjānī, about the year 658 (1260). The author's account of the reign of Sulṭān Maḥmūd is very brief and uninstructive, but in other parts of his work he has given quotations from earlier authorities bearing upon the history of the Ghaznawids and the relations of Sulṭān Maḥmūd with the Ghūrids, the Seljukids and the Khāns of Turkistān.

In 710 (1310–11) Rashīdu'd-Dīn Faḍlu'llāh b. 'Imādu'd-Dawlah Abu'l-Khair b. Muwaffaqu'd-Dawlah 'Alī completed his general history, named *Jāmi'u't-Tawārīkh*. It is a voluminous work but as an authority on the reign of Sulṭān Maḥmūd it is absolutely of no value. The brief chronological summary of universal history in it is an epitome of Ibnu'l-Athīr, and the account of Sulṭān Maḥmūd is an unacknowledged verbatim copy of Jurbādhqānī's translation of 'Utbī's *Kitābu'l-Yamīnī*. It is a glaring instance of plagiarism in Oriental literature.[1]

About the year 730 (1329–30), Ḥamdu'llāh b. Abū Bakr b. Aḥmad b. Naṣr al-Mustawfī composed two works on history, namely, *Ta'rīkh-i-Guzīda* and the metrical *Ẓafar Nāmah* which was intended to be a continuation of Firdawsī's *Shāhnāmah*. *Ta'rīkh-i-Guzīda* does not furnish any valuable material for the history of Sulṭān Maḥmūd though the author mentions among his sources the *Maqāmāt-i-Abū Naṣr-i-Mushkānī* and *Mujalladāt* of Baihaqī, and *Mashāribu't-Tajārib* of Ibn Funduq. The last ten years of the reign of the Sulṭān receive very scanty notice, while the events of the

1 See Appendix A (1).

earlier period are given too briefly to be useful.[1] The *Ẓafar Nāmah* deals with the history of the Muslim rulers down to the time of the author but it adds nothing of value to the account in *Ta'rīkh-i-Guzīda*.

A universal history under the title of *Majma'u'l-Ansāb*[2] was composed by Muḥammad b. 'Alī b. 'Alī b. ash-Shaikh Muḥammad b. Ḥusain b. Abū Bakr in 733 (1332–3) in the reign of Sulṭān Abū Sa'īd, a great-grandson of Hulāgū Khān. *Majma'u'l-Ansāb* is the only known history that gives a connected story of the predecessors of Sulṭān Maḥmūd and contains the full text of the *Pand-Nāmah* or the Counsel of Subuktigīn to his son Maḥmūd. The reign of the Sulṭān is dealt with at some length but the manuscript being defective and confused at many places, it is not possible to utilise it to any great extent. The style and language of its account of the Ghaznawids show that it was taken from Baihaqī or some other writer of the same period.

About the year 800 (1397–8), 'Abdu'r-Raḥmān b. Muḥammad b. Khaldūn, commonly known as Ibn Khaldūn, wrote his universal history named *Kitābu'l-'Ibar*. Ibn Khaldūn has based his account of Sulṭān Maḥmūd on Ibnu'l-Athīr whose scattered notices he has collected into a continuous narrative without any valuable additions or alterations.

Āthāru'l-Wuzarā, which contains biographical sketches of the important wazīrs of the Muslim sovereigns, was written about the middle of the ninth century A.H. by Saifu'd-Dīn Ḥājjī b. Niẓām al-Faḍlī. In his account of the lives of the wazīrs of Sulṭān Maḥmūd, the

1 It is stated in E. and D. iii, 60, that *Ta'rīkh-i-Guzīda* is "the best general history of the East", that "implicit confidence is to be placed in it", and that "it contains much matter not found elsewhere", but as regards the period of Sulṭān Maḥmūd it does not deserve such fulsome praise.

2 The account of the Ghaznawids is omitted from all manuscripts of this work except the one in the Bibliothèque Nationale, Paris (Supplément persan, 1278).

author has given long quotations from the lost *Maqāmāt-i-Abū Naṣr-i-Mushkānī*[1] which furnish useful information for the history of the Sulṭān, his method of transacting state business and his relations with his wazīrs and other ministers.

Mujmal-i-Faṣīḥī, which is a chronological compendium of prominent events, was composed about the middle of the ninth century A.H. by Faṣīḥu'd-Dīn Aḥmad b. Muḥammad, known as Faṣīḥī al-Khwāfī. Like *Āthāru'l-Wuzarā* this work gives some quotations from the lost *Maqāmāt-i-Abū Naṣr-i-Mushkānī*, but otherwise it is not reliable. Its dates are usually wrong and it does not deserve the unbounded confidence which Major Raverty bestows upon it.[2]

3. LATER WORKS

Passing on to later works, the earliest in point of time is the universal history named *Rawḍatu'ṣ-Ṣafā* which was composed about the year 900 (1494–5) by Muḥammad b. Khwānd Shāh b. Maḥmūd, surnamed Mīr-Khwānd. The author has enumerated the *Mujalladāt* of Baihaqī among his authorities, but he does not give any information particularly derived from it. He has appropriated without acknowledgment a large portion of Jurbādhqānī's translation of *Kitābu'l-Yamīnī*[3] and, for the later period of the Sulṭān's reign, has made a verbatim translation of Ibnu'l-Athīr.

A few years after Mīr-Khwānd, his nephew Ghiyāthu'd-Dīn b. Humāmu'd-Dīn surnamed Khwānd-Amīr wrote two works on history, named *Khulāṣatu't-*

1 Apart from internal evidence, it is probable that these extracts were taken from Baihaqī's lost works, because those passages that have been quoted from Baihaqī's *Ta'rīkh-i-Mas'ūdī* are almost a verbatim copy of the original. Cf. Baihaqī, p. 171, and *Āthāru'l-Wuzarā*, f. 106 a.

2 *Tab. Nāṣ.* p. 40, note, and p. 46, note 4.

3 See Appendix A (2).

Tawārīkh and *Ḥabību's-Siyar* but both are based on *Rawḍatu's-Ṣafā*.

In 993 (1585) Mullā Aḥmad Thatawī and Āṣaf Khān composed *Ta'rīkh-i-Alfī*, which is a chronological compendium covering a period of 1000 years. The authors have achieved cheap originality by reckoning, not from the Hijra, but from the death of the Prophet.[1] This work is mainly a compilation from Ibnu'l-Athīr and *Rawḍatu's-Ṣafā*, the very words of which have sometimes been copied with a few verbal alterations.[2]

Ṭabaqāt-i-Akbarī was composed about the beginning of the eleventh century A.H. by Niẓāmu'd-Dīn Aḥmad b. Muḥammad Muqīm al-Harawī. The account of Sulṭān Maḥmūd as given in this work is an unacknowledged epitome of Gardīzī's *Zainu'l-Akhbār*.

Gulshan-i-Ibrāhīmī, commonly known as *Ta'rīkh-i-Firishta*, was written in 1015 (1606) by Muḥammad Qāsim Hindū Shāh surnamed Firishta. This work gives a detailed account of the expeditions of Sulṭān Maḥmūd. Firishta has enumerated *Zainu'l-Akhbār* of Gardīzī among his authorities, and has made references to Baihaqī's *Mujalladāt, Ta'rīkh-i-Yamīnī* and *Maqāmāt*. But it is difficult to ascertain how many, if any, of these authorities Firishta actually consulted because, with the exception of one quotation from Baihaqī's *Ta'rīkh-i-Yamīnī*, he does not give any material exclusively derived from these works. He has, however, utilised *Zainu'l-Akhbār* extensively; for, besides a direct quotation regarding Sulṭān Maḥmūd, his chapter on Sulṭān Mas'ūd is a copy of Gardīzī's account of that sovereign, with a few insignificant alterations.

Among other works which deserve only a passing

1 In E. and D. v. 156, great tribute is paid to the compilers of *Ta'rīkh-i-Alfī* for having consulted all the known historical works in Arabic or Persian, but evidently they had not utilised the *Zainu'l-Akhbār* of Gardīzī.

2 See Appendix A (3).

notice, the most celebrated is the *Mir'āt-i-Mas'ūdī*, dealing with the life of the Sālār Mas'ūd-i-Ghāzī who is said to have been a nephew of Sulṭān Maḥmūd. *Mir'āt-i-Mas'ūdī* was composed about 1020 (1611) by 'Abdu'r-Raḥmān Chishtī. It is a history mixed with a liberal supply of pious fiction. The author claims to have based his work on a history by Mullā Muḥammad-i-Ghaznawī who is alleged to have been attached to the court of Sulṭān Maḥmūd, but this so-called contemporary history is not mentioned by any previous writer.

Another work which has gained much celebrity[1] is Sujān Rāy's *Khulāṣatu't-Tawārīkh* which was composed in 1086 (1675). The author mentions *Ta'rīkh-i-Mawlānā 'Unṣurī* among his authorities but 'Unṣurī appears to be an obvious error for 'Utbī because firstly, the poet 'Unṣurī is not credited with the authorship of a work of this name, and secondly, Sujān Rāy does not furnish any new material for the history of Sulṭān Maḥmūd from this unique work. His account of the Sulṭān is an ornate abridgment of *Rawḍatu'ṣ-Ṣafā* and *Ta'rīkh-i-Firishta*.

There are several other more or less important works which deal with the times of Sulṭān Maḥmūd but they do not furnish any valuable historical material. A chronological list of some of them is given below:

(1) *Jāmi'u'l-'Ulūm* by Fakhru'd-Dīn Muḥammad b. 'Umar ar-Rāzī, composed about the beginning of the seventh century A.H.

(2) *Mukhtaṣaru'd-Duwal* by Gregory Abu'l-Faraj b. Hārūn, alias Bar Hebraeus, composed about 658 (1260).

(3) *Mir'ātu'l-Jinān* by Abū Muḥammad 'Abdu'llāh b. As'ad b. 'Alī al-Yāfi'ī, composed about the middle of the 8th century A.H.

(4) *Al-Bidāya wa'n-Nihāya* by Ismā'īl b. 'Umar 'Imādu'd-Dīn Abu'l-Fidā, Ibn Kathīr, composed about the middle of the eighth century A.H.

1 See E. and D. viii, 8.

(5) *'Uyūnu't-Tawārīkh* by Muḥammad b. Shākir b. Aḥmad al-Kutubī ash-Shāfi'ī, composed about the middle of the eighth century A.H.

(6) *Ta'rīkh-i-Ja'farī* by Ja'far b. Muḥammad al-Ḥusain, composed about 820 (1417).

(7) *Sīratu'l-Khulafā wa's-Salāṭīn* by Ibrāhīm b. Muḥammad b. Duqmāq, composed about 840 (1436–7).

(8) *Ta'rīkh-i-Muḥammadī* by Muḥammad Bihāmad Khānī, composed in 842 (1438–9).

(9) *Ta'rīkh-i-Khairāt* of unknown authorship, composed about 850 (1446).

(10) *Rawḍatu'l-Jannāt fī Awṣāfi'l-Harāt* by Mu'īnu'z-Zamajī al-Asfizārī, composed in 897 (1492).

(11) *Ta'rīkh-i-Ṣadr-i-Jahān* by Faḍlu'llāh b. Zainu'l-'Ābidīn, composed about 907 (1501–2).

(12) *Dastūru'l-Wuzarā* by Khwānd-Amīr, composed about 925 (1519).

(13) *Ta'rīkh-ī-Abu'l-Khair Khānī* by Mas'ūdī b. 'Uthmān Kūhistānī, composed in 960 (1553).

(14) *Akhbāru'd-Duwal wa Āthāru'l-Uwal* by Aḥmad b. Yūsuf al-Qaramānī, composed about 1007 (1598–9).

(15) *Muntakhabu't-Tawārīkh* by Ḥasan b. Muḥammad-i-Khākī, composed in 1019 (1610).

(16) *Taqwīmu't-Tawārīkh* by Ḥājjī Khalīfa, composed in 1075 (1664–5).

(17) *Tuḥfatu'l-Kirām* by Mīr 'Alī Shēr Qānī, composed in 1183 (1769–70).

These are almost all the important works which deal with the reign of Sulṭān Maḥmūd. It is to be regretted that no Hindū sources are available to correct or supplement the statements of the Muslim writers. The Hindūs did not possess any historical sense and their so-called histories are nothing more than collections of legends. The Solankhī Rājās who ruled Kāthiāwār at the time of the invasion of Sulṭān Maḥmūd were fortunate in having some Jain monks as their chroniclers, but they have drawn a veil over the doings of this furious invader although he subverted some of their powerful dynasties and mingled with the dust many of their ancient gods. Thus it is exclusively on Muslim authorities that the present work has been based.

4. ARCHAEOLOGICAL RECORDS

The archaeological evidence on this period is very scanty and of little value, probably because Afg͟hānistān, the cradle of the empire of Sulṭān Maḥmūd, has not yet been opened up to antiquarian research. Moreover, about a hundred years after the death of the Sulṭān, G͟hazna was completely destroyed by Sulṭān 'Alā'u'd-Dīn of G͟hūr, "the World-Incendiary", and nothing is said to have escaped his fury except the tombs of Sulṭān Maḥmūd and Sulṭān Mas'ūd and two minarets which mark the site of the ancient town of G͟hazna. The gates of the tomb of Sulṭān Maḥmūd which, under a grave misapprehension, were taken to India by the orders of Lord Ellenborough, are now lodged in the fort at Agra. The inscriptions on these monuments were published in the *Journal of the Asiatic Society of Bengal*, xii, 76–7, and more recently in *Syria*, vi, 61–90. The inscriptions, which are in Cufic characters, have been so damaged by atmospheric influences that they cannot be properly deciphered, but apparently they contained nothing of value except the titles of the Sulṭān. The inscription on the marble sarcophagus is still intact and records the titles of the Sulṭān and the date of his death.

More enduring than the architectural remains of his time are his coins. The inscriptions on them corroborate or correct the statements of the historians as to the dates at which different titles were conferred on him. This subject has been thoroughly investigated by E. Thomas in his paper on "The Coins of the Kings of Ghazni".[1]

Unfortunately even the assiduity of the archaeologist

1 *JRAS*. xvii, 138–90.

has not been able to determine with any approach to exactness the names of the various contemporary Hindū rājās. All that has so far been accomplished, and that is not much, has been summarised by Sir V. A. Smith in his *Early History of India*. The inscriptions bearing on the period of Sulṭān Maḥmūd, which have so far been discovered, have been published in the *Journal of the Asiatic Society of Bengal*, *The Epigraphia Indica* and the *Indian Antiquary*, but taken together their historical value is almost negligible.

CHAPTER II

THE MUSLIM WORLD IN THE FOURTH CENTURY A.H.

ISLAM came as a blessing to Arabia. Its unifying forces welded together the heterogeneous clans of the desert into a nation of world-conquerors; and, within a century of the death of the Prophet Muḥammad, the surging tide of Muslim conquest had swept over the East and the West. The banks of the Jaxartes and the shores of the Atlantic alike resounded with the call of *Allāh Akbar*, God is Great.

But the disruptive tendencies which have led to the downfall of so many Oriental dynasties were at work even in the early stages of the Islamic state. After the death of 'Alī in 40 (660–1), a successful *coup d'état* placed the supreme power in the hands of Mu'āwiyah; while the Shī'ites, the legitimists of Islam, claimed the Caliphate for the descendants of the Prophet from his daughter Fāṭima, the wife of 'Alī. This was the beginning of the schism which still divides the world of Islam and has been responsible for the shedding of pools of innocent blood.

The cause of the Shī'ites was espoused by the Persians. The ancient monarchy of Persia had fallen before the Muslim arms at the battle of Nihāwand. It was a political as well as a religious triumph, and the Persians as a nation embraced the religion of their conquerors. But instead of conciliating them and assuaging their injured feelings by giving them a position of equality in the universal brotherhood of Islam, the Umayyads treated them with contempt and allowed them very little share in the administration of their country. The government became a monopoly of the Arabs whose narrow tribal sympathies, coupled with their irritating pride of race and nationality, brought home to the humbled nation the full significance of its fall. The vanquished were for a time stunned with the magnitude of the catastrophe but when the stupefying effects of the first blow had passed they made frantic efforts to shake off the foreign yoke, and, in their search for a rallying point, they were attracted towards the descendants of ʻAlī, presumably by reverence for their noble descent, personal valour and heroic indifference to changing fortunes of war.

The ʻAbbāsids, the descendants of ʻAbbās, an uncle of the Prophet, also made common cause with the Shīʻites by pretending devotion to the "Family of the Prophet", and these three forces began to act concertedly for the downfall of their common enemy, the Umayyads. It was accomplished by the adroit machinations of Ibrāhīm, the ʻAbbāsid, and the valour of Khurāsān. Nihāwand was avenged on the Zāb. The "House of Hāshim" triumphed; but power passed into the hands of the ʻAbbāsids, and the unfortunate descendants of ʻAlī found in their former allies enemies even more relentless than the Umayyads. It was however a Persian triumph, and Arab rule was replaced by a truly Muslim government in which the claims of the subject race to an equal share in the commonwealth were thoroughly vindicated.

But the empire thus established began in its turn to show symptoms of decay and disintegration. The single-hearted devotion of the earlier Muslims to the cause of Islam had been replaced by a narrow spirit of self-aggrandisement and lust of power, so that after a short spell of unprecedented vigour and magnificence, rapid decay set in. Spain, North Africa, Egypt, and Syria fell off from the empire; while in Persia independent principalities cropped up in all directions, presaging a harvest of trouble for the already distracted Caliph. Power passed into the hands of the Turkish praetorians who tendered only a qualified obedience to the "Commander of the Faithful". Bereft of almost all political significance and detested alike by the Arabs and the Persians, the Caliph found himself in a "splendid isolation".

The process of disintegration of the 'Abbāsid empire had begun early. In 138 (755–6) a member of the Umayyad Dynasty made himself independent master of Spain. In 172 (788–9) a descendant of 'Alī, named Idrīs, established a dynasty in Morocco which lasted till 364 (974–5). About the same time, Ibrāhīm b. Aghlab, a lieutenant of Hārūnu'r-Rashīd, assumed independence in Tunis. Egypt was lost to the empire in 254 (868) when Aḥmad b. Ṭūlūn, the governor, cast off the yoke of the 'Abbāsids. The Ṭūlūnids were supplanted about 323 (934–5) by the Ikhshīds, and the Ikhshīds were succeeded in 358 (969) by the Fāṭimids who had established their power in North Africa in the middle of the third century A.H. The Fāṭimids claimed descent from Fāṭima, the daughter of the Prophet, and contended with the 'Abbāsids for the allegiance of "the Faithful" till 567 (1171–2) when they were supplanted by Sulṭān Ṣalāḥu'd-Dīn.

The province of Yaman became independent in the beginning of the third century A.H. under its governor Muḥammad b. Ziyād whose family ruled there till the beginning of the fifth century A.H.

In Syria and Mesopotamia, the Ḥamdānid family established its power in the beginning of the fourth century A.H. but their rule did not last long. Mesopotamia was conquered by 'Aḍudu'd-Dawlah about 368 (978–9) and Syria was absorbed by the Fāṭimids in 369 (979–80), while the outlying provinces became independent under the Marwānids of Diyār Bakr and the 'Uqailids of Mawṣil.

Persia was also split up into numerous independent principalities, the first of which was established by

Ṭāhir to whose military genius al-Ma'mūn owed his elevation to the Caliphate. Ṭāhir was made governor of Khurāsān in 205 (820–1) and, on his death two years later, the governorship of the East became hereditary in his family. His dynasty ended in 259 (872–3) when Ya'qūb the Ṣaffārid, ruler of Sīstān and Bust, defeated Muḥammad, the last of the Ṭāhirids, and annexed Khurāsān. Ya'qūb now became so powerful that he threatened the Caliph himself, but his march on Baghdād was arrested by his timely death in Shawwāl 265 (June 879). His brother and successor 'Amr conciliated the Caliph who, however, fearing his power, played him off against Ismā'īl the Sāmānid. 'Amr was defeated and Khurāsān passed under the sway of the Sāmānids. The Ṣaffārids still held their own in Sīstān and made spasmodic efforts to regain their power till 300 (912–13) when they were finally crushed. A few years later the dynasty was revived in the person of Aḥmad, a descendant of Ya'qūb, who was appointed governor of Sīstān by the Sāmānid Naṣr. After his death, his son Khalaf ruled in Sīstān till 393 (1002) when he was defeated and taken prisoner by Sulṭān Maḥmūd.

In the provinces bordering on the southern shore of the Caspian Sea, i.e. Dailam, Gīlān and Ṭabaristān, the descendants of 'Alī had long maintained a spiritual hold on the people. About the middle of the third century A.H. the 'Alids took possession of Ṭabaristān and ruled there till 316 (928) when it was conquered by Naṣr the Sāmānid. Shortly after that, Mardāwīj b. Ziyār who traced his genealogy to Argūsh Farhādwand, an old Persian king of Gīlān, acquired power in Ṭabaristān. His brother Washmgīr and, after him, his two sons, Bihistūn and Qābūs, ruled the province till their power was greatly curtailed by the encroachments of the Buwaihids, who ultimately forced Qābūs into exile. Qābūs regained his ancestral kingdom in 388 (998) and ruled till 402 (1011–12). The dynasty lost all importance after the death of his son and successor Mīnūchihr in 420 (1029).

About the middle of the fourth century A.H. Ḥasanawaih b. Ḥusain, chief of a tribe of Kurds, made himself master of a large part of Kurdistān. After his death about 369 (979–80) 'Aḍudu'd-Dawlah conquered Kurdistān but he allowed Badr, son of Ḥasanawaih, to rule the country as his deputy. Badr consolidated his power during the disturbances in Raiy following the death of Fakhru'd-Dawlah. He died in 405[1] (1014–15) and was succeeded by his son Ẓahīr who was defeated and put to death by Shamsu'd-Dawlah b. Fakhru'd-Dawlah.

The Buwaihids rose to power in the first quarter of the fourth century A.H. In the year 319 (931) Mardāwīj b. Ziyār gave the governorship of Karaj to their ancestor 'Alī b. Buwaih who traced his genealogy to Bahrām Gūr. From Karaj 'Alī and his brothers, Ḥasan and Aḥmad, extended their power over the whole of Western Persia and 'Irāq and acquired control of Baghdād, but after a short period of brisk conquest and vigorous rule decay set in and their kingdom was conquered by Sulṭān Maḥmūd and the Seljuks.

The Sāmānids first came into prominence in the time of the Caliph al-Ma'mūn at whose command the four sons of Asad b. Sāmān were given the government of important towns in Transoxiana. About the end of the third century A.H. their power extended from the Jaxartes to Baghdād, and from Khwārizm and the Caspian Sea to the borders of India. In the year 389 (999) the dynasty came to an end when Sulṭān Maḥmūd and Īlak Khān conquered Khurāsān and Bukhārā respectively.

In the lands on the other side of the Jaxartes the Qarā-Khānid Dynasty of Turkomāns held sway up to the borders of China. One of them named Abū Mūsā Hārūn Bughrā Khān took Bukhārā in 382 (992) but he

1 For an account of Badr, see *Mujmal*, ff. 258 a–261 b.

was forced to return to his country as the climate did not agree with him. His successor Ilak Khān conquered Bukhārā in 389 (999) and put an end to the Sāmānid Dynasty. The Qarā-Khānids, in their various branches, continued to rule till the middle of the sixth century A.H.[1]

1 Besides these, there were the kingdoms of Jurjāniyyah, Khwārizm, Gharshistān, and Jūzjānān which were nominal dependencies of Bukhārā.

CHAPTER III

THE PREDECESSORS OF SULṬĀN MAḤMUD

I. ALPTIGĪN

ALPTIGĪN, the founder of the kingdom of Ghazna, was born about 267[1] (880–1). He was sold as a slave to Aḥmad b. Ismā'īl the Sāmānid who enrolled him in his body-guard.[2] Naṣr b. Aḥmad emancipated him,[3] and Nūḥ b. Naṣr gave him the command of some troops,[4] from which position he rose to be the Ḥājibu'l-Ḥujjāb.[5] After the death of Nūḥ, Alptigīn acquired great influence over the youthful 'Abdu'l-Malik. When Bakr b. Malik, commander of the troops of Khurāsān, came to Bukhārā in Ramaḍān 345 (December 956) Alptigīn fell upon him and stabbed him to death.[6] To reward him for his services or perhaps to remove him from the capital, the Amīr bestowed upon Alptigīn the government of the province of Balkh, but as this did not satisfy his ambition, the Amīr appointed him commander of the troops of Khurāsān. Alptigīn took over charge of his new government on 20th Dhu'l-Ḥajja, 349[7] (10th February, 961).

On the death of Amīr 'Abdu'l-Malik in Shawwāl 350 (November 961), Abū 'Alī Bal'amī, the wazīr, who was a partisan of Alptigīn, wrote to ask his opinion as to the most suitable candidate for the succession. Alptigīn favoured the son of the late Amīr[8] who was a minor, but before his reply was received, the army had sworn allegiance to Manṣūr, the late Amīr's brother.

1 Faṣīḥī, f. 207 b.
2 *Guzīda*, p. 381; *Ṣubḥ-i-Ṣādiq*, f. 998 a.
3 Faṣīḥī, f. 207 b.
4 *Guzīda*, p. 384.
5 Gardīzī, p. 42.
6 *Ibid.* p. 41.
7 *Ibid.* p. 42.
8 *Ibid.* p. 43; and *Ṭab. Nāṣ.* p. 42.

Alptigīn now resolved to enforce his will at the point of the sword. He struck up an alliance with Abū Manṣūr Muḥammad, his predecessor in office and at that time governor of Ṭūs, and, leaving him in charge of Khurāsān, marched on Bukhārā in Dhu'l-Qa'da 350 (December 961). The Amīr cleverly alienated Abū Manṣūr from Alptigīn by restoring to him the province of Khurāsān and commanded him to prevent the passage of the river Oxus.[1] Alptigīn gained the bank of the river, but there he was apprised of the danger of his position. Hemmed in on both sides by the enemy and afraid of treason in his own camp, as the Amīr had won over some of his officers, Alptigīn gave up his proposed advance on Bukhārā and, setting fire to his encampment, fell back on Balkh.[2] The Amīr despatched after him an army of 12,000 horse under the command of Ash'ath b. Muḥammad[3] who overtook him near the Khulam pass. The two armies met in the middle of Rabī' i 351 (April 962). Alptigīn was victorious and captured, besides other important officers, a maternal uncle of the Amīr.[4] With a view to establishing himself somewhere beyond the reach of his offended suzerain, Alptigīn marched to Ghazna, defeated Abū Bakr Lawīk, the ruler,[5] captured the fort after a siege of four months[6] and proclaimed himself king.

Amīr Manṣūr however did not let him rest in peace. He sent against him Abū Ja'far at the head of an army 20,000 strong. Alptigīn inflicted a crushing defeat on

1 Gardīzī, p. 43.

2 *Ibid.* pp. 43–4; and *Majma'u'l-Ansāb*, f. 223 a.

3 Narshakhī, p. 97; Gardīzī, p. 44, has Babdāḥ.

4 *Tajārib*, ii, 192; and Ibnu'l-Athīr, viii, 404.

5 *Ṭab. Nāṣ.* p. 71. *Guzīda*, p. 385, incorrectly says that Alptigīn put Abū Bakr Lawīk to death. Abū Bakr had taken refuge with the king of Kābul.

6 *Majma'u'l-Ansāb*, f. 224 a. It is mentioned in *Zīnatu'l-Majālis*, f. 91 a; *Ṣubḥ-i-Ṣādiq*, f. 999 a; *Jannātu'l-Firdaws*, f. 37 b, that the fort of Ghazna fell on Monday, 13th Dhu'l-Ḥajja, 351 (12th January, 963).

him and forced him to return.[1] The Amīr now made the best of the situation by becoming reconciled to Alptigīn and conferring upon him the government of the territories which he had conquered.[2]

Alptigīn then conquered Bust and a part of the kingdom of Kābul but he did not enjoy his sovereignty for long. He died on 20th Sha'bān, 352[3] (13th September, 963).

2. ABŪ ISḤĀQ IBRĀHĪM

Alptigīn was succeeded by his son Abū Isḥāq Ibrāhīm[4] who was a weakling. The army got out of control and, taking advantage of this state of affairs, Abū 'Alī Lawīk, son of Abū Bakr Lawīk, advanced on Ghazna, defeated Ibrāhīm and occupied the country. Ibrāhīm fled to Bukhārā to seek the assistance of Amīr Manṣūr[5] and returned the following year with a large force, put Abū 'Alī Lawīk to flight on 27th Shawwāl, 354[6] (26th September, 965) and entered Ghazna, but he died shortly after this on 25th Dhu'l-Qa'da, 355[7] (12th November, 966).

1 *Guzīda*, p. 385.

2 *Ṭab. Nāṣ.* p. 43. The account of Alptigīn's rebellion is given differently in *Majma'u'l-Ansāb*, f. 223 a; while that given in *Siyāsat Nāmah*, pp. 98–106, is full of blunders and contradictory statements.

3 *Majma'u'l-Ansāb*, f. 224 a; *Ṣubḥ-i-Ṣādiq*, f. 999 a; *Zīnatu'l-Majālis*, f. 91 a; and *Jannātu'l-Firdaws*, f. 37 b. Sir Denison Ross (*The Heart of Central Asia*, p. 112) incorrectly says that he died in 366 (976–7), and that Subuktigīn was his immediate successor.

4 Ibn Ḥawqal, p. 13; and Gardīzī, p. 41.

5 *Ṭab. Nāṣ.* p. 71; and 'Utbī, p. 14.

6 Faṣīḥī, f. 289 b; and *Jahān Ārā*, f. 82 a.

7 *Majma'u'l-Ansāb*, f. 224 b; *Zīnatu'l-Majālis*, f. 92 a; and *Ṣubḥ-i-Ṣādiq*, f. 999 b. It is said in *Ṭab. Nāṣ.* p. 72, that he died one year after his return from Bukhārā.

3. BILKĀTIGĪN

As Ibrāhīm left no son capable of taking his place,[1] the nobles chose Bilkātigīn, a slave of Alptigīn and commander of his body-guard,[2] to be their ruler. Bilkātigīn was a famous soldier and is said to have won the regard of his subjects by the purity of his private life and the strict administration of justice. After a reign of ten years he died in 364 (974–5) while he was engaged in the siege of Gardīz.[3]

4. PIRĪTIGĪN

Bilkātigīn was succeeded by another slave of Alptigīn named Pirī or Pirītigīn.[4] He soon made himself obnoxious to his subjects, who invited Abū ʿAlī Lawīk to be their king. Abū ʿAlī accompanied by "the son of the king of Kābul" promptly advanced on Ghazna.[5] Subuktigīn met the invaders in the vicinity of Charakh,[6] with a body of 500 slaves and inflicted a crushing defeat on them. Both Abū ʿAlī and "the son of the king of Kābul" were taken prisoners and put to death.[7] Pirītigīn was deposed and, by the unanimous consent of the nobility, Subuktigīn was raised to the throne on 27th Shaʿbān, 366[8] (20th April, 977).

1 ʿUtbī, p. 15.

2 *Ṭab. Nāṣ.* p. 73. Browne, i, 372, incorrectly says that both Abū Isḥāq and Bilkātigīn were sons of Alptigīn. Cf. also E. and D. ii, 479, and *JRAS.* xvii, 145.

3 *Ādābu'l-Mulūk*, f. 75 a; *Jahān Ārā*, f. 82 b; and *Zīnatu'l-Majālis*, f. 92 a.

4 ʿAwfī, f. 391 b. Sir W. Haig, p. 11, calls him Pīrāi, but there is no authority for it.

5 *Ṭab. Nāṣ.* p. 73.

6 It is situated on the road from Ghazna to Kābul.

7 *Ṭab. Nāṣ.* p. 73. A different account is given in *Majmaʿu'l-Ansāb*, f. 225 a. Raverty, *Notes*, p. 677, incorrectly places this battle in 363 (973–4). For the chronology of the predecessors of Subuktigīn, see Appendix B.

8 *Ṭab. Nāṣ.* p. 73; and Ibnu'l-Athīr, viii, 503. ʿUtbī does not, as is generally supposed, altogether ignore the successors of Abū Isḥāq Ibrāhīm; see his *Kitābu'l-Yamīnī*, p. 15.

5. ABŪ MANṢŪR SUBUKTIGĪN

Abū Manṣūr Subuktigīn was born about 331[1] (942–3). His father, named Jūq, was the chieftain of a small principality in Turkistān and was a man of extraordinary physical strength.[2] One day a hostile neighbouring tribe carried out a raid on his town and captured Subuktigīn, his third son, who was then only twelve years of age. After remaining a prisoner in the hands of that tribe for four years, he was sold as a slave to Naṣr the Ḥājjī.[3] Subuktigīn however fell ill and Naṣr was compelled to leave him at Nakhshab for three years. During this period he managed to learn the art of fighting and swordsmanship, which pleased Naṣr so much that he placed him in command of his other slaves.[4] Subuktigīn was brought to Bukhārā, probably in 348 (959), and was purchased by Alptigīn, the Ḥājibu'l-Ḥujjāb of Amīr 'Abdu'l-Malik.[5] Alptigīn was so well disposed towards him that he promoted him rapidly to higher ranks without making him go through the usual grades in the service of the slaves.[6] After the death of Alptigīn, Subuktigīn became the Ḥājibu'l-Ḥujjāb and "the most trusted officer" of Abū Isḥāq Ibrāhīm,[7] and gained the hand of a daughter of Alptigīn in marriage.[8] During the reigns of Bilkātigīn and Pirītigīn, he continued to enjoy dignity and honour,[9] till by the

1 The date is inferred from *Ṭab. Nāṣ.* p. 75, and *Majma'u'l-Ansāb*, f. 227 a.

2 *Majma'u'l-Ansāb*, f. 226 b.

3 Subuktigīn embraced Islam probably after he had fallen into the hands of Naṣr the Ḥājjī. See Baihaqī, p. 107; *Ṭab. Nāṣ.* p. 70; and *Majma'u'l-Ansāb*, f. 227 a.

4 Subuktigīn's *Pand-Nāmah*, as given in *Majma'u'l-Ansāb*, ff. 226 b *et seq.* A different and apparently incorrect account of Subuktigīn's early history is given in *Jāmi'u't-Tawārīkh*, f. 204 b.

5 *Majma'u'l-Ansāb*, f. 227 b; and *Ṭab. Nāṣ.* p. 71.

6 *Siyāsat Nāmah*, pp. 95–7.

7 'Utbī, p. 15.

8 *Guzīda*, p. 393.

9 *Ṭab. Nāṣ.* pp. 71–3; and *Majma'u'l-Ansāb*, ff. 224 b–225 a.

unanimous consent of the nobility, he was raised to the throne on Friday, 27th Sha'bān, 366[1] (20th April, 977).

During the first year or two after his accession, Subuktigīn added Bust and Quṣdār to his kingdom[2] and then turned his attention to India. The whole territory from Lamaghān to the river Chināb was ruled by Jaipāl of the Hindūshāhiyya Dynasty.[3] To retaliate for a raid of Subuktigīn, Jaipāl advanced with a large force to attack Ghazna about the year 376[4] (986–7). Subuktigīn met him near a hill called Ghūzak, between Ghazna and Lamaghān. The Hindūs fought bravely but a sudden snowstorm created consternation among them and Jaipāl was forced to sue for peace. Maḥmūd was in favour of carrying on the war till Jaipāl was beaten but Subuktigīn, fearing that if the Hindūs, as they had threatened to do in despair, burnt themselves with all their valuables, he would lose the rich peace-offerings, consented to come to terms. Jaipāl promised to pay an indemnity of 1,000,000 *dirhems* and 50 elephants and to cede some forts and towns on the frontier. As a security for the fulfilment of these terms, Jaipāl left some of his kinsmen as hostages and returned to his kingdom. Once back in safety, Jaipāl repudiated his promise and took prisoners the officers of Subuktigīn who had been sent to take charge of the ceded forts and towns.[5]

1 *Ṭab. Nāṣ.* p. 73; and Ibnu'l-Athīr, viii, 503. In *Majma'u'l-Ansāb*, f. 225 a, it is incorrectly given as 363 (973–4).

2 Khwānd-Amīr, *Khulāṣatu't-Tawārīkh*, f. 216 a, says 367 (977–8). Cf. also 'Utbī, pp. 17–19, 20–1.

The kingdom of Quṣdār roughly corresponded with Balūchistān. The town of Quṣdār is most probably modern Khuzdār.

3 See my article in *JRAS.* 1927, pp. 491–2. Raverty, *Notes*, p. 320, and Smith, p. 396, say that it extended to the river Hakra. They have evidently confused Waihand, the capital of the Hindūshāhiyya Dynasty, with Bhatinda, and hence the error.

4 'Utbī, pp. 9, 22, says that Maḥmūd was fifteen years of age at this time. I have conjectured the date from this statement.

5 'Utbī, pp. 21–4.

When Subuktigīn got news of this outrage, he marched at the head of a large army and captured many towns in Lamaghān. Jaipāl in retaliation organised a league of Hindū rājās against Subuktigīn and marched on Ghazna at the head of a great host which is said to have been swelled to the enormous number of 100,000 cavalry and infantry by the contingents furnished by the rājās of Northern India.[1] Subuktigīn put him to the rout, annexed the districts between Lamaghān and Peshāwar, and introduced Islam among the people. The Khaljīs and Afghāns who inhabited this region submitted to him and were recruited in the army.[2]

Subuktigīn and the Sāmānids. When Subuktigīn succeeded to the throne at Ghazna, the power of the Sāmānids had declined and the governors of the outlying parts of the empire were frequently in rebellion against them. Subuktigīn however maintained the respect due to Amīr Nūḥ as his overlord and helped him to crush the insurgents. When Fā'iq and Abū 'Alī Sīmjūrī[3] made common cause against their overlord Amīr Nūḥ, he appealed to Subuktigīn who quickly responded to the call, hastened over the mountain passes and advanced to Herāt where the rebels had mustered in strength. By negotiations he prevailed on them to make peace with the Amīr and to pay an indemnity of 15,000,000 *dirhems*. Shortly after this Abū 'Alī broke the peace. Subuktigīn attacked him near Herāt on 15th Ramaḍān, 384[4] (23rd October, 994). Abū 'Alī fought bravely but his forces were routed by a timely attack led by Maḥmūd. Abū 'Alī fled to Raiy and took refuge with Fakhru'd-Dawlah. The victors

1 Firishta, p. 20, mentions the Rājā of Ajmer among them, but Ajmer was not founded at that time, see *infra*, p. 215.

2 'Utbī, pp. 21–6.

3 Sir W. Haig, p. 12, incorrectly calls him "Abu 'Alī Sūnjūr".

4 'Utbī, p. 80; Gardīzī, p. 55; and Baihaqī, p. 235.

entered Herāt where the grateful Amīr rewarded Subuktigīn with the title of *Nāṣiru'd-Dīn wa'd-Dawlah* and
the province of Bal<u>kh</u>, and Maḥmūd with the title
of *Saifu'd-Dawlah* and the command of the troops of
<u>Kh</u>urāsān.[1] Maḥmūd entered Nī<u>sh</u>āpūr but he was sur-
prised by Abū 'Alī and Fā'iq who captured the town
and forced him to take shelter at Herāt. Hearing news
of this disaster, Subuktigīn advanced to Ṭūs and met
Abū 'Alī in battle on 20th Jumādī ii, 385 (22nd July,
995). Abū 'Alī fought desperately but the day was
decided against him by a vigorous attack delivered by
Maḥmūd. Both Abū 'Alī and Fā'iq, being tired of this
fruitless struggle, made overtures of peace to Amīr Nūḥ.
When their messengers arrived in Bu<u>kh</u>ārā, the Amīr,
with a view to breaking up their alliance, imprisoned
the one sent by Fā'iq while he showed honour to Abū
'Alī's ambassador. Fā'iq fled to Īlak <u>Kh</u>ān for assistance,
and Abū 'Alī was thrown into prison when he came to
Bu<u>kh</u>ārā in 386 (996) and handed over to Subuktigīn
for safe custody.[2]

Fā'iq in the meantime prevailed on Īlak <u>Kh</u>ān to
attack Bu<u>kh</u>ārā. Amīr Nūḥ, hearing news of this, again
appealed for assistance to Subuktigīn, who came at the
head of a large force; but the Amīr gave him offence by
refusing, on the advice of his wazīr 'Abdu'llāh b.
Muḥammad b. 'Uzair, to take part in the struggle with
Īlak <u>Kh</u>ān. Instead of fighting, therefore, Subuktigīn
made peace with Īlak <u>Kh</u>ān by ceding to him all the
Sāmānid territories to the east of Qaṭwān, and despatched Maḥmūd to Bu<u>kh</u>ārā at the head of 20,000
horse, to procure the dismissal of the obnoxious wazīr.
The frightened Amīr dismissed 'Abdu'llāh and accepted
in his place a minister nominated by Subuktigīn.[3]

1 Subuktigīn already had the title of *Mu'īnu'd-Dawlah*. See
al-Bīrūnī, *The Chronology of Ancient Nations*, p. 130.
2 'Utbī, pp. 75–101. Abū 'Alī died in 387 (997).
3 'Utbī, pp. 98–100.

Shortly after this Abu'l-Qāsim, brother of Abū 'Alī Sīmjūrī, taking advantage of the absence of Subuktigīn and Maḥmūd from K̲h̲urāsān, captured Nīs̲h̲āpūr but he was forced to evacuate it at the approach of Maḥmūd and his uncle Bug̲h̲rājuq.[1]

The Death of Subuktigīn. Subuktigīn now returned to Balk̲h̲. About this time, one of his sisters and some other relatives died. He grieved at this so much that he himself became ill.[2] He then marched towards G̲h̲azna to recover his health in its bracing climate, but on the way he breathed his last at the village of Mādrū Mūy, on the frontier of Balk̲h̲, in S̲h̲a'bān 387[3] (August 997).

Thus passed away Subuktigīn, loved by his soldiers whose hardships he had always shared and by his people who had profited from his benevolent administration. His name is immortalised by the title of *Amīr-i-'Ādil*, the Just Amīr, which the historians confer upon him. He was resolute and resigned in adversity, and humane and benevolent in prosperity. He had many sons of whom two, Ḥasan and Ḥusain, are said to have died young, while Maḥmūd, Ismā'īl, Naṣr and Yūsuf survived him. He was very affectionate to his children and seems to have devoted special attention to their education. After his rise to power, he sent for his mother, brothers and sisters and allowed them to participate in his prosperity.[4] His relations with his overlord Amīr Nūḥ were praiseworthy. His ready assistance to him in crushing the power of the recalcitrant nobility and stemming the tide of conquest from Turkistān, stands in conspicuous contrast with the treason and perfidy which characterised the dealings of the Buk̲h̲ārite nobility towards their suzerain. He

1 'Utbī, pp. 102–3.
2 *Ibid.* pp. 106–7.
3 *Ibid.* p. 107; Gardīzī, p. 58; and *Ṭab. Nāṣ.* p. 75.
4 *Majma'u'l-Ansāb*, f. 229 b.

was a great statesman and strengthened his position by securing for his son Maḥmūd the hand of a princess of the Farīghūnid house, which was connected by marriage with the Sāmānids.[1] Towards the end of his career, he had become so powerful that foreign princes eagerly desired his friendship.

1 Gardīzī, p. 48; and 'Utbī, p. 227.

CHAPTER IV

THE EARLY LIFE OF MAḤMŪD

ABU'L-QĀSIM MAḤMŪD,[1] the eldest son of Subuktigīn,[2] was born on the night between the 9th and 10th Muḥarram, 361[3] (1st and 2nd November, 971). His mother was the daughter of a nobleman of Zābulistān.[4]

1 The following pedigree of Maḥmūd is given in *Ṭab. Nāṣ.* p. 70, on the authority of *Ta'rīkh-i-Mujadwal*:

Maḥmūd b. Subuktigīn b. Jūq b. Qarā Bajkam b. Qarā Arslān b. Qarā Mallāt b. Qarā Nu'mān b. Fīrūz-i-Bam Sinjān b. Yazdagird, the last Sāsānid monarch. In *Jāmi'u't-Tawārīkh*, f. 204 b, Maḥmūd is connected with the Sāmānids, but this does not seem to be correct.

2 'Utbī, p. 114. Briggs, Firishta, i, 29, footnote, stigmatises Maḥmūd as the illegitimate son of Subuktigīn, but there is absolutely no authority for this allegation. See also note 4, below.

3 *Ṭab. Nāṣ.* p. 76; 'Awfī, f. 256 b, where Baihaqī is quoted; and Ibn Khallikān, ii, 113. Ibnu'l-Athīr, ix, 281, gives 10th Muḥarram, 360 (13th November, 970), and Sibṭ Ibnu'l-Jawzī, f. 219 b, quoting aṣ-Ṣābī's *Dhail*, gives 14th Dhu'l-Ḥajja, 361 (26th September, 972), but both are probably errors of copyists.

Historians have connected the birth of Sulṭān Maḥmūd with some extraordinary occurrences. It is stated in *Ṭab. Nāṣ.* p. 76, that the birth of Maḥmūd synchronised with the falling down of an idol-temple at Waihand, and that shortly before his birth Subuktigīn saw in a dream a tree issuing out of the chafing-dish in his room and spreading out rapidly so as to overshadow the whole world, thus presaging the future iconoclast and conqueror. But this is not peculiar to the historians of Sulṭān Maḥmūd. The birth of Alexander the Great is also said to have been marked by somewhat similar events. See Plutarch's *Lives*, ii, 104.

4 *Siyāsat Nāmah*, p. 108; and *Guzīda*, p. 395. Maḥmūd is for this reason called "Maḥmūd-i-Zābulī" by his court-poets. Zābulistān was the name of the district round Ghazna, between the Helmund and the Khwāsh-rūd.

In the satire which is attributed to Firdawsī, Maḥmūd is called "the son of a slave-girl", but if his mother had really been a slave-girl, his court-poets would not have called him Maḥmūd-

Only a few stray facts are known about his early life. He received the usual scholastic education of an eastern prince under the tutorship of a learned man, "the father of Qāḍī Bū 'Alī of Ṣīniyya",[1] and was well grounded in different branches of the sacred learning.[2] He knew the *Qur'ān* by heart[3] and was familiar with Muslim Law and Tradition.[4] The political side of his education was not neglected. Subuktigīn himself instructed him in the principles of successful sovereignty and put them in the form of a *Pand-Nāmah*.[5] Maḥmūd had also acquired great experience of administrative work. It is stated that when Subuktigīn went to war in Bust, he left Maḥmūd, who was then barely seven years of age, as his deputy at Ghazna, with Bū 'Alī Kirmānī as his wazīr[6] and, a few years later, assigned to him the government of the province of Zamīn Dāwar.[7]

Besides this, Maḥmūd was drilled in the military arts of the time. He was known to be an excellent swordsman, and his skill as a marksman and a lance-fighter could not be equalled.[8] He gained experience of warfare in the company of his father. As a boy he distinguished himself in a punitive expedition against

i-Zābulī. Professor Maḥmūd Khān Shīrānī has conclusively shown in a series of scholarly articles in the quarterly journal *Urdū* (1921–3) that this satire is apocryphal. See also *infra*, p. 158, note 1.

1 Baihaqī, p. 609. Amīn Aḥmad Rāzī, *Haft Iqlīm*, f. 100 b (Brit. Mus. Add. 24,092), erroneously makes the famous traditionist, Abū Bakr Baihaqī, the preceptor of Sulṭān Maḥmūd. Ṣīniyya was a place between Wāsiṭ and Ṣālīq.

2 'Utbī, p. 8.

3 Baihaqī, p. 609; and Farrukhī, f. 23 a.

4 Ḥājjī Khalīfa, ii, 327. He is even supposed to have composed a book on Muslim Law. See *infra*, pp. 156–7.

5 The full text of it has been preserved in the *Majma'u'l-Ansāb*, ff. 226 b–229 a. There is a reference to this *Pand-Nāmah* in *Āthāru'l-Wuzarā*, f. 88 a.

6 'Awfī, ff. 142 a, 391 b; and *Majma'u'l-Ansāb*, f. 226 a.

7 Baihaqī, pp. 123, 126.

8 *Ādābu'l-Mulūk*, f. 80 a.

Ghūr[1] and, when only fifteen years of age, he took a prominent part in a battle near Lamaghān in 376 (986–7) between his father and Jaipāl.[2]

In 380 (990–1) some factious persons created a breach between father and son, as a consequence of which Maḥmūd was imprisoned in the fort of Ghazna, but the misunderstanding was short-lived and, after some months, he was released and restored to favour.[3] A few years later in 384 (994), Maḥmūd fought on the side of his father in his war against Fā'iq and Abū 'Alī Sīmjūrī and displayed remarkable skill as a warrior and general. The grateful Amīr recognised his services by bestowing on him the title of *Saifu'd-Dawlah* and appointing him to the command of the troops of Khurāsān in place of Abū 'Alī Sīmjūrī.

But shortly after Maḥmūd had taken possession of Nīshāpūr, Abū 'Alī and Fā'iq, finding that Subuktigīn had left him with inadequate resources, attacked him in Rabī' i 385 (April 995). Maḥmūd evacuated Nīshāpūr at their approach, encamped three miles out of the

1 This fact has been omitted by all historians. There are only two references to it in contemporary writers. 'Unṣurī, p. 76, in a *qaṣīda* in praise of Sulṭān Maḥmūd, says:

ور از شجاعت گوئی بکودکی در غور

به پشت اسپ مبارز به بود پیش پدر

"And if you talk of his valour, in his boyhood, he (Maḥmūd) fought in Ghūr, on horseback, side by side with his father."

Abū 'Āmir an-Najdī, in a *qaṣīda* ('Utbī, p. 82) written to congratulate Maḥmūd on his getting the title of *Saifu'd-Dawlah*, says:

فالهند و الغور قد شابت شعورهم

لما راوا منك من باسٍ و قد فشلوا

"The people of India and Ghūr have become old and decrepit (with grief or fear) since they have witnessed your prowess."

2 See *supra*, p. 29; and 'Awfī, f. 488 b.

3 *Majma'u'l-Ansāb*, f. 245 a; and Faṣīḥī, f. 303 b. These are the only two works that mention this fact. Baihaqī, p. 257, and Farrukhī, f. 25 a, probably make a reference to it.

town and awaited reinforcements from his father, but Abū 'Alī and Fā'iq engaged him in battle, defeated his army, captured his elephants and took possession of Nīshāpūr. Subuktigīn hastened to his help and gave battle to their allied armies on 20th Jumādī ii, 385 (22nd July, 995). After a desperate battle the enemy broke and fled. Many officers of Abū 'Alī fell prisoners into the hands of the victors and were exchanged for the elephants which he had captured.[1]

The rapid growth of their power occasioned frequent intrigues against father and son. Amīr Nūḥ's wazīr, 'Abdu'llāh b. Muḥammad b. 'Uzair, advised him to deprive them of some portion at least of the vast territories which he had granted to them, but the Amīr refused to give offence to such powerful allies.[2] When Īlak Khān advanced to Bukhārā in 386 (996), 'Abdu'llāh again offended Subuktigīn[3], who sent Maḥmūd at the head of 20,000 picked troops to turn him out of office and replace him by a friendly wazīr. This was done, as has already been mentioned,[4] but during his absence in Bukhārā, Abu'l-Qāsim, brother of Abū 'Alī Sīmjūrī, strengthened himself in Kūhistān and captured Nīshāpūr. Maḥmūd, assisted by his uncle Bughrājuq, advanced to Nīshāpūr and Abu'l-Qāsim evacuated the town without giving battle. Having crushed all opposition, Maḥmūd consolidated his power in Khurāsān. Shortly after this, however, Subuktigīn died, and Maḥmūd was called to Ghazna to struggle for the throne with his brother Ismā'īl.[5]

1 'Utbī, pp. 90–1.
2 *Ibid.* p. 83.
3 See *supra*, p. 31.
4 See *supra*, p. 31.
5 'Utbī, pp. 102–3.

CHAPTER V

THE STRUGGLE FOR THE THRONE

SUBUKTIGĪN died in Sha'bān 387 (August 997) on his way from Balkh to Ghazna. Shortly before his death, he nominated Ismā'īl, a younger son by a daughter of Alptigīn,[1] as his successor in the provinces of Ghazna and Balkh, made his noblemen swear allegiance to him[2] and entrusted to him the care of his family and dependents.[3] Ismā'īl hurried to Balkh, proclaimed himself king, did homage to Amīr Abu'l-Ḥārith Manṣūr b. Nūḥ, the Sāmānid,[4] and, to secure the loyalty of his soldiers in view of the forthcoming struggle with his brother Maḥmūd, he lavished on them the treasures accumulated by the assiduity of his father.[5]

It is difficult to ascertain the considerations which induced Subuktigīn to nominate Ismā'īl in preference to Maḥmūd as his successor. He might have been influenced by Ismā'īl's connection with Alptigīn, by his presence at the death-bed,[6] by a desire to provide for all his three grown-up sons,[7] or merely by paternal affection, but it cannot be denied that he displayed lack of political foresight in assuming that Maḥmūd, the eldest and obviously the most capable of his sons, would let Ismā'īl enjoy the suzerainty which the possession of Ghazna implied for its master.

1 *Guzīda*, p. 393; and *Majma'u'l-Ansāb*, f. 229 b.

2 'Utbī, p. 110.

3 *Ibid.* Baihaqī, p. 306, says that Subuktigīn commended his infant son, Yūsuf, to the care of Maḥmūd.

4 *Catal. of Or. Coins in Brit. Mus.* by S. Lane-Poole, ii, 130.

5 'Utbī, p. 114.

6 *Ibid.*

7 Subuktigīn had secured the command of the troops of Khurāsān for Maḥmūd and had given charge of the province of Bust to Naṣr. By his will, he left the provinces of Ghazna and Balkh to Ismā'īl.

Maḥmūd did not acquiesce in this settlement. He desired to have his own superior claims vindicated without depriving Ismā'īl of his share in the patrimony. When he received the news of his father's death, he sent Abu'l-Ḥasan Ḥamūlī to Ismā'īl with a letter of condolence, in which he assured Ismā'īl of his fraternal affection and of his willingness to deliver to him the province of Balkh or Khurāsān if he surrendered Ghazna in recognition of Maḥmūd's superior rights. He further pointed out that he would not have disputed the will of his father if Ismā'īl had possessed the requisite experience of warfare and administration. Ismā'īl rejected this proposal. At this juncture, Abu'l-Ḥārith Farīghūnī,[1] ruler of Jūzjānān and father-in-law of Maḥmūd, endeavoured to induce the brothers to settle their differences in a parley, but Ismā'īl, probably suspecting the good offices of the mediator, turned a deaf ear to his suggestion. Maḥmūd therefore marched on Ghazna to enforce his will at the point of the sword. From Herāt he made another attempt at reconciliation but Ismā'īl again declined to listen to him.[2]

Maḥmūd now made preparations for the struggle. He won over his brother Abu'l-Muẓaffar Naṣr, ruler of Bust, and his uncle Bughrājuq, governor of Herāt and Fūshanj, who, with their armies, joined him at Herāt,[3] while his father-in-law Abu'l-Ḥārith Farīghūnī brought the whole weight of his position to bear in his favour. Thus strengthened he resumed his march on Ghazna. Ismā'īl moved down from Balkh to protect it. Before hostilities actually began, Maḥmūd made a final attempt at compromise, but Ismā'īl, interpreting Maḥmūd's solicitude for peace as a symptom of weakness, set his face against reconciliation.[4]

1 For a brief account of the Farīghūnids, see Appendix C.

2 'Utbī, pp. 114–16.

3 *Ibid.* p. 116.

4 See Appendix D, for a discussion of Elphinstone's remark on the alleged weakness of Maḥmūd's title to the throne.

Maḥmūd was now forced to refer the dispute to the arbitrament of the sword—*ultima ratio regum*. He marshalled his army in battle array in front of Ismā'īl's position.[1] The two armies were equally matched except in the relative skill of their commanders. One was an inexperienced youth whose time had been spent chiefly in the society of scholars and literary men, the other was a man of ripe age and mature experience whose cool courage and furious charge had shattered the ranks of the impetuous Turkomāns with the same facility as those of the heterogeneous hosts of the effete Hindūs. And this disparity between the commanders made all the difference in the battle that followed.

The two armies met on the plain of Ghazna in Rabī' i 388[2] (March 998). Ismā'īl held his own for the whole day, but towards the evening his army broke and fled before a fierce charge led by Maḥmūd in person. Maḥmūd won the day, and with it the throne of Ghazna. Ismā'īl took refuge in the fort but realising that it would be impossible to sustain a long siege with the surrounding country in the hands of his brother, he surrendered himself when Maḥmūd promised to treat him kindly.[3] His reign had lasted only seven months.[4]

1 'Unṣurī, p. 76, says that Ismā'īl had strengthened his position by a line of 200 elephants.

2 This date is inferred from the fact that Ismā'īl's reign lasted only for seven months.

3 'Utbī, p. 118. Sir W. Haig, p. 11, incorrectly says that Ismā'īl was surrendered to Maḥmūd by his nobles.

4 Ibnu'l-Athīr, ix, 92. Raverty, *Ṭab. Nāṣ.* p. 51, note 6, and p. 75, note 6, incorrectly says that Ismā'īl was dethroned in 389 (999).

Ismā'īl was a man of gentle disposition and scholarly habits. He was the author of several short treatises and poems in Arabic and Persian. He was a devout Muslim and during his short rule he is said to have followed the practice of the Orthodox Caliphs in leading the Friday prayer. See Ibn Funduq, f. 39 b; Ibnu'l-Athīr, ix, 92; and as-Subkī, *Ṭabaqātu'sh-Shāfi'iyya*, iv, 14.

Ismā'īl was now placed in nominal confinement but was allowed every indulgence consistent with his position.[1] About the close of 389[2] (999), however, Ismā'īl abused the confidence of his brother and plotted against his life. Maḥmūd got an inkling of the plot and ordered Nūshtigīn Kāj, the chief agent, to be executed.[3] Ismā'īl was now removed from Ghazna and sent to Amīr Abu'l-Ḥārith at Jūzjānān where he ended his days in peace.[4]

1 'Utbī, pp. 128, 131, 132.

2 *Ibid.* p. 131, says that it happened shortly after Maḥmūd's victory over 'Abdu'l-Malik b. Nūḥ in Jumādī i 389.

3 The way in which Maḥmūd came to know of the plot is stated thus in 'Utbī, p. 132:

One day Maḥmūd went out hunting in the direction of Marv-Rūd, accompanied by Ismā'īl and Nūshtigīn Kāj. On casting a chance glance towards them, Maḥmūd saw that Nūshtigīn, with his hand on the hilt of his sword, was looking towards Ismā'īl for some pre-arranged signal to strike at Maḥmūd; but Ismā'īl, perhaps suspecting that Maḥmūd had noticed Nūshtigīn's action, pretended to appear unconcerned.

Ismā'īl may have been secretly encouraged in this plot by the Sāmānid Amīr Abu'l-Ḥārith Manṣūr with whom Maḥmūd's relations were strained about this time.

4 'Utbī, p. 132; but Faṣīḥī, f. 309 a, incorrectly says that Ismā'īl was sent to the "fort of Kālanjar, now called Talwāra".

Part Two

THE WARS OF SULṬĀN MAḤMŪD

CHAPTER VI

WARS IN CENTRAL ASIA

A. *Relations with the* Sāmānids

AFTER the capture of Ghazna, Maḥmūd proceeded to Balkh and did homage to Amīr Abu'l-Ḥārith Manṣūr, son and successor of Amīr Nūḥ.[1] The Amīr congratulated him on his victory over Ismā'īl and confirmed him in possession of the provinces of Balkh, Herāt, Tirmidh, Bust, etc., but with regard to Khurāsān, he regretted that he had already given it to Begtūzūn,[2]

1 For a brief account of the early history of the Sāmānids, see Appendix E.

2 Col. Malleson, *History of Afghanistan*, p. 57, makes the unfounded statement that Amīr Nūḥ "nominated...Tūzan Bēg to the governorship of Ghaznī".

The events which led to the appointment of Begtūzūn in place of Maḥmūd are given below:

On the death of Amīr Nūḥ in Rajab 387 (July 997), 'Abdu'llāh b. Muḥammad b. 'Uzair, the former wazīr, found an opportunity of wreaking vengeance on Maḥmūd. He persuaded Abū Manṣūr of Isfījāb to accompany him to Kāshghar to induce Īlak Khān to attack Bukhārā and, after its conquest, to demand from him the command of the troops of Khurāsān which was then held by Maḥmūd. At their invitation Īlak Khān marched on Bukhārā, but at Samarqand he ordered both 'Abdu'llāh and Abū Manṣūr to be imprisoned, and sent Fā'iq to Bukhārā at the head of 3000 troops as his advance-guard. Abu'l-Ḥārith left Bukhārā and crossed the Oxus. Fā'iq occupied Bukhārā, but he was so much touched by the miserable condition of the Sāmānids that he sent a deputation of the notables of the town to the Amīr to induce him to return. The Amīr did so, but he found that the two powerful nobles, Fā'iq and Begtūzūn, neither of whom he dare offend, were not on good terms with each other. He therefore separated them by giving to Begtūzūn the command of the troops of Khurāsān. Maḥmūd was at this time engaged in the struggle for succession with Ismā'īl.

a military commander who was in power at Bukhārā. Maḥmūd sent Abu'l-Ḥasan Ḥamūlī to Bukhārā to plead his cause but the Amīr refused to revise his order.

Despairing of getting back Khurāsān by peaceful means, Maḥmūd resolved to take it by force and advanced on Nīshāpūr. Begtūzūn evacuated the town and sent for reinforcements. The Amīr himself hurried to his relief and encamped near Sarakhs. Maḥmūd evacuated Nīshāpūr without giving battle,[1] and withdrew to Marv-Rūd.[2] Begtūzūn occupied Nīshāpūr and marched to Sarakhs to join forces with the Amīr.

Fā'iq and Begtūzūn now suspected the Amīr of sympathising with Maḥmūd and formed a plot to depose him.[3] When the Amīr was returning from a hunting party on 12th Ṣafar, 389 (2nd February, 999), Begtūzūn met him on the way, and, on the pretext of discussing an important matter regarding Maḥmūd, brought him to his camp where he was made a prisoner. Fā'iq and Begtūzūn now raised to the throne Abu'l-Fawāris 'Abdu'l-Malik, a younger brother of the late Amīr.[4]

Maḥmūd took up the cause of the fallen monarch and marched to Sarakhs to punish Fā'iq and Begtūzūn, who fled to Marv on his approach. Maḥmūd pressed in pursuit and encamped in front of Marv, but before hostilities began peace was made by the terms of which Maḥmūd was confirmed in the possession of Herāt, Balkh, etc., while Begtūzūn was allowed to hold the command of the troops of Khurāsān. Maḥmūd thus lost the object to gain which he had taken up arms,

1 'Utbī, p. 124, says that Maḥmūd withdrew because he hated to be the one to give the last blow to the Sāmānid power.

2 It was situated at a place where the river Murghāb debouches into the plains. See Le Strange, pp. 404–5.

3 Baihaqī, p. 804, says that Fā'iq and Begtūzūn were afraid that Abu'l-Ḥārith might hand them over to Maḥmūd, as his father Amīr Nūḥ had handed over Abū 'Alī Sīmjūrī to Subuktigīn.

4 Gardīzī, p. 60; and Baihaqī, p. 804.

but he is said to have been so pleased that he distributed 2000 *dīnārs* as a thanksgiving among the poor.[1] The peace, however, was short-lived. Dārā b. Qābūs, who had not agreed to the peace, instigated some of the followers of the Amīr to fall upon the rear of Maḥmūd's army which was under the command of Naṣr, and plunder his baggage. This furnished Maḥmūd with a *casus belli*.[2]

Maḥmūd at once faced about and marshalled his forces in battle array. He put Naṣr in charge of the right wing with 10,000 cavalry and 30 elephants, some of his trusted officers in charge of the left wing with 12,000 cavalry and 40 elephants, while he himself commanded the centre with 10,000 cavalry and 70 elephants, and advanced to attack the united forces of Amīr 'Abdu'l-Malik, Fā'iq, Begtūzūn and Abu'l-Qāsim Sīmjūrī. The battle took place near Marv on 27th Jumādī i, 389 (16th May, 999). Maḥmūd was victorious and Amīr 'Abdu'l-Malik fled to Bukhārā, leaving 2000 dead on the field and 2500 prisoners in the hands of the victors.[3] Abu'l-Qāsim escaped to Kūhistān and Begtūzūn took refuge at Nīshāpūr. When Maḥmūd advanced to prevent a junction of their forces, Begtūzūn fled towards Jurjān. Maḥmūd now placed Ṭūs under the command of Abu'l-Ḥārith Arslān Jādhib[4] with instructions to chase Begtūzūn out of Khurāsān, but he evaded his pursuers and, after an unsuccessful attempt to stir up rebellion against Maḥmūd in Khurāsān, crossed over to Bukhārā by way of the Ghuzz desert.[5]

Maḥmūd next turned his attention to Abu'l-Qāsim

1 Gardīzī, p. 60; and Baihaqī, p. 805. Why Maḥmūd was so pleased at this apparently unsatisfactory peace is not explained.

2 'Utbī, pp. 126–7; and Baihaqī, p. 805.

3 *Tajārib*, iii, 342–3, from the Sulṭān's letter to the Caliph.

4 Reynolds, p. 362, calls Arslān Jādhib "a well-known and celebrated man of Multan", and has been followed by Raverty, *Ṭab. Nāṣ.* p. 321, note 7!

5 'Utbī, p. 131.

Sīmjūrī, who had managed to strengthen himself in Kūhistān, and ordered Arslān Jādhib to proceed against him. Abu'l-Qāsim was defeated and forced to fly to Ṭabas.[1]

Maḥmūd now became the master of Khurāsān. He appointed his brother Naṣr to the command of the troops of this province and returned to Balkh to watch the course of events at Bukhārā. He sent a report of his victory over 'Abdu'l-Malik to the Caliph al-Qādir Bi'llāh who granted to him the patent of the sovereignty of the territories which he had conquered and bestowed upon him the title of *Yamīnu'd-Dawlah wa Amīnu'l-Millah* in Dhu'l-Ḥajja 389[2] (November 999).

In the meantime Amīr 'Abdu'l-Malik was making great preparations for a struggle with Maḥmūd for the possession of Khurāsān, but the death in Sha'bān 389[3] (July–August 999) of Fā'iq, the most skilful of his generals, forced him to suspend his activities. A little later, on Monday, 10th Dhu'l-Qa'da[4] (23rd October, 999), Īlak Khān took Bukhārā, captured 'Abdu'l-Malik, together with all the scions of the royal family, and put an end to the Sāmānid Dynasty.

But a son of Amīr Nūḥ, named Abū Ibrāhīm Ismā'īl al-Muntaṣir, escaped from the custody of Īlak Khān and made spasmodic efforts to regain the kingdom of his ancestors. He crossed over to Khwārizm and was joined by the nobles who were still loyal to the Sāmānid cause. After an abortive attempt on Bukhārā, he advanced to Nīshāpūr, defeated Naṣr on 28th Rabī' i, 391 (25th February, 1001) and forced him to fall back on Herāt.[5] Maḥmūd however soon arrived with

1 'Utbī, p. 131.
2 *Ibid.* pp. 133–4; and Gardīzī, pp. 62–3.
3 'Utbī, p. 134; and Baihaqī, p. 806.
4 Gardīzī, p. 61.
5 'Utbī, p. 137; and Gardīzī, p. 63. Gardīzī adds that after this battle "Hindū-bacha'ī", i.e. a Hindū boy, fell prisoner into the hands of Muntaṣir.

reinforcements and Muntaṣir fled to Jurjān, but he returned to Khurāsān in Shawwāl 391 (September 1001), and, at his approach, Naṣr again evacuated Nīshāpūr and sent for reinforcements. Maḥmūd despatched Abū Sa'īd Altūntāsh to his assistance. Thus strengthened, Naṣr marched to Nīshāpūr, defeated Muntaṣir and forced him to fly to Jurjān, but within a short time Muntaṣir returned and took Sarakhs. Naṣr defeated him in the vicinity of Sarakhs, captured many of his officers including Abu'l-Qāsim Sīmjūrī, and sent them as prisoners to Ghazna.[1]

Muntaṣir again crossed over to Transoxiana to try his luck there, but, being unable to gain a footing he returned to Marv, the governor of which, however, drove him to Abīward, on the edge of the Ghuzz desert. Harassed on all sides and tired of the uniform failure that had attended his attempts, Muntaṣir appealed for help to Maḥmūd, who ordered the governor of Herāt to join forces with him; but, without waiting for reinforcements, Muntaṣir again advanced to Bukhārā. After an unsuccessful struggle with Īlak Khān in Sha'bān 394 (June 1004), he returned to Khurāsān and marched across the desert to Pul-i-Zāghūl.[2]

Disgusted with the disturbance which the activities of Muntaṣir were causing to the peace of his newly acquired territories and growing apprehensive of his designs on Khurāsān, Sulṭān Maḥmūd sent a large force against him under Farīghūn b. Muḥammad. Muntaṣir fled to Jurjān, followed by Naṣr, Arslān Jādhib and Ṭughānjuq, governor of Sarakhs. Failing to get any support in Jurjān, Muntaṣir returned to Nasā and after another unsuccessful attempt on Bukhārā, took refuge in the Ghuzz desert, in the camp of Ibn Buhaij, chief

1 'Utbī, p. 141.

2 *Ibid.* p. 146. Yāqūt, ii, 907, says that Zāghūl was the name of a town in the district of Marv-Rūd. Pul-i-Zāghūl, or the Bridge of Zāghūl, was probably situated somewhere near it.

of a settlement of the Arabs in that desert. Ibn Buhaij treacherously murdered him in Rabī' i 395[1] (December 1004), at the instigation of Abū 'Abdu'llāh Māh-Rūy Bundār who was the 'Āmil of that region. Thus ended the stormy career of the last of the Sāmānids, who had shown a fortitude and tenacity of purpose deserving of a better fate.

When Maḥmūd heard the news of the assassination of the unfortunate prince, he ordered both Abū 'Abdu'llāh and Ibn Buhaij to be put to death, and the camp of the Arabs to be plundered and destroyed, as a punishment for the crime.[2]

B. Sulṭān Maḥmūd *and the* Khāns *of* Turkistān

It has already been stated that shortly after Maḥmūd had conquered Khurāsān, Īlak Khān took Bukhārā and put an end to the Sāmānid Dynasty.[3] The two sovereigns exchanged friendly messages and agreed to maintain the river Oxus as their boundary line. To strengthen their friendly relations, Maḥmūd solicited and obtained the daughter of Īlak Khān in marriage.[4] In Muḥarram

1 'Utbī, p. 148; but according to Gardīzī, p. 65, Rabī' ii.

2 For further details see 'Utbī, pp. 135–48; and Gardīzī, pp. 63–5.

3 See *supra*, p. 45. These Khāns are called Afrāsiyābī Turks by Muslim historians and Qarā-Khānids by modern writers. Very little is known about their early history and even the tribe to which they belonged is not definitely known. 'Utbī, Gardīzī and Baihaqī have ignored them almost completely, except for some scattered references. The account of them in Ibnu'l-Athīr too is very confused. Among the few modern scholars who have attempted to construct their history, Sir H. H. Howorth (*JRAS.* 1898, pp. 467–502), and Major Raverty (*Ṭab. Nāṣ.* pp. 900–6) have made numerous misstatements. See also Bretschneider, *Medieval Researches*, i, 251–63; *Ta'rīkh-i-Rashīdī*, pp. 286–8, and 361–3; and Zambaur, pp. 206–7. Barthold, pp. 278–86, gives a scholarly discussion of some disputed points about the history of these Khāns.

4 She was probably the one called Mahd-i-Chigal in some stories.

390[1] (December 999) he sent Abu'ṭ-Ṭayyib Sahl b. Muḥammad b. Sulaimān aṣ-Ṣu'lūkī, chief doctor of the Shāfi'ites, and Ṭughānjuq,[2] governor of Sarakhs, as his representatives to Ūzgand where the nuptials were celebrated with great splendour. The bride was brought to Khurāsān about the middle of the same year.[3]

WAR WITH ĪLAK KHĀN

These cordial relations however soon came to an end. Īlak Khān coveted the province of Khurāsān and was waiting for an opportunity to conquer it.[4] When Sulṭān Maḥmūd went on his expedition to Multān in 396 (1005–6), Īlak Khān despatched two divisions of his army, one under his brother Chaghartigīn[5] to take Balkh and the other under his kinsman Subāshītigīn to conquer Khurāsān. Chaghartigīn and Subāshītigīn captured Balkh and Herāt respectively,[6] and the whole of Khurāsān passed under the sway of Īlak Khān.

Before his departure to Multān, the Sulṭān, in view of such an attack, had left instructions for his officers, in obedience to which Arslān Jādhib concentrated his forces at Ghazna, while Abu'l-'Abbās Faḍl b. Aḥmad, the wazīr, strengthened all the approaches to the capital and posted strong detachments along the road to Balkh across Panjhīr and Bāmiyān. When Sulṭān Maḥmūd received information of this attack, he left the task of subjugating the outlying parts of Multān to his officers,[7] returned post-haste to Ghazna and with an army con-

1 Jamāl al-Qarashī (Barthold, *Texts*), f. 39 a.

2 'Utbī, p. 192. On coin No. 518 d, described in *Additions to the Oriental Collection of Coins in the British Museum* by Lane-Poole, ii, 218, his name is given Tughānchūq.

3 'Utbī, pp. 192–3.

4 'Awfī, f. 357 b.

5 'Utbī says Ja'fartigīn.

6 Baihaqī, p. 688, says that the Bāzār-i-'Āshiqān or the Lovers' Market, which had been constructed at the special order of Sulṭān Maḥmūd, was burnt to the ground at this time.

7 Ibnu'l-Athīr, ix, 133, and 'Unṣurī, p. 80, say that Maḥmūd came to Ghazna without making a halt on the way.

siderably increased by the contingents furnished by the Khaljīs, marched across the Hindū Kush mountains to Balkh.[1] Chaghartigīn evacuated the town and fled to Tirmidh. Sulṭān Maḥmūd ordered Arslān Jādhib, with 10,000 soldiers, to proceed against Subāshītigīn, who took to flight on his approach. Arslān followed in pursuit. Subāshītigīn fled to Bukhārā but finding his way blocked by floods in the river Murghāb, he turned towards Marv and then wheeled round to Sarakhs (as the Ghuzz desert that stretched between him and Bukhārā was impassable owing to excessive heat),[2] defeated Muḥassin b. Ṭāriq, chief of the Ghuzz tribe, who had attempted to block his passage, and escaped to Jurjān, probably with a view to seek the assistance of Qābūs. But being disappointed, he returned to Nasā and, leaving all his heavy baggage there, set out for Marv across the desert. The Sulṭān despatched Abū 'Abdu'llāh Muḥammad b. Ibrāhīm aṭ-Ṭā'ī, commander of the Arabs, who surrounded Subāshītigīn in the desert, inflicted a crushing defeat on him and captured his brother with 700 soldiers. Subāshītigīn escaped and crossed over to Bukhārā.[3]

In the meantime Īlak Khān had despatched Chaghartigīn with 12,000 soldiers to create a diversion in favour of the hard-pressed Subāshītigīn by attacking Balkh, which the Sulṭān allowed him to occupy. When Subāshītigīn was finally crushed and forced to leave Khurāsān, the Sulṭān turned his attention to Balkh. Chaghartigīn evacuated it on his approach and fled to Bukhārā. Thus about the beginning of the year 397 (September–October 1006) Khurāsān was cleared of the enemy.[4]

1 It was probably at this time that Anandpāl of the Hindūshāhiyya Dynasty offered his services to Maḥmūd. See al-Bīrūnī, ii, 13.

2 'Utbī, p. 215. It shows that this event took place about the end of 396 (July–August 1006).

3 *Ibid.* p. 216; and Gardīzī, p. 68.

4 'Utbī, pp. 216–17. See also *Majma'u'l-Ansāb*, f. 232 a.

But Īlak Khān did not relinquish his ambition to conquer Khurāsān, and made great preparations for another struggle. He prevailed on his kinsman Qadir Khān,[1] ruler of Kāshghar, to come to his assistance, and with an imposing army numbering 50,000 warriors,[2] he again crossed the Oxus. The Sulṭān advanced to meet him, at the head of an army consisting of Khaljīs, Afghāns, Kurds, Ghuzz Turkomāns and Indians, encamped on the plain of Katar,[3] about twelve miles from Balkh and disposed his army in battle array. He posted Altūntāsh on the right wing, Arslān Jādhib on the left, Naṣr, Abū Naṣr Farīghūnī, ruler of Jūzjānān and Abū 'Abdu'llāh Muḥammad aṭ-Ṭā'ī in the centre, and strengthened his front by a line of 500 elephants. Īlak Khān's right wing was commanded by Qadir Khān, the left by Chaghartigīn, while he himself occupied the centre. The two armies met on 22nd Rabī' ii,

1 His name has been differently written as Qadr Khān by 'Utbī, Yūsuf Qadr Khān by Gardīzī, Quṭūr Khān in *Jāmi'u't-Tawārīkh*, and Qaidū Khān in *Guzīda*. His real name however was Yūsuf Qadir Khān (یوسف قدِر خان). Qadir was a Turkish adjective meaning "most despotic among kings", and distinct from Qadr, the Arabic substantive. Farrukhī, f. 22 b, confirms this in the following lines:

بجاه و منزلت و قدر تا جهان بوده است
ندید خان چو قدر خان زمین ترکستان
بهر شمار قدر خان ازو فزون‌تر بود
درین سخن نه همانا که کس بود بگمان

Qadir, and not Qadr, fits in the metre of these lines. See also *Dīwān Lughātu't-Turk*, i, 304, and Barthold, p. 273, note 5.

2 'Utbī, p. 217; but Gardīzī limits their number to 40,000.

3 Gardīzī, p. 69. Farrukhī often mentions Katar in reference to this battle. For example, he says on f. 168 a:

آنچه او کرد بترکستان با لشکر خان
شاه کرد است بدان لشکر در دشت کتر

398¹ (5th January, 1008). Ilak K͟hān fought bravely.
With a small body of 500 slaves he delivered such a
furious charge on the centre that the warriors of
Maḥmūd began to waver, and another attack would
have ended in a complete rout. At this critical moment,
Sulṭān Maḥmūd revived the courage of his soldiers by
seeking divine assistance. Leaving the field of battle,
he climbed a hillock, prostrated himself on the ground
in fervent prayer to the "God of Victories" and rose
with a confidence which inspired his soldiers. Their
drooping spirits thus raised, the Sulṭān led a counter-
attack on the centre of Ilak K͟hān and rushed into the
thick of the battle. His personal intrepidity was soon
rewarded. Imitating his example, the commanders of
other divisions made repeated impetuous charges on
the enemy, and the execution wrought in their ranks
by the Sulṭān's elephants completed their demoralisa-
tion. One of the elephants, lifting Ilak K͟hān's standard-
bearer in his trunk, hurled him into the air and then
catching him on his steel-clad tusks, cut the wretch in
two, while others threw down riders from their horses
and trampled them to death. The huge army of the
K͟hān was seized with consternation and fled. Many
were captured and thousands perished in their attempt
to cross the Oxus. Immense booty fell into the hands
of the victors. In spite of the severe winter, the Sulṭān
followed the fugitives,² but about this time, news
arrived of the rebellion of Sukhpāl at Multān and he
hurried back to G͟hazna.³

1 Gardīzī, p. 69, and 'Awfī, f. 357 b; but in 'Utbī, p. 219,
Ibnu'l-Athīr, ix, 135, *Majma'u'l-Ansāb*, f. 232 b, it is placed in A.H.
397. In *Alfī*, f. 373 a, the battle is said to have taken place towards
the close of 397 (August 1007), i.e. in summer, and a few lines
below is mentioned the story of the Sulṭān's pursuit of the fugitive
K͟hān in severe winter, and the anecdote of the jester Walc͟hak.

2 Firis͟hta, pp. 25–6 (probably on the authority of Baihaqī's
Ta'rīk͟h-i-Yamīnī), relates the story of the severe winter and the
retort of the court-jester Walc͟hak which persuaded the Sulṭān
to give up the pursuit. 3 'Utbī, p. 223.

Īlak Khān now retired to his country and made great efforts to retrieve his reputation. He entered into a secret alliance with the ruler of Quṣdār[1] and tried to induce his brother Aḥmad Ṭughān Khān and Qadir Khān to make common cause with him in a final struggle with Sulṭān Maḥmūd. Īlak Khān probably intended to attack Khurāsān simultaneously with the rebellion of the ruler of Quṣdār[2] but his plan failed. Qadir Khān rejected the proposal and Ṭughān Khān not only refused to join but also sent an ambassador to Sulṭān Maḥmūd to cultivate friendly relations with him.[3] Īlak grew so furious at this that in 401 (1010), he invaded the country of his brother. He had not, however, proceeded far beyond Ūzgand when he was forced to return by a heavy fall of snow. He started again in the following spring (March 1011) but probably the brothers came to an understanding, as about this time they referred their dispute for arbitration to Sulṭān Maḥmūd, who is stated to have brought about a reconciliation between them.[4]

Relations with Qadir Khān

Īlak Khān died in 403[5] (1012–13) and was succeeded by his brother Aḥmad Ṭughān Khān, who maintained

1 Ibnu'l-Athīr, ix, 159. Probably Shāh Muḥammad, the younger Shār of Gharshistān, was also in secret alliance with Īlak Khān. See 'Utbī, p. 255.

2 See *infra*, p. 74.

3 'Utbī, p. 226, says that in the beginning of 400 (August 1009) an ambassador arrived in Ghazna from Ṭughān Khān.

4 *Ibid.* pp. 248–50; and Ibnu'l-Athīr, ix, p. 156.

5 'Utbī, p. 291. Sir H. H. Howorth, *JRAS.* 1898, p. 480, on the authority of Sachau's *Geschichte von Khwarezm*, ii, 12–14, says that Īlak Khān lived up to 407 (1016–17), because Baihaqī, p. 844, refers to an Īlak Khān as the ruler of some territories in Transoxiana in that year. But Īlak was a title and not a name. Baihaqī, p. 631, makes Sulṭān Mas'ūd, in the year 426 (1035), address the ambassador of 'Alītigīn's son thus: "How is our brother Īlak?", meaning by "Īlak" the son of 'Alītigīn.

friendly relations with Sulṭān Maḥmūd. On his death in 408[1] (1017–18) his kingdom passed to his brother Abū Manṣūr Arslān Khān, known as *al-Aṣamm*, the Deaf. He gave one of his daughters to Mas'ūd, son of Sulṭān Maḥmūd.[2] Arslān died probably in 414[3] (1023) and two of his kinsmen, namely Qadir Khān, ruler of Kāshghar and Ṭughān Khān, a brother of 'Alītigīn of Bukhārā,[4] fought for the possession of his kingdom. Ṭughān Khān was victorious and took possession of Balāsāghūn,[5] the capital of the late Arslān Khān.[6]

Hearing of this struggle, Maḥmūd came to Balkh about the middle of 415[7] (September 1024) to watch the course of events in Transoxiana. When he received news of the success of Ṭughān Khān, he became apprehensive of the growing power of the brothers, 'Alītigīn and Ṭughān Khān who, with Bukhārā and Balāsāghūn in their hands, might menace the security of Khurāsān. He therefore took steps to crush them before their power was consolidated. A pretext for invasion was not wanting. The people of Transoxiana, it is stated, brought to Maḥmūd complaints of the

1 Ibnu'l-Athīr, ix, p. 210.

2 'Utbī, pp. 293–4. The account of Ibnu'l-Athīr, ix, 210–11, is very confused and unintelligible. He says that Qadir Khān and Arslān Khān invaded Khurāsān in 410 (1019–20), but were defeated by the Sulṭān near Balkh. Maḥmūd, however, was busy in A.H. 410 in India, see *infra*, p. 111. Cf. also Barthold, p. 280.

3 Baihaqī, p. 655, says that the Khānate of Turkistān was in dispute before the departure of Maḥmūd to Somnāth, i.e. about A.H. 414, which is the probable date of the death of Arslān Khān.

4 It is stated in *Majma'u'l-Ansāb*, f. 236 b, that 'Alītigīn was "the son of the brother of the father of Qadir Khān," that is, nephew of Bughrā Khān. See Barthold, pp. 280–2, 284–5.

5 It was situated on or near the head-waters of the Karāgaty branch of the river Chū in Moghalistān, N.E. of Aulie-ata, in Lat. 43° 0' N., Long. 73° 40' E. See *Ta'rīkh-i-Rashīdī*, p. 361, note, and Barthold, p. 514.

6 There are numerous vague references to these events in 'Utbī, pp. 247–50, 291–4; and Baihaqī, pp. 98, 348, 417–18, 655.

7 Gardīzī, p. 81.

highhandedness of 'Alītigīn, and Sulṭān Maḥmūd resolved to cross the Oxus, ostensibly to punish 'Alītigīn for his alleged oppression.[1]

Sulṭān Maḥmūd had made all the necessary preparations for the occasion beforehand, and he acted swiftly. The river Oxus was spanned with a bridge of boats[2] and the whole army crossed over to the other side before 'Alītigīn was aware of it. The Sulṭān then advanced on Samarqand where 'Alītigīn had taken up his position. On his way the Sulṭān received the allegiance of several petty chieftains and was joined by Altūntāsh, the Khwārizmshāh, who brought large reinforcements. Sulṭān Maḥmūd encamped near Samarqand, disposed his army in battle array and strengthened his front by a line of 500 elephants. 'Alītigīn evacuated Samarqand without giving battle and retreated to the steppes. The Sulṭān despatched the chamberlain Bilkātigīn in pursuit. 'Alītigīn himself escaped, but his wife and children, while they were on their way to join him, fell into the hands of Bilkātigīn and were brought to Samarqand. The Sulṭān treated them with the respect and consideration due to their position.[3]

Shortly after this, Qadir Khān of Kāshghar came

1 Gardīzī, p. 81. It is, however, mentioned in *Rawḍah*, p. 777, that by arrogating to himself the dignity of the Grand Khān, 'Alītigīn had offended Qadir Khān, who induced Sulṭān Maḥmūd to invade Transoxiana by pointing out to him that 'Alītigīn might become a danger to Khurāsān if he were allowed to gather power. The Sulṭān therefore went to Samarqand where Qadir Khān came to meet him. Ibnu'l-Athīr is very confused at this point.

2 Gardīzī, p. 81, gives the process of the construction of the bridge, thus: The boats were wrapped in huge filaments of date-palm trees which had been brought on camels from Sīstān. These filaments were held in position by iron chains covered with cow-hide. The inside of the boats was stuffed with straw to enable the army to pass over them. According to Farrukhī, f. 22 b, the bridge was completed in one week.

3 Gardīzī, pp. 84–5; and Farrukhī, f. 22 b. Firishta, p. 32, incorrectly says that 'Alītigīn himself was captured and sent as a prisoner to a fort in India.

to Samarqand to make an alliance of friendship with Sulṭān Maḥmūd. The two sovereigns met on Thursday, 27th Ṣafar, 416[1] (29th April, 1025), and the occasion was marked by great splendour and magnificence.[2] To strengthen the bond of friendship a matrimonial alliance was made, according to which Sulṭān Maḥmūd betrothed his daughter Zainab to Yaghāntigīn[3] (afterwards known as Bughrā Khān), son of Qadir Khān, and Qadir Khān gave one of his daughters to prince Muḥammad.[4] The Sulṭān now returned to Ghazna leaving Samarqand in the hands of Qadir Khān, but shortly after his departure, 'Alītigīn came out of his retreat, defeated Qadir Khān and took possession of Samarqand. Qadir Khān sent Yaghāntigīn to seek the assistance of Sulṭān Maḥmūd but he had to return disappointed as, in the meantime, the Sulṭān had made up his mind to lead an expedition to Somnāth.[5]

On his return from Somnāth in 417 (1026), the Sulṭān sent Abū Bakr Ḥaṣīrī with a large force to the assistance of Qadir Khān who defeated 'Alītigīn and forced him to come to terms.[6]

Qadir Khān maintained friendly relations with Sulṭān Maḥmūd. He died in 423[7] (1032).

1 This date is given by al-Bīrūnī in his unique and hitherto unknown work named *Ghurratu'z-Zījāt*, f. 2 a. Baihaqī, p. 246, however, says that the meeting took place on Naw Rūz, the Persian New Year's Day, which fell on 5th Muḥarram, 416 (8th March, 1025) according to Baihaqī, pp. 666 and 708.

2 It is said in *Ṭab. Nāṣ.* p. 116, that it was at this time that Qadir Khān requested the Sulṭān to remove "the son of Saljūq" and his followers to Khurāsān.

3 Baihaqī, p. 230; and Barthold, p. 284, note 7.

4 Baihaqī, pp. 230–1. Gardīzī, pp. 83–4, gives a detailed account of the presents that were exchanged and the ceremonies that were observed on this occasion. See also Barthold, p. 283.

5 Baihaqī, pp. 98, 655.

6 *Ibid.* p. 655, and Farrukhī, f. 168 a, make vague references to this event. It is not mentioned in any other work.

7 Baihaqī, p. 525; and Ibnu'l-Athīr, ix, 290. For the details of these events, see Barthold, pp. 279–85.

The fame of Sulṭān Maḥmūd had by this time spread far into the East, and in 417[1] (1026) he received embassies from Qatā Khān,[2] ruler of Qatā,[3] and Īghur Khān,[4] ruler of Qūchū.[5] They made a proposal to enter into a matrimonial alliance with the Sulṭān but he rejected it on the ground that the Khāns were not Muslims.[6]

C. *The* Ma'mūnids *and the Conquest of* Khwārizm *and* Jurjāniyyah

The Ma'mūnids, as the rulers of Jurjāniyyah[7] were called, were the feudatories of the Sāmānids. Nothing is mentioned about them by Muslim historians till 382[8] (992) when Ma'mūn b. Muḥammad b. 'Alī, ruler of Jurjāniyyah, is stated to have assisted Amīr Nūḥ b. Manṣūr, the Sāmānid, during the period of his exile

1 Gardīzī, p. 87.

2 *Ibid.* p. 87, reads Qayā Khan; al-Bīrūnī, *Qānūnu'l-Mas'ūdī*, f. 92 a, has Qatā Khān. Cf. *Jahān Nāmah*, f. 205.

3 Al-Bīrūnī, *op. cit.* f. 92 a, says that Qatā was situated to the north-west of China, and places it in Lat. 29° 40′ N. (which is most probably a mistake for 39° 40′), Long. 113° 40′ E. (modern 88° 5′ E.). According to *Jahān Nāmah*, f. 205 a, Qatā, also called Khiṭā, was the name of a town in Māchīn or Greater China. It was probably the same as modern Kuchā, Lat. 41° 42′ N., Long. 82° 55′ E. See *Serindia*, p. 1238.

4 Gardīzī, p. 87, reads Bughar or Lughar Khān; al-Bīrūnī, *op. cit.* f. 96 b, reads Īghur Khān which probably means "the Khān of the Uigurs". According to 'Awfī (Brit. Mus. Or. 2676), f. 66, Īghur and Qatā were two provinces of China, and Īghur was the name of a tribe of the Ghuzz Turkomāns.

5 Al-Bīrūnī, *op. cit.* f. 96 b, places it in Lat. 42° 0′ N., Long. 111° 20′ E. (modern 85° 45′ E.), and adds that it was also known as حسابحكت. Qūchū was the capital of the Uigur Turks of Turfān, and its ruins are still shown at Karā-Khoja, Lat. 42° 52′ N., Long. 89° 30′ E. See the *Indian Antiquary*, vol. I, pp. 17–19; and Sir Aurel Stein's *Serindia*, p. 473, and *Ruins of Desert Cathay*, ii, 359.

6 Gardīzī, p. 87.

7 Gurgānj of Persian writers, and modern Urganj.

8 'Utbī, p. 77; and Gardīzī, p. 53. Mīrzā Muḥammad, *Chahār Maqāla*, p. 241, incorrectly says 380 (990).

from Bu<u>kh</u>ārā. To punish Abū 'Abdu'llāh, the <u>Kh</u>wār-izm<u>sh</u>āh, for his treachery to Abū 'Alī Sīmjūrī, Ma'mūn attacked him in 385 (995), took him prisoner and annexed the kingdom of <u>Kh</u>wārizm.[1] Ma'mūn was assassinated in 387 (997) and was succeeded by his son Abu'l-Ḥasan 'Alī, who married Kah-Kāljī, a sister of Sulṭān Maḥmūd.[2] Abu'l-Ḥasan died about 399[3] (1008–9) and was succeeded by his brother Abu'l-'Abbās Ma'mūn, a young man of 25 years of age. He married Kah-Kāljī, the widow of his brother,[4] and professed to have great consideration for Sulṭān Maḥmūd, so much so that when the Caliph al-Qādir Bi'llāh bestowed upon him the title of '*Ainu'd-Dawlah wa Zainu'l-Millah*, he did not assume it openly for fear of offending the Sulṭān as it had been received without his intervention.[5]

But these good relations did not last long. The Sulṭān asked Abu'l-'Abbās to read the <u>kh</u>uṭbah in his name and to acknowledge him as his overlord. Abu'l-'Abbās called a council of his officers to consult them in this matter. They unanimously refused to submit to the control of a foreign potentate. When the army got information of this it became mutinous and was pacified only by a lavish distribution of gold among the commanders. This lulled for some time the storm which burst out in full fury a little later. Abu'l-'Abbās dare not offend the army any more, and to secure his position against a possible hostile move of the Sulṭān, he tried to enter into a secret alliance with the <u>Kh</u>āns of Turkistān[6].

When the spies of the Sulṭān reported the news of this secret alliance to him, he marched to Bal<u>kh</u> at the

1 'Utbī, pp. 78, 94–6. 2 Baihaqī, p. 838.
3 See Appendix F.
4 Gardīzī, p. 73; and Baihaqī, p. 838. Raverty, *Ṭab. Nāṣ.* p. 120, note 5, wrongly makes Abu'l-'Abbās son-in-law of Sulṭān Maḥmūd.
5 Baihaqī, p. 838. 6 *Ibid.* pp. 840–6.

head of a huge army of 100,000 horse and 500 elephants[1] and threatened Khwārizm. The Khāns of Turkistān intervened and persuaded the Sulṭān to withdraw his forces, which he promised to do if the Khwārizmshāh recognised him as his suzerain. Abu'l-'Abbās was now constrained to comply with this demand and ordered the *khuṭbah* to be read in the name of the Sulṭān in the districts of Nasā and Farāwah. This satisfied the Sulṭān, and he returned to Ghazna.[2]

The army, particularly that stationed at Hazārasp under the command of Alptigīn of Bukhārā,[3] regarded Abu'l-'Abbās's submission to the Sulṭān as a deliberate insult to the honour of their country. They advanced on the capital and began by a series of murders which culminated in the assassination of Abu'l-'Abbās Ma'mūn on 15th Shawwāl, 407[4] (17th March, 1017). After this they raised one of his sons,[5] who was only seventeen years of age, to the throne. Alptigīn, the leader of the regicides, acted as a dictator and terrorised Khwārizm for a period of four months.

When Sulṭān Maḥmūd heard the news of the tragic end of his brother-in-law and vassal, he resolved to attack Khwārizm in order to punish the regicides.[6] But before giving out his plans, he arranged for the safe return of his sister, the widow of Abu'l-'Abbās, and, by diplomacy and tact, secured the neutrality of the Khāns of Turkistān.[7] After this he marched to Balkh at the head

1 Baihaqī, p. 846.

2 *Ibid.* p. 846.

3 Baihaqī, Gardīzī, and Ibnu'l-Athīr, but 'Utbī reads Niyālastigīn, or, in some copies, Niyāltigīn.

4 Baihaqī, p. 848, and Gardīzī, p. 73.

5 'Utbī, p. 301; but Baihaqī, p. 848, says that one of his nephews named Abu'l-Ḥārith Muḥammad b. 'Alī b. Ma'mūn, was raised to the throne.

6 *Āthāru'l-Wuzarā*, ff. 95 b–101 b, in which a long passage is cited from the lost *Maqāmāt-i-Abū Naṣr-i-Mushkānī*. See also *infra*, p. 128, for the proceedings of a council which the Sulṭān called on this occasion.

7 Baihaqī, pp. 849–50.

of a large army. The regicides now made overtures of peace but the Sulṭān proposed such stringent terms that they refused to accept them. Accordingly they made preparations for defence and collected an army of 50,000 warriors.[1]

The Sulṭān marched from Balkh to Tirmidh where he embarked his army in boats, sailed down the Oxus to Khwārizm and advanced on Jurjāniyyah or Gurgānj, the capital. The first action with the enemy was disastrous. The advance-guard of the Sulṭān under Abū 'Abdu'llāh Muḥammad aṭ-Ṭā'ī, which was encamped on the outskirts of a desert, was surprised by Khumār Tāsh and put to rout, while the soldiers were engaged in their morning prayer. The disgrace of this defeat was, however, wiped out by the Sulṭān's body-guard who followed Khumār Tāsh and defeated and captured him.[2] The next day, Alptigīn himself advanced at the head of a strong army to check the advance of the Sulṭān. The two armies met on 5th Ṣafar, 408[3] (3rd July, 1017), and a desperate battle followed. The Khwārizmians put up a strong fight but they were utterly defeated and dispersed. No further resistance was offered, and the Sulṭān entered Jurjāniyyah in triumph.[4]

The young Amīr and many scions of the Ma'mūnid family were placed in custody,[5] and a terrible vengeance was taken for the assassination of Abu'l-'Abbās. Alptigīn and many other regicides were captured, and lashed, dismembered, gibbeted or trampled to death by ele-

1 Baihaqī, p. 850; Gardīzī, p. 73; and *Āthāru'l-Wuzarā*, ff. 95 b–101 b.

2 Baihaqī, p. 850; Gardīzī, p. 73; and *Āthāru'l-Wuzarā*, f. 100 a.

3 Gardīzī, p. 74.

4 'Utbī, pp. 301–2; Baihaqī, pp. 850–1; and *Āthāru'l-Wuzarā*, f. 100 b.

5 Farrukhī, f. 35 a, says that they were sent to the forts of Ūk, Ṭāq and Sipahbud (or Iṣpahbud) in Sīstān.

phants. Their corpses, after being paraded in the streets, were hanged on gibbets close to the tomb of their victim, the late Amīr.[1]

The Sulṭān now appointed Altūntāsh to the chief command of Khwārizm and Jurjāniyyah, with the title of *Khwārizmshāh* and, leaving Arslān Jādhib to help him in reducing the country to order and submission, he returned to Ghazna. Shortly after his departure, Abū Isḥāq, father-in-law of the late Abu'l-'Abbās, collected an army and tried to free Khwārizm from foreign domination but he was defeated and forced to flee. Arslān Jādhib and Altūntāsh then crushed all spirit of resistance among the people by savage punishments and indiscriminate massacres, and Khwārizm henceforth became a peaceful part of the empire of Sulṭān Maḥmūd.[2]

D. *Conquest of* Gharshistān

When Sulṭān Maḥmūd conquered Khurāsān from the Sāmānid 'Abdu'l-Malik at Marv in Jumādī i 389 (May 999), he sent Abū Naṣr Muḥammad al-'Utbī, the author of *Kitābu'l-Yamīnī*, on a diplomatic mission to Gharshistān,[3] calling upon its ruler Abū Naṣr Muḥammad b. Asad ash-Shār[4] to recognise him as his

1 'Utbī, p. 303; Baihaqī, pp. 851–2; and Gardīzī, p. 74.

2 Baihaqī, pp. 852–3.

3 Also called Gharjistān and Gharj-ash-Shār. *Gharj* meant "mountain" in the local dialect, and *Shār* was the title of the rulers of Gharshistān, so that the full name meant "The Mountains of the Shārs". It lay to the east of the modern district of Bādghīs, at the head of the upper Murghāb. See Le Strange, p. 415. Some scholars, like D'Herbelot (Muqaddasī, transl. by G. S. A. Ranking, p. 41, note) and Raverty (*Ṭab. Nāṣ.* Index, p. 189) have confused it with Gurjistān or modern Georgia, in the Caucasus.

4 The word *Shār*, according to 'Utbī, p. 251, meant "the Powerful Lord". According to the *Ency. of Islam*, i, 643, it is derived from the old Persian word khshathriya. The first Shār mentioned in Muslim histories was Abū Naṣr Muḥammad b.

overlord. The S̲h̲ār consented and read the <u>k̲h̲uṭbah</u> in the name of Maḥmūd in place of the Sāmānid Amīr 'Abdu'l-Malik.[1]

Some time after this, the younger S̲h̲ār named S̲h̲āh Muḥammad b. Abū Naṣr Muḥammad, offended the Sulṭān by refusing to accompany him on an expedition, and by behaving arrogantly when called upon to explain this action.[2] The Sulṭān ordered Altūntās̲h̲, Arslān Jād̲h̲ib and Abu'l-Ḥasan al-Manī'ī, governor of Marv-Rūd, to attack G̲h̲ars̲h̲istān.[3] In spite of the difficulties of the way they penetrated to Afs̲h̲īn, the capital.[4] Abū Naṣr Muḥammad, the elder S̲h̲ār, submitted but his son S̲h̲āh Muḥammad offered resistance and took refuge in an almost inaccessible hill-fort. The invaders followed him thither, laid siege to the fort and with battering rams made a breach in the outer walls. The garrison defended the inner fortifications with heroism but they were ultimately overpowered and forced to surrender. S̲h̲āh Muḥammad, the younger S̲h̲ār, with many of his officers, was taken prisoner and

---

Asad. He was a man of literary tastes, and when his son S̲h̲āh Muḥammad grew up to manhood, he abdicated in his favour and betook himself to study. When Abū 'Alī Sīmjūrī rebelled against Amīr Nūḥ, he tried to persuade the S̲h̲ārs to acknowledge him as their overlord. On their refusal, he invaded their territory, and drove them to a remote part of the country. When Abū 'Alī was constrained to flee from K̲h̲urāsān after his defeat by Subuktigīn, the S̲h̲ārs returned to their capital. For further details of their history, see 'Utbī, pp. 251–9.

Major Raverty, Ṭab. Nāṣ. p. 341, has committed numerous blunders in a short note on their history.

1 'Utbī, p. 254.

2 From his attitude towards the Sulṭān, it appears that the younger S̲h̲ār was probably in secret alliance with Īlak K̲h̲ān who, about the year 400 (1009–10), intended to make another attempt to conquer K̲h̲urāsān.

3 About the beginning of the year 403 (July–August 1012).

4 Afs̲h̲īn was situated on the eastern bank of the upper Murg̲h̲āb, about fifty miles above Marv-Rūd. See Le Strange, p. 416.

sent to Mastang[1] where he died a few years later.[2] His wazīr was forced under pain of the rack to disgorge the treasures which he was suspected of having concealed. The kingdom of Gharshistān was annexed in 403[3] (1012) and was placed under the command of Abu'l-Ḥasan al-Manī'ī, governor of Marv-Rūd.[4]

Abū Naṣr Muḥammad, the elder Shār, was taken to Ghazna where he was treated with great respect and was assigned a place of honour at the court. The Sulṭān paid him the value of his private territorial property in Gharshistān which had been seized at the time of the conquest. Aḥmad b. Ḥasan al-Maimandī, the wazīr of the Sulṭān, had great respect for him and did all in his power to mitigate the degradation of his fall. He died in 406[5] (1015–16).

E. Sulṭān Maḥmūd *and the* Seljukids

A section of the Ghuzz tribe[6] separated from their fellow-tribesmen and, under their chief named Seljuk, son of Duqāq,[7] migrated to Muslim territory in Transoxiana in the latter half of the fourth century A.H.[8]

1 Gardīzī, p. 71. Mastang is in Balūchistān. See Le Strange, p. 347.

2 Ibnu'l-Athīr, ix, 104, says that Shāh Muḥammad died some time before the death of his father which took place in 406 (1015–16).

3 Gardīzī, p. 71.

4 'Utbī, p. 257.

5 *Ibid.* p. 259; and Ibnu'l-Athīr, ix, 104. Abū Naṣr Muḥammad was a man of great learning and profound knowledge of Arabic. Ibnu'l-Athīr, *loc. cit.*, says that he transcribed the Arabic lexicon *Kitābu't-Tahdhīb* of Muḥammad b. Aḥmad al-Azharī, and read it with the author himself. His love of learning attracted many scholars to his court. In al-Maqdisī, p. 309, note, Abū Naṣr Muḥammad, is called *al-Faqīh*, i.e. the Jurisconsult, in obvious reference to his great learning.

6 Barthold, p. 257; and *Ency. of Islam*, ii, p. 168.

7 According to Rāwandī, p. 88, his name was Luqmān.

8 Ibnu'l-Athīr, ix, 321; *Guzīda*, p. 437; and Barthold, pp. 254–6.

About 375[1] (985–6) they settled at Nūr in Bukhārā and occasionally helped the Sāmānids in their wars with their neighbours in Turkistān.[2] The political conditions in Transoxiana were favourable for the development of their power. In the beginning of the fifth century A.H., Isrā'īl,[3] son of Seljuk, acquired great influence at Bukhārā which he had helped 'Alītigīn to conquer either from Īlak Khān or his successors.[4]

When Sulṭān Maḥmūd crossed over to Transoxiana, 'Alītigīn and Isrā'īl both fled from Bukhārā. 'Alītigīn managed to escape into the steppes, but Isrā'īl was captured in 416[5] (1025) and sent as a prisoner to the

1 *Guzīda*, p. 434; and Faṣīḥī, f. 301 a.

2 'Utbī, pp. 73, 143, 146.

3 Gardīzī, p. 84; and Rāwandī, p. 89; but Ibnu'l-Athīr, ix, 323, calls him Arslān.

4 Ibnu'l-Athīr, ix, 323. The account of Ibnu'l-Athīr is, however, so vague that the details of these events cannot be ascertained.

For the early history of the Seljukids, see Ibnu'l-Athīr, ix, 266–8 and 321 *et seq.*; *Ṭab. Nāṣ.* pp. 116 *et seq.*; *Guzīda*, pp. 434–5; *Rawḍah*, pp. 775–7; *Ency. of Islam*, articles on "Seldjuks", and "Ghuzz"; Rāwandī, pp. 86–94; and Barthold, pp. 254–7, 297–300 and numerous scattered notices.

5 Gardīzī, p. 84. A different version of these events is given in Ibnu'l-Athīr, ix, 261, 323; Rāwandī, pp. 88–9; *Guzīda*, p. 435; and *Majma'u'l-Ansāb*, ff. 236 b–237 a, thus: It is said that when Sulṭān Maḥmūd came to Transoxiana, Qadir Khān complained to him of the annoyance which the Seljuks were causing and requested him to take them to Khurāsān. The Sulṭān agreed to do so and cultivated friendly relations with Isrā'īl so that he was induced to come to him on a visit. During the course of conversation, Isrā'īl told the Sulṭān the effect that the sending of his arrow and bow would have in collecting an army. This made the Sulṭān so suspicious of his power that he ordered him to be captured when in a state of intoxication, and sent him as a prisoner to Kālanjar where he remained for seven years. He once attempted to escape but was captured and brought back to the fort. On this occasion, he sent word to his followers to make war on Sulṭān Maḥmūd and to conquer his country. When Isrā'īl died his followers, with a view to create trouble, requested the Sulṭān to allow them to settle in Khurāsān.

fort of Kālanjar in the Kashmīr hills.[1] His tribesmen are then said to have approached Sulṭān Maḥmūd with a request to allow them to settle in Khurāsān on the plea that they were oppressed by their generals in Transoxiana. The Sulṭān consented, hoping that they would furnish recruits for his army. Arslān Jādhib, however, fearing that they might menace the peace of Khurāsān, advised the Sulṭān to order a general massacre of them or at least to cut off each man's thumb so that he could no longer draw the bow.[2] Maḥmūd rejected this inhuman and probably impracticable proposal. Consequently four thousand Ghuzz families under their chieftains crossed the Oxus and were allowed to settle on the outskirts of the desert in the provinces of Sarakhs, Farāwah and Abīward,[3] but as a precaution, the Sulṭān forbade them to bear arms of any kind and required them to settle in scattered places.[4]

Sulṭān Maḥmūd, however, soon realised that he had made a mistake in bringing the Seljuks into Khurāsān. They made themselves so obnoxious in the neighbourhood that towards the close of the year 418 (close of 1027) the people of Nasā and Abīward were forced to complain to the Sulṭān of their violence.[5] The Sulṭān despatched Arslān Jādhib, governor of Ṭūs, to

1 This Kālanjar was situated to the north of Jhelum, in the pass leading into Kashmīr. It was therefore different from the fort named Kālinjar in Bundhelkhand. See Baihaqī, pp. 88, 211, 664; and Kalhana, vol. ii, 433, and Bk vii, l. 1256, note. Most of the Muslim historians who mention the fact of Isrā'īl's imprisonment say that Kālanjar was situated near Multān. This wrong indication as to its position has misled Dr M. Iqbāl (Rāwandī, pp. 478–9) in his attempts to locate it. See also *infra*, p. 106 note.

2 Gardīzī, p. 85. Ibnu'l-Athīr, ix, 323, says that Arslān suggested that they should be drowned in the Oxus. See also Baihaqī, p. 597.

3 Gardīzī, p. 85.

4 Ibnu'l-Athīr, ix, 323; and *Ṭab. Nāṣ.* p. 120.

5 Gardīzī, p. 89.

punish them but they were too strong for him, and all his attempts to crush them proved unsuccessful.[1] The Sulṭān severely reprimanded him for his incapacity but, as Arslān stated in excusing himself, the Seljuks had grown so strong that the resources of a provincial governor were not adequate to crush their power.[2]

Consequently Sulṭān Maḥmūd, in spite of his illness, personally moved against the Seljuks in 419 (1028). He marched to Ṭūs and furnished Arslān Jā<u>dh</u>ib with necessary reinforcements to fight the enemy. Arslān was more successful this time and was able to inflict a crushing defeat on the Seljuks at Ribāṭ-i-Farāwah. Thousands of them were captured and put to the sword.[3] Some of the survivors took refuge in Dihistān and the Bal<u>kh</u>ān mountains while others fled to Kirmān, the ruler of which, Qawāmu'd-Dawlah Abu'l-Fawāris b. Bahā'u'd-Dawlah, received them kindly and promised them assistance but as he died in <u>Dh</u>u'l-Qa'da 419[4] (December 1028), they moved on to Iṣfahān. 'Alā'u'd-Dawlah Abū Ja'far b. Kākawaih, the ruler of Iṣfahān, treated them with consideration as they offered to enlist in his army, but they did not enjoy his favour for long. A messenger from Sulṭān Maḥmūd arrived at their heels with instructions for 'Alā'u'd-Dawlah to annihilate the Seljuks. 'Alā'u'd-Dawlah accordingly tried to entrap them by asking their leaders to a dinner, ostensibly to enrol them in the army. On their arrival, however, they got information of 'Alā'u'd-Dawlah's secret design from one of his Turkish slaves and began to leave hurriedly. 'Alā'u'd-Dawlah's men tried to intercept them but they fought their way out, defeated a

1 Gardīzī, p. 89. Rāwandī, p. 93, incorrectly says that the Seljuks kept their peace till the death of Sulṭān Maḥmūd.

2 Gardīzī, p. 89.

3 *Ibid.* p. 90. Ibnu'l-A<u>th</u>īr, ix, 266, makes a passing reference to this battle but places it in A.H. 420.

4 Ibnu'l-A<u>th</u>īr, ix, 259, 266.

detachment of Kurds which was sent after them and fled to Ādharbā'ijān and the Balkhān mountains.[1]

But this did not end the troubles of the Sulṭān. From their mountain fastnesses the Seljuks continued to carry out raids on the adjoining provinces, so that the Sulṭān had again to send after them Arslān Jādhib, who chased them up and down the country for two years. In spite of his weakness and infirmity, the Sulṭān himself joined in the pursuit and followed them from Nīshāpūr to Dihistān and Jurjān, till they were completely swept out of Khurāsān.[2] This triumph was however temporary. Within a decade of the death of the Sulṭān, the Seljuks became the masters of Khurāsān.

1 Gardīzī, p. 90; and Ibnu'l-Athīr, ix, 266, 267, 324.

2 Baihaqī, p. 71; and Ibnu'l-Athīr, ix, 267. Those of the Seljuks who had fled to the Balkhān mountain were permitted by Sulṭān Mas'ūd to return to Khurāsān.

CHAPTER VII

WARS IN ĪRĀN, SĪSTĀN AND ADJOINING LANDS

A. *Conquest of* Sīstān

WALIYYU'D-DAWLAH ABŪ AḤMAD KHALAF B. AḤMAD, a descendant of Ya'qūb the Ṣaffārid and governor of Sīstān, became independent about the middle of the fourth century A.H. at the break-up of the Sāmānid empire.[1] Khalaf was not on good terms with his neighbour Subuktigīn, and had tried on various occasions to induce Īlak Khān to invade Ghazna.[2] In 388 (998) Khalaf sent his son Ṭāhir to occupy the province of Fūshanj which had been left undefended as Bughrājuq, the governor, had been called by Maḥmūd to help him in his struggle with Ismā'īl. When Maḥmūd ascended the throne, he supplied Bughrājuq with the necessary reinforcements to enable him to recover his province. Ṭāhir was defeated and forced to flee, but Bughrājuq, being flushed with victory, drank heavily and, while in a state of intoxication, rode in pursuit of the enemy. Ṭāhir, finding him helplessly drunk, turned back and put him to the sword.[3]

Maḥmūd now resolved to punish Khalaf. In the beginning of 390 (December 999) he marched to Sīstān at the head of a large army. Khalaf retired to the fort of Iṣpahbud. Maḥmūd laid siege to it. Khalaf sued for peace and offered to pay an indemnity of 100,000 *dīnārs*. Maḥmūd accepted these terms and returned to Ghazna.[4]

1 For an account of the early Ṣaffārids, see Appendix G.
2 'Utbī, p. 152.
3 *Ibid.* pp. 154–5. An-Nuwairī, f. 7 b, incorrectly places this event in A.H. 390.
4 'Utbī, pp. 155–6; and Gardīzī, p. 63.

A little later Khalaf quarrelled with his son Ṭāhir, and, after an unsuccessful attempt to defeat him in battle, planned a stratagem to circumvent his ruin. He sent an affectionate message to him, beseeching him to come and take possession of the treasure, as he felt his end to be near. The unsuspecting Ṭāhir came and, while Khalaf was holding him in his embrace, a hundred soldiers who were hidden in the rank growth of vegetation close by, fell upon him, bound him hand and foot and carried him a prisoner to the fort where he was put to death a few days afterwards.[1]

This was too much even for the ferocious nobility of those times, and, in horror and disgust at the foul deed, Ṭāhir b. Yazīd, the commander, and other officers invited Maḥmūd to come and be their ruler.[2] Maḥmūd consequently marched to Sīstān in Muḥarram 393[3] (November 1002). Khalaf retired to an almost impregnable fort named Ṭāq[4] which had seven fortifications and was surrounded by a deep and wide ditch. Maḥmūd laid siege to the fort and ordered the ditch to be filled in. The besiegers then crossed over in the face of a shower of stones and missiles, and attacked the gates of the fort, which crashed down under the furious charge of the elephants. The assailants rushed in to occupy the outer fortifications. The defenders fought bravely and contested every inch of the ground, but when Khalaf saw Maḥmūd's elephants trampling his

1 *Tajārib*, iii, 385–6. 'Utbī, p. 159, however, says that Khalaf had abdicated in favour of Ṭāhir but as Ṭāhir became disobedient to him, he feigned illness and called upon Ṭāhir to come and take charge of the treasure.

2 Sir W. Haig, p. 14, says that Khalaf had rebelled against Maḥmūd. This is not supported by any authority.

3 'Utbī, p. 160; and Gardīzī, p. 66. In *Guzīda*, p. 396, the date is incorrectly given as 374 (984).

4 'Utbī calls this fort *Madīnatu'l-'Adhrā*, i.e. the Virgin Fort, probably because of its supposed impregnability.

men to death, he was so disconcerted that he offered submission, and surrendered the fort.[1]

Khalaf was now brought a prisoner before Maḥmūd. He threw himself at his feet[2] and presented costly pearls and precious stones. Maḥmūd spared his life, allowed him to keep all his wealth and, at his own request, sent him to Jūzjānān.[3] The Sulṭān placed Sīstān in charge of the Ḥājib Qinjī and returned to Ghazna.[4]

A few months after his departure, news was received of a formidable rising against his authority. The Sulṭān marched to Sīstān in Dhu'l-Qa'da 393 (September 1003) at the head of 10,000 warriors and was accompanied by his brother Naṣr, Altūntāsh and Abū 'Abdu'llāh Muḥammad aṭ-Ṭā'ī. The rebels took refuge in the strong fort of Ūk[5] which the Sulṭān invested.

1 'Utbī, pp. 160–2.

2 It is mentioned in *Mujmal*, f. 264 b, and *Guzīda*, p. 396, that, while imploring Maḥmūd for mercy, Khalaf addressed him as Sulṭān. This so pleased Maḥmūd that he spared his life. 'Utbī and Gardīzī, however, do not mention this. In *Siyāsat Nāmah*, p. 44, and Ibnu'l-Athīr, ix, 92, it is said that Maḥmūd was the first to be called Sulṭān, while the author of the *Ṭab. Nāṣ*. p. 75, adds that he was the first ruler who received the title of Sulṭān from the Caliph, but cf. Barthold, p. 271.

3 Sir W. Haig, p. 14, incorrectly says that Khalaf was rewarded with the government of a district.

Khalaf lived at Jūzjānān till 397 (1006–7) when it was found that he was in secret correspondence with Īlak Khān who was then at war with Sulṭān Maḥmūd. He was therefore removed to Gardīz where he died in Rajab 399 (March 1009). The Sulṭān restored all his private property to his son Abū Ḥafṣ.

In spite of his callousness, Khalaf was a man of versatile genius with a well-developed taste in literature and great love for the learned. Bākharzī, f. 80 b, mentions him among the poets. His court was one of the centres of learning to which were attracted the *literati* of the age. He is said to have spent 30,000 *dīnārs* on the compilation of a stupendous commentary on the *Qur'ān* in 100 volumes. See 'Utbī, pp. 163–66; Jurbādhqānī, p. 253; and Ibnu'l-Athīr, ix, 123.

4 'Utbī, p. 168.

5 Gardīzī, p. 67; and Raverty, *Ṭab. Nāṣ*. p. xlv. 'Utbī, and Yāqūt, i, 210, call it Ark.

On Friday, 15th Dhu'l-Ḥajja (15th October, 1003), the rebels made a sortie on the besiegers and after an indecisive action retired to the fort. The Sulṭān ordered an escalade to be attempted under cover of darkness and captured the fortifications before the enemy were aware of it. The garrison were seized with panic and fled for their lives. Many were captured and thousands were put to the sword.

The Sulṭān now placed the province of Sīstān in charge of his brother Naṣr and returned to Ghazna.[1]

B. *Conquest of* Ghūr

The whole stretch of hilly country situated to the east and south-east of Herāt and south of Gharshistān and Jūzjānān, was called Ghūr or Ghūristān.[2] The outlying parts of this region had submitted to Muslim conquerors but the interior had remained independent on account of its inaccessibility.[3] After some unsuccessful attempts, Subuktigīn was able to extend his influence to eastern Ghūr and was recognised as suzerain by Ibn Sūrī,[4] ruler of Mandīsh.[5] After the death of Subuktigīn, Ibn Sūrī adopted a hostile attitude, occasionally withheld the stipulated tribute, waylaid the

1 'Utbī, pp. 168–70; and Gardīzī, p. 67.

2 Le Strange, p. 416. According to Iṣṭakhrī, pp. 272, 281, only the inhabitants of the outlying parts had accepted Islam and the people of the interior were still heathens.

3 Gardīzī, pp. 46–7, and Baihaqī, p. 134, say that about 369 (979–80) Amīr Nūḥ b. Manṣūr, the Sāmānid, sent Abū Ja'far Zubaidī to conquer Ghūr, but he was forced to retire after taking a few forts.

4 *Ṭab. Nāṣ.* pp. 74, 320. 'Utbī calls him Ibn Sūrī, that is, son of Sūrī, but in *Rawḍah* and some other histories he is called Muḥammad b. Sūrī.

5 *Ṭab. Nāṣ.* p. 318, and *infra*, p. 72, note 2. Mandīsh was the name of a fort. Sulṭān Muḥammad was sent there as a prisoner after his deposition. See Baihaqī, p. 11.

caravans and levied blackmail on the subjects of Sulṭān Maḥmūd in the adjacent provinces.[1]

The governors of these provinces carried on a desultory warfare with Ibn Sūrī, but on their approach he always managed to take shelter behind his inaccessible hills. In 401[2] (1011) the Sulṭān personally set out for Ghūr and sent Altūntāsh, governor of Herāt, and Arslān Jādhib, governor of Ṭūs, in command of the advance-guard. The news of this invasion spread rapidly and the people of Ghūr began to pour out of their villages to defend their mountain home. Altūntāsh was defeated, but the Sulṭān soon came to his assistance and scattered the Ghūrīs in a series of well-contested actions. This cleared the way into Ghūr, and the invaders marched on Āhangarān,[3] the capital. Ibn Sūrī, despising the shelter of his fort, entrenched himself in inaccessible hills and ravines and opposed the Sulṭān with an army of 10,000 warriors. The battle raged fiercely till noon. All that valour and military skill could accomplish failed to dislodge the Ghūrīs from their advantageous position. The Sulṭān then had recourse to a ruse. He feigned flight, and the simple mountaineers rushed out of their entrenchments to pursue an apparently defeated enemy. When they reached the plain, the Sulṭān faced about and made a charge on their disorderly ranks. The Ghūrīs fled for their lives, leaving huge booty on the field of battle. Ibn Sūrī, with his son Shīth and many important officers, fell prisoner into the hands of the conquerors.[4]

The Sulṭān now placed Mandīsh under Abū ʻAlī, son

1 ʻUtbī, p. 243; Ibnu'l-Athīr, ix, 155; and *Ṭab. Nāṣ.* p. 320.

2 Probably in June 1011.

3 See Mustawfī, *Nuzhatu'l-Qulūb*, p. 154, for its locality. Raverty, *Ṭab. Nāṣ.* p. 321, note, has confused it with Dih-i-Āhangarān which was the name of a suburb of Ghazna.

4 ʻUtbī, p. 244.

of Ibn Sūrī[1] and sent Ibn Sūrī and S͟hīt͟h as prisoners to G͟hazna. Ibn Sūrī, preferring death to a life of captivity, sucked poison which had been set beneath his signet ring and died on the way at Kīdān.[2]

So far only eastern G͟hūr had been conquered. In 405[3] (1015) the Sulṭān marched to K͟hwābīn, which was most probably the name of the south-western district of G͟hūr,[4] captured some forts and returned to G͟hazna.[5]

A few years later, Sulṭān Maḥmūd sent his son Mas'ūd, governor of Herāt, to subjugate the north-western part of G͟hūr, known as Tab.[6] Mas'ūd left Herāt on 10th Jumādī i, 411 (1st September, 1020) and in about six days reached the frontier of G͟hūr where he was joined by Abu'l-Ḥasan K͟halaf[7] and

1 Abū 'Alī is said to have been friendly to Sulṭān Maḥmūd during the time of his father Ibn Sūrī. He was a good ruler and maintained loyal relations with Sulṭān Maḥmūd. When Ibn Sūrī committed suicide, S͟hīt͟h was sent back to him for custody. Abū 'Alī treated him well. Abū 'Alī was assassinated about 421 (1030) by his nephew 'Abbās, son of S͟hīt͟h. See Ṭab. Nāṣ. pp. 329–30.

2 'Utbī, p. 244; and Ṭab. Nāṣ. p. 321. Kīdān was situated somewhere on the road between Bāmiyān and G͟hazna. I have been able to determine its position roughly by comparing Ṭab. Nāṣ. pp. 342–3, 415 and 431–2 where Kīdān is mentioned several times in different connections. The position of Kīdān on the north-western side of G͟hūr gives an idea of the position of Mandīs͟h.   3 Probably in May 1015.

4 According to Baihaqī, p. 127, K͟hwābīn was situated to the north of Bust and Zamīn Dāwar, and Abu'l-Ḥasan K͟halaf who accompanied Prince Mas'ūd on his expedition against G͟hūr in 411 (1020), was the ruler of some part of G͟hūr. See infra, p. 73, note 1.

5 Baihaqī, p. 127. This expedition is not given by any other authority.

6 Ibid. p. 129. I have not been able to locate this place, as the description of this region in the Muslim geographers is very meagre. It was however near G͟hars͟histān (ibid. p. 133), which fixes its position roughly.

7 Baihaqī, p. 795, says that the territories of Abu'l-Ḥasan lay between Herāt and G͟hazna. He was probably ruler of K͟hwābīn.

Shīrwān,[1] chieftains of the south-western and north-eastern parts of G̲h̲ūr respectively. Thus strengthened, Mas'ūd marched along the right bank of the Harī-rūd, captured the hill-forts of Bartar and Razān[2] and advanced into the interior of Tab. Mas'ūd now sent an ambassador to the ruler of Tab demanding submission, but he returned an insolent reply. He therefore continued his march on Tab, captured many strong forts that offered resistance and appeared before the capital. This frightened the ruler into submission, and he promised to surrender all the forts which he had captured on the side of G̲h̲ars̲h̲istān.[3]

Mas'ūd now proceeded against another fort called Tūr,[4] captured it after a week's hard fighting, placed it in charge of his officers and returned to Herāt. On his way back, at Mārābād,[5] he received the tribute, consisting chiefly of arms,[6] which the rulers of G̲h̲ūr had sent according to the terms of their submission. The whole of G̲h̲ūr, possibly with the exception of the inaccessible interior, was thus brought under the sway of the Sulṭān.[7]

1 Baihaqī, p. 128, says that the territories of Shīrwān adjoined G̲h̲ars̲h̲istān.

2 Baihaqī, p. 129 and 'Unṣurī, p. 82. No geographer mentions the names of these places, probably because they were not situated on any of the important routes.

3 Baihaqī, pp. 128–33. This expedition is not mentioned by any other authority. In the *Ency. of Islam*, ii, 141, this expedition is wrongly stated to have been undertaken against G̲h̲ars̲h̲istān in the year 401 (1010–11).

4 Baihaqī, p. 133. Tūr is perhaps the same place as Gud̲h̲ar or Kudar which is mentioned by 'Unṣurī, p. 82. It is not mentioned by any geographer.

5 Baihaqī, p. 134, says that Mārābād was situated about 10 *farsak̲h̲* or nearly 35 miles from Herāt. See Le Strange, p. 410.

6 G̲h̲ūr was famous for its arms in those times.

7 Baihaqī, pp. 133–4.

C. Sulṭān Maḥmūd *and the Ruler of* Quṣdār

The kingdom of Quṣdār, corresponding roughly to the north-eastern half of modern Balūchistān, was a dependency of Ghazna. In 401 (1010–11) the ruler of Quṣdār adopted a hostile attitude at the instigation of Īlak Khān[1] and withheld the annual tribute. The Sulṭān marched against him in Jumādī i 402[2] (December 1011) and laid siege to Quṣdār. The ruler offered submission and, in addition to the annual tribute, promised to deliver fifteen elephants and to pay an indemnity of 15,000,000 *dirhems*.[3] The Sulṭān accepted these terms, allowed him to retain his kingdom as a feudatory chieftain and returned to Ghazna.[4]

D. *Conquest of the Valleys of the Rivers* Nūr *and* Qīrāt

It was reported to Sulṭān Maḥmūd that the people of "the pleasant valleys"[5] of the rivers Nūr and Qīrāt[6]

1 Ibnu'l-Athīr, ix, 159.

2 *Ibid.* The date of this expedition is not mentioned in the printed editions of 'Utbī, but it is given in al-Manīnī, ii, 132, and some manuscripts of 'Utbī.

3 'Utbī, pp. 250–1, but the amount seems to be greatly exaggerated.

4 *Ibid.* and Ibnu'l-Athīr, ix, 159. This expedition is omitted by Gardīzī.

5 Gardīzī, p. 78, says قیرات جای منزه است which Raverty, *Notes*, p. 135, has incorrectly translated "Qīrāt was a place of sanctity."

6 These were the names of two rivers in modern Kāfiristān to the north of Lamaghān. See al-Bīrūnī, i, 259; Raverty, *Notes*, pp. 108, 135; and Map of the Sulaiman Mountains on the Afghan Frontier of India, in *PRGS*. January 1879. Raverty in *Ṭab. Nāṣ*. p. xlv, has wrongly made these rivers fall into the Kābul river at Darūntha which is much lower down. Firishta, p. 31, wrongly calls these valleys, "Nārdīn and Qīrāt", and has confused this expedition with the one against "Nārdīn" or Nandana. Cunningham, *Ancient Geography*, pp. 338–44, has incorrectly identi-

worshipped the lion.[1] He therefore resolved to conquer these valleys and introduce Islam among their people. In the beginning of 411[2] (May–June 1020) he marched thither and ordered artisans such as stone-hewers, diggers, carpenters and blacksmiths to make a road for the army across the unknown and difficult country. The ruler of the Qīrāt valley offered submission and embraced Islam with a large number of his followers. The Sulṭān treated him with due respect and confirmed him in the government of his kingdom as a feudatory ruler.[3]

The people of the Nūr valley, on the contrary, adopted a defiant attitude and the Sulṭān despatched his chamberlain 'Alī b. Īl-Arslān al-Qarīb[4] against them. 'Alī reduced them to obedience and left a garrison there under 'Alī b. Qadr-i-Rājūq,[5] to keep the country in hand.

The Sulṭān now appointed teachers to instruct the converts in the rudiments of Islam and returned to Ghazna.[6]

fied "Nūr" with Narāyanpūr in Alwar State, and "Qīrāt" with Vairāt or Matsya which was the name of an ancient kingdom and of a town between Delhi and Jaipūr.

1 Gardīzī, p. 78. From Ibn Ḥawqal and other geographers, it appears that Buddhism was the prevailing religion in these regions. The worship of "the Lion" refers most probably to the Sākiya Sinha (Lion), the Buddha.

2 *Ibid.* Firishta, p. 31, wrongly mentions it after A.H. 412.

3 Gardīzī, p. 78.

4 *Ibid.* On the death of Sulṭān Maḥmūd, this 'Alī raised Prince Muḥammad to the throne. See Baihaqī, p. 12. Firishta, p. 31, calls him 'Alī b. Arslān Jādhib.

5 Gardīzī, p. 78. Firishta, p. 31, calls him 'Alī b. Qadr-i-Saljūqī.

6 Gardīzī, pp. 78–9.

E. *Expedition against the* Afghāns

The Afghāns,[1] inhabiting the mountainous region between Ghazna and the Indus, used to carry out plundering raids on the frontier districts of Sulṭān Maḥmūd and blackmail the caravans as they passed between Khurāsān and India.[2] In 409 (1019) they waylaid his troops as they were returning in detachments over the hill-passes from Kanauj. The Sulṭān therefore marched against them about the end of the same year, shortly after his return from Kanauj,[3]

> While his standard was still covered with the dust of the way, like the wild rose,
> And his sword, with the fresh blood on it, was still like the pomegranate blossom.[4]

In order to take them unawares, the Sulṭān gave out that he was going in a different direction but he turned round, surrounded them in their mountain haunts and did terrible execution among them, so that very few are said to have escaped except women and children.[5] The Sulṭān then returned to Ghazna.[6]

1 Col. Malleson, *History of Afghanistan*, p. 66, has confused this expedition with the one against Ghūr. He calls the people against whom this expedition was undertaken, "Ghilzais, inhabitants of Ghor". They were neither "Ghilzais" nor inhabitants of "Ghor" but Afghāns, as stated by 'Utbī, p. 317. See also al-Bīrūnī, i, 208, and *Ṭab. Nāṣ.* p. 74, note 2.

2 Ibnu'l-Athīr, ix, 218; *Guzīda*, p. 399; and *Chahār Maqāla*, p. 18.

3 'Utbī, p. 317; and Ibnu'l-Athīr, ix, 218. Probably in Dhu'l-Ḥajja 409 (April 1019).

4 Farrukhī, f. 2 a, in a *qaṣīda* regarding an expedition which was undertaken shortly after the return from Kanauj.

5 'Utbī, p. 317; and Ibnu'l-Athīr, ix, 218.

6 'Utbī, p. 317. Faṣīḥī, f. 324 a, gives another expedition against the Afghāns in the year 414 (1023–4), but it is not mentioned by any other writer.

F. *Relations of* Sulṭān Maḥmūd *with the* Ziyārids

S̲h̲amsu'l-Ma'ālī Abu'l-Ḥasan Qābūs b. Was̲h̲mgīr b. Ziyār,[1] ruler of Jurjān and Ṭabaristān, who succeeded his brother Bihistūn in Rajab 367 (February 978), was defeated by Mu'ayyidu'd-Dawlah b. Ruknu'd-Dawlah the Buwaihid, at Astarābād in Jumādī i 371 (November 981) and forced to take refuge with Amīr Nūḥ b. Manṣūr the Sāmānid.[2] The Amīr tried many times but was not successful in reinstating him in his kingdom. In 387 (997) Subuktigīn, who had promised to help him to recover his ancestral kingdom and even asked Īlak K̲h̲ān to supply him with reinforcements for this purpose, died before his plans could mature.[3] Maḥmūd now promised to accomplish the wish of his father, but he wanted Qābūs to pay the cost of the expedition within a few months of his being reinstalled in his kingdom. When Qābūs asked for longer time Maḥmūd refused to grant it, as he himself was

1 Mardāwīj b. Ziyār, the founder of this dynasty, was a lieutenant of Asfār b. S̲h̲īrawaih who had captured Raiy from Mākān b. Kākī about 315 (927–8). Mardāwīj put Asfār to death in 316 (928–9) and became master of Qazwīn and Raiy, and shortly after that took Ṭabaristān and Jurjān from Mākān and extended his sway to Iṣfahān, but before his death in 323 (934–5) the provinces of Iṣfahān and Hamadān had become independent under 'Alī b. Buwaih. Mardāwīj was succeeded by his brother Was̲h̲mgīr who recognised the Sāmānids as his overlords. On his death in D̲h̲u'l-Ḥajja 356 (November 967) his son Bihistūn came to the throne. Bihistūn died in Rajab 367 (February 978) and was succeeded by his brother Qābūs. In 369 (979–80) Qābūs offended Mu'ayyidu'd-Dawlah and 'Aḍudu'd-Dawlah by giving shelter to their brother Fak̲h̲ru'd-Dawlah. Consequently Mu'ayyidu'd-Dawlah marched against him, defeated him at Astarābād in Jumādī i 371 (November 981) and forced him to take refuge in K̲h̲urāsān. For further details regarding their early history, see scattered notices in *Tajārib*, vols. i and ii; 'Utbī, pp. 35–9, 170–4, 274–6; Ibn Isfandiyār, pp. 225–36; and *Guzīda*, p. 414.

2 *Tajārib*, iii, 15; and 'Utbī, p. 35.

3 'Utbī, p. 171.

making preparations for a struggle for the throne with his brother. Qābūs was offended, and, for the rest of his life, he cherished hatred against Maḥmūd.[1]

About this time, however, taking advantage of the disturbance caused by the death of Fakhru'd-Dawlah, Qābūs occupied Jurjān in Sha'bān 388[2] (August 998). He then gradually extended his sway over Ṭabaristān and Jibāl. In 402 (1011–2) he was deposed for cruelty by his army, and his son Mīnūchihr was raised to the throne.[3]

Sulṭān Maḥmūd supported the claim of Dārā,[4] another son of Qābūs, who had quarrelled with his father and taken refuge at Ghazna, and sent an army under Arslān Jādhib to place him on the throne, but Mīnūchihr disarmed the hostility of the Sulṭān by recognising him as his overlord and promising to pay an annual tribute of 50,000 *dīnārs*. Shortly after this, Sulṭān Maḥmūd gave one of his daughters to him in marriage.[5]

Mīnūchihr remained loyal to the Sulṭān and, like other feudatory princes, occasionally sent troops to accompany him on his expeditions.[6] In the year 420 (1029) when Sulṭān Maḥmūd went to Jurjān to await the issue of events at Raiy,[7] Mīnūchihr welcomed him in his kingdom and made him a present of 40,000 *dīnārs*. Shortly after this, news arrived that Majdu'd-Dawlah had been taken prisoner, and the Sulṭān left Jurjān and marched to Raiy. The fall of Raiy filled

1 'Utbī, pp. 171–2.

2 *Ibid.* pp. 172–4.

3 *Ibid.* pp. 274–7; Ibnu'l-Athīr, ix, p. 167; and Ibn Isfandiyār, pp. 231–3. Qābūs was put to death in 403 (1012–3), that is, one year after his deposition. *Mujmal*, f. 261 b, and Rabino, *Māzandarān and Astarābād*, p. 141, note 2, incorrectly place the death of Qābūs in 409 (1018–19) and 424 (1033) respectively.

4 For an account of Dārā, see 'Utbī, pp. 282–4, and scattered notices.

5 Baihaqī, pp. 245–6; and 'Utbī, pp. 278–80, 283.

6 'Utbī, p. 278.

7 See *infra*, p. 82.

Mīnūchihr with apprehension that the Sulṭān might next turn his arms against his kingdom. He therefore assumed a hostile attitude, closed the road to Ghazna which passed through his territory, destroyed all the bridges and laid the surrounding country waste. The Sulṭān became furious when he learnt this and resolved to teach Mīnūchihr a lesson before returning to Ghazna. In spite of the difficulty of the way and his growing infirmity, he made straight for Jurjān. This unexpected display of energy so cowed Mīnūchihr that he made profuse apologies for his conduct and secured pardon by paying a fine of 500,000 *dīnārs*.[1] The Sulṭān then returned to Ghazna.

Mīnūchihr died a few months later, about the end of 420[2] (1029).

G. Sulṭān Maḥmūd *and the Rulers of* Mukrān

The kingdom of Mukrān which was originally a dependency of the Buwaihids,[3] comprised the strip of sea-coast from the Gulf of 'Umān to Sind and a part of Kirmān and Balūchistān. When the power of the Buwaihids declined, Ma'dān, ruler of Mukrān,[4] trans-

1 Ibnu'l-Athīr, ix, 262. Farrukhī, f. 37 b, seems to make a vague reference to this.

2 Ibnu'l-Athīr, ix, 278. In Ibn Isfandiyār, p. 235, and *Ḥabību's-Siyar*, vol. ii, pt iv, p. 59, it is incorrectly given as 424 (1033). Ibn Khaldūn, iv, 426, wrongly says that Mīnūchihr died in 426 (1035), and that his son and successor did homage to Sulṭān Maḥmūd who had died in 421 (1030).

The history of the later Ziyārids is very confused. Baihaqī, Ibn Isfandiyār, Ibnu'l-Athīr, an-Nuwairī, Khwānd-Amīr and Ẓahīru'd-Dīn contain scattered references to them. Sir E. Denison Ross (*Asia Major*, ii, 209–13) has tried to throw some light on their history. H. L. Rabino, *Māzandarān and Astarābād*, p. 141, has also given a brief note on the House of Ziyār.

3 *Tajārib*, ii, 299.

4 The capital of Mukrān was named Kīz, near the modern town of Turbat, see Le Strange, p. 333.

ferred his allegiance to Subuktigīn and, after his death, to his son Maḥmūd.[1] In 416 (1025–26), during the absence of the Sulṭān on his expedition to Somnāth, Ma'dān died leaving two sons named 'Īsā and Abu'l-Mu'askar, who struggled for the succession. Abu'l-Mu'askar was defeated and forced to take refuge in Sīstān.[2]

When Sulṭān Maḥmūd returned from Somnāth in 417 (1026), Abu'l-Mu'askar went to Ghazna and was received into favour. 'Īsā now becoming apprehensive that the Sulṭān might help Abu'l-Mu'askar to the throne, recognised Sulṭān Maḥmūd as his overlord and sent a deputation of the notables of Mukrān to explain the cause of his quarrel with his brother Abu'l-Mu'askar. This disarmed the hostility of the Sulṭān, who confirmed 'Īsā in the government of Mukrān and required him to provide for the maintenance of his brother.[3]

In 420 (1029), finding the Sulṭān harassed by the Seljuks, 'Īsā adopted a hostile attitude and declared himself independent. When Sulṭān Maḥmūd got news of this, he resolved to place Abu'l-Mu'askar on the throne, but he died before this design could be put into practice.[4]

H. *Conquest of* Raiy, Hamadān *and* Iṣfahān

Fakhru'd-Dawlah, the Buwaihid ruler of Raiy,[5] died in 387 (997) and was succeeded by his son Majdu'd-Dawlah, who was only nine years of age.[6] Majdu'd-

1 Baihaqī, p. 292. 2 *Ibid.* p. 291.

3 *Ibid.* pp. 291–3.

4 *Ibid.* Sulṭān Mas'ūd, shortly after his accession to the throne, fulfilled the wish of his father and sent a large army to Mukrān. 'Īsā was defeated and put to death and Abu'l-Mu'askar was raised to the throne. See Baihaqī, pp. 71–2, 293–5; Gardīzī, p. 97; and Ibnu'l-Athīr, ix, 281.

5 For a brief account of the Buwaihids, see Appendix H.

6 Majdu'd-Dawlah was born in Rabī' ii 379 (July 989) according to *Mujmal*, f. 257 b, and Ibnu'l-Athīr, ix, 48; but in

Dawlah's mother Sayyida who was a sister of Ispahbud Rustam b. Marzubān, ruler of Shahrbār, became the regent.[1] When Majdu'd-Dawlah grew up to manhood, he tried to throw off his mother's tutelage but Sayyida refused to relinquish power and, in the struggle that followed, Majdu'd-Dawlah was defeated and taken prisoner in 397[2] (1006–7). After a short time, he was released on consenting to remain in the background and allowing his mother to act as ruler.[3] Majdu'd-Dawlah henceforth spent his time in the pursuit of knowledge and the pleasures of the harem,[4] so much so that when, on the death of Sayyida in 419 (1028), the government of the country devolved upon him, he found himself unequal to the heavy responsibilities. His administrative capacity, if he ever possessed any, had been blunted during his long retirement and his devotion to literary pursuits had so softened his disposition that the army which was accustomed to stern discipline, grew restless under his mild control. The Dailamite troops terrorised the inhabitants of Raiy and even threatened the life of Majdu'd-Dawlah,[5] who in despair implored the assistance of Sulṭān Maḥmūd.[6]

Maḥmūd had been eagerly waiting for such an opportunity[7] and he grasped it with alacrity. He im-

Tajārib, iii, 297, and Ibnu'l-Athīr, ix, 93, it is stated that Majdu'd-Dawlah was four years of age at the time of his accession which is incorrect. Cf. also 'Utbī, pp. 61 and 284.

1 'Utbī, p. 173; and Jurbādhqānī, p. 261, note.

2 Ibnu'l-Athīr, ix, 144.

3 See Appendix H.

4 Majdu'd-Dawlah had fifty wives who had borne him thirty children. See Ibn Jawzī, f. 177 b; *Mujmal*, f. 262 b; and Ibnu'l-Athīr, ix, 262.

5 Ibnu'l-Athīr, ix, 261; *Guzīda*, p. 429. It is further stated in *Mujmal*, f. 261 a, that the army even plundered the treasury of Majdu'd-Dawlah.

6 Ibnu'l-Athīr, ix, 261; *Guzīda*, p. 429; but Abu'l-Fidā, i, 165, says that the army of Majdu'd-Dawlah had sent the invitation to Sulṭān Maḥmūd.

7 Baihaqī, p. 319, further adds that the Sulṭān had intentionally avoided attacking Raiy during the lifetime of Sayyida.

mediately despatched a force of 8000 horse under the command of the Ḥājib 'Alī with instructions to take Majdu'd-Dawlah prisoner,[1] and, in spite of his declining health, he himself marched to Jurjān, probably to prevent any help coming to Majdu'd-Dawlah from the Seljuks.[2] 'Alī reached Raiy in Rabī' ii 420[3] (May 1029). Majdu'd-Dawlah played himself into the hands of the enemy. He came out of the town with a small guard of 100 soldiers to welcome 'Alī but when he dismounted from his horse as a mark of respect to hear the Sulṭān's message, he was placed under surveillance in the Ghaznawid camp. 'Alī then promptly despatched his officers to occupy the gates of Raiy[4] and sent news of this success to Sulṭān Maḥmūd, who hurried from Jurjān and entered the town of Raiy on Monday, 9th Jumādī i, 420 (26th May, 1029) without any opposition.[5] Immense booty fell into his hands consisting, among other things, of 1,000,000 *dīnārs*, jewels of half that value, 6000 dresses and innumerable vessels of gold and silver.[6]

After this, Majdu'd-Dawlah was brought into the presence of the Sulṭān and an interesting dialogue took place between them. "Have you read the *Shāhnāmah* and the *Ta'rīkhu't-Ṭabarī*?" asked the Sulṭān. "Yes", answered Majdu'd-Dawlah. "But your conduct was not like one who had read them. And do you play chess?" asked the imperious catechiser. "Yes", replied the other. "Did you ever see one king approach the other

1 Ibnu'l-Athīr, ix, 261.
2 *Ibid.* p. 267; and Baihaqī, pp. 152, 258.
3 Ibnu'l-Athīr, ix, 261.
4 Gardīzī, p. 91.
5 *Mujmal*, f. 262 a; and Gardīzī, p. 91. Ibn Jawzī, f. 177 b, says Monday, 16th Jumādī i (2nd June). Lord Curzon, *Persia*, i, 348, wrongly gives A.D. 1027 as the date of the conquest of Raiy.
6 Gardīzī, p. 91; Ibn Jawzī, f. 177 b; *Mujmal*, f. 262 b; and Ibnu'l-Athīr, ix, 261.

king in a game of chess?" continued the Sulṭān. "No", was the brief reply of the fallen monarch. "What induced you then", was the swift rejoinder of Sulṭān Maḥmūd, "to call to your kingdom one who is superior to you in power?" The unfortunate prince hung his head in confusion.[1] Majdu'd-Dawlah and his son Abū Dulaf were sent as prisoners to India.[2]

The Sulṭān now began to persecute the Carmathians, the Bāṭinis and the Mu'tazilites, and thousands of them were gibbeted, stoned to death or carried in chains to Khurāsān to languish in captivity.[3] Their houses were searched and all books dealing with their heretical beliefs were cast into the flames, while those dealing with topics more acceptable to the Sulṭān's puritan views were transported to Ghazna.[4]

The Sulṭān stayed at Raiy for some time and appointed officers to carry on the administration of the country. The rulers of the neighbouring states came to offer allegiance, with the exception of Ibrāhīm b. Marzubān of Dailam, generally known as "Sālār", ruler of Zanjān, Abhar, Sarjahān and Shahrazūr.[5] To punish the Sālār for his hostility, the Sulṭān sent a large army against him under Marzubān b. Ḥasan who was an old rival of the Sālār and had taken refuge with the Sulṭān. Marzubān made an alliance with some of the Dailamite chieftains, advanced against the Sālār and

1 Ibnu'l-Athīr, ix, 262.

2 Gardīzī, pp. 91, 97. It is stated in *Guzīda*, p. 429, and Faṣīḥī, f. 335 a, that they were put to death but this is incorrect. According to Gardīzī, pp. 91, 97, they were brought from India to Ghazna by the order of Sulṭān Mas'ūd and were treated with honour. Raverty, *Ṭab. Nāṣ.* p. 87, note, has followed the error of *Guzīda* and Faṣīḥī.

3 Gardīzī, p. 91; Farrukhī, f. 39 a; *Mujmal*, f. 262 b; and Ibnu'l-Athīr, ix, 262.

4 Ibn Jawzī, f. 178 a; Ibnu'l-Athīr, ix, 262; and *Mujmal*, f. 262 b. Fifty camel-loads of books are said to have been burnt under the trees on which the Carmathians had been gibbeted. See also Yāqūt, *Irshād*, ii, 315; and *infra*, p. 160.

5 For the position of these localities, see Le Strange, p. 221.

took Qazwīn, but when the Sulṭān returned to Ghazna, the Sālār came out of his retreat, defeated Marzubān and re-occupied Qazwīn.[1]

The Sulṭān placed the newly conquered province in charge of Mas'ūd and directed him to conquer the remaining provinces still under the Buwaihids.[2] Mas'ūd first turned his attention to the Sālār and, accompanied by Marzubān, laid siege to the strong fort of Sarjahān where he had taken refuge. Having failed to reduce it by force of arms, Mas'ūd had recourse to an artifice. By promises of rich rewards, he won over some officers of the Sālār, who guided a detachment of the besiegers to the vulnerable point of the fort. Finding himself thus betrayed, the Sālār came out of the fort and engaged the besiegers in battle on 1st Ramaḍān, 420 (13th September, 1029) but he was defeated and taken prisoner. His son offered submission and promised to pay tribute.[3]

Mas'ūd now returned to Raiy and proceeded to complete the conquest of Hamadān and Iṣfahān. He attacked Hamadān first, put the deputy of 'Alā'u'd-Dawlah b. Kākawaih[4] to flight and occupied the province. After this he advanced to Iṣfahān. 'Alā'u'd-Dawlah fled to Tustar and Mas'ūd took the town in the beginning of the year 421[5] (January 1030). 'Alā'u'd-Dawlah then prevailed on the Caliph, through his kins-

1 Ibnu'l-Athīr, ix, 262.

2 Baihaqī, p. 359; *Ṭab. Nāṣ.* p. 87. Baihaqī, p. 258, and Farrukhī, f. 125 a, however, say that the Sulṭān left Mas'ūd at Raiy with an ill-equipped army numbering 2000.

3 Baihaqī, p. 259; and Ibnu'l-Athīr, ix, 263.

4 His full name was Abū Ja'far Muḥammad b. Dushmanziyār and he was commonly known as Ibn-i-Kākawaih. Abū 'Alī b. Sīnā, the famous philosopher, lived at his court. See Ibnu'l-Athīr, ix, 146, 279; and al-Qifṭī, *Ta'rīkhu'l-Ḥukamā*, pp. 419–26.

5 Sibṭ Ibnu'l-Jawzī, f. 218 b; Baihaqī, p. 259; and Ibnu'l-Athīr, ix, 279. Sykes, *History of Persia*, ii, 96, erroneously attributes the conquest of Iṣfahān to Sulṭān Maḥmūd in person, and places it before his return to Ghazna in 420 (1029).

man Jalālu'd-Dawlah who was then in power at Baghdād, to ask Mas'ūd to permit him to remain as his deputy at Iṣfahān.[1] While these negotiations were in progress, Mas'ūd received on 20th Jumādī i, 421 (26th May, 1030) the news of the death of his father. Anticipating a struggle for the throne with his brother,[2] he regarded the Caliph's recommendation as opportune and allowed 'Alā'u'd-Dawlah to keep the government of Iṣfahān on condition that he paid an annual tribute of 20,000 *dīnārs*.[3]

Mas'ūd then returned to Raiy, placed it in charge of Ḥasan-i-Sulaimānī[4] and marched to Nīshāpūr to claim the throne of his father.

1 Ibnu'l-Athīr, ix, 279; and Baihaqī, pp. 14–15.
2 Baihaqī, p. 11.
3 *Ibid.* pp. 14–16.
4 *Ibid.* pp. 19–25.

CHAPTER VIII

WARS IN INDIA

A. *Relations with the* Rājās *of the* Hindūshāhiyya Dynasty *of* Waihand

INDIA had early attracted the attention of Alptigīn and his successors but the details of their wars with the Rājās of the Hindūshāhiyya Dynasty of Waihand[1] are available only from the accession of Subuktigīn who fought numerous battles with Rājā Jaipāl and extended the frontier of his kingdom, on the side of India, to Lamaghān.[2] Maḥmūd continued the forward policy of his father and, when he was recognised as an independent sovereign by the Caliph of Baghdād in 389 (999), he resolved to lead an expedition to India every year.[3]

I. CAPTURE OF SOME FRONTIER FORTS

In pursuance of this resolution, Maḥmūd marched towards India about the close of the year 390[4] (September 1000), took "many forts", probably in the vicinity of Lamaghān, and returned to Ghazna.[5]

1 For an account of the Hindūshāhiyya Dynasty, see Appendix I. Waihand is modern Hund. It is called Udabhānda by Kalhana. See Cunningham, *Ancient Geography*, pp. 53–4; and Kalhana, ii, 336–8. Raverty, *Ṭab. Nāṣ.* p. 79, note, has wrongly identified it with Bhatinda.

2 See *supra*, pp. 29–30.

3 'Utbī, p. 134, simply says, "He made it obligatory on himself to undertake every year an expedition to Hind." Elliot's translation of this passage (E. and D. ii, 24) is misleading as it implies that the Sulṭān *vowed* to undertake a holy war to Hind every year and gives to his expeditions a touch of religious fanaticism.

4 The date is inferred from Gardīzī, p. 63.

5 Gardīzī is the only contemporary authority to mention this expedition. Firishta and Niẓāmu'd-Dīn, the only two among later writers to give this expedition, have most probably taken it from Gardīzī, but both have made mistakes in copying it. Sir W. Haig, p. 13, erroneously regards this expedition as apocryphal.

2. BATTLE OF PESHĀWAR AND WAIHAND

The following year Maḥmūd made greater preparations for an attack on Jaipāl, Rājā of Waihand.[1] He marched from Ghazna in Shawwāl 391[2] (September 1001), at the head of 15,000 cavalry and a large number of volunteers and encamped near Peshāwar. Jaipāl advanced to meet him with an army numbering 12,000 horse, 30,000 foot and 300 war-elephants and took up his position in front of Maḥmūd's camp. The two armies met on Thursday, 8th Muḥarram, 392[3] (27th November, 1001) and the conflict raged fiercely till noon when the Hindūs, unable to withstand the repeated cavalry charges of the Muslims, broke and fled leaving 5000 dead on the field of battle.[4]

The spoils captured satisfied the most fantastic expectations of the conquerors. Fifteen necklaces of pearls, one of which was valued at 80,000 *dīnārs* and other booty "beyond all bounds of calculation" fell into their hands. Jaipāl himself with fifteen of his sons and grandsons was taken prisoner[5] and sent to a place named Mīrand.[6] Peace was concluded between them by the terms of which Jaipāl promised to pay 250,000 *dīnārs* as ransom and to deliver 50 elephants.[7] Jaipāl was allowed to return to his kingdom, but one son and

1 It is stated in *Majma'u'l-Ansāb*, f. 231 b, that on the death of Subuktigīn, Jaipāl tried to take back what Subuktigīn had conquered of his kingdom and attacked Maḥmūd who marched from Ghazna to repel the invasion.

2 Firishta, p. 24.

3 'Utbī, p. 158; and Gardīzī, p. 66.

4 Gardīzī, p. 66, and 'Utbī, p. 157.

5 Gardīzī, p. 66.

6 'Unṣurī (Asiatic Society of Bengal MS). In *Ṭab. Nāṣ.* p. 82 it is called Man-Yazīd. See also my article in *JRAS*. July 1927, pp. 493–5.

7 'Utbī, p. 158; and *Majma'u'l-Ansāb*, f. 231 b. It is implied from the account given in the latter work that "the sale of Jaipāl", to which 'Unṣurī (*loc. cit.*) makes a reference, meant only the fixing of Jaipāl's ransom.

one grandson of his were detained as hostages till the conditions should be fulfilled.[1]

After this victory, Maḥmūd advanced to Waihand, the capital of the Hindūshāhiyya Dynasty, and spent the remaining winter months in reducing the adjoining territories.[2] He returned to Ghazna in the beginning of spring[3] (April 1002).

Jaipāl did not long survive this humiliation, and, shortly after his return to the Punjāb, he burnt himself to death probably in the beginning of 393[4] (1002–3). He was succeeded by his son Anandpāl.[5]

3. BATTLE ON THE INDUS

In spring 396 (March–April 1006), Sulṭān Maḥmūd marched to Multān[6] but as it was not safe to cross the river Indus lower down, he resolved to cross it near Peshāwar and asked Anandpāl to let him pass through his territories.[7] Anandpāl refused to do so and taking up the cause of Dā'ūd, the ruler of Multān, advanced towards Peshāwar to prevent the passage of the river. The Sulṭān inflicted a crushing defeat on him and pursued him as far as the river Chināb[8] where Anandpāl

1 'Utbī, p. 158.

2 'Utbī, p. 159, and Gardīzī, p. 56, distinctly mention that the Sulṭān's march to Waihand was undertaken in continuation with the preceding expedition, but Reynolds, p. 282, incorrectly makes it a distinct expedition.

3 'Utbī, p. 159; Gardīzī, p. 56. The capital of the Hindūshāhiyya kingdom was now probably shifted to Nandana. According to *Guzīda*, p. 396, Maḥmūd was called *Ghāzī* after this victory.

4 'Utbī, p. 159. See also Appendix I.

5 Anandpāl was at that time governor of Lahore. For details, see *JRAS*. July 1927, pp. 493–5 and Appendix I.

6 'Utbī, p. 211. See also *infra*, p. 97.

7 'Utbī, p. 211. It is implied from this fact that the Sulṭān and Anandpāl were at peace, for otherwise this request would have been meaningless. Gardīzī, p. 67, says that the reason for the request was that the Sulṭān wanted to take Dā'ūd unawares.

8 Firishta, p. 25.

eluded the Sulṭān by escaping into the Kashmīr hills.[1] The Sulṭān relinquished the pursuit and resumed his march to Multān.[2]

4. BATTLE OF WAIHAND AND CAPTURE OF NAGARKOT

Anandpāl was now filled with serious apprehension at the growing power of the Sulṭān whose advance he and his father had failed to check single-handed. He therefore appealed to the neighbouring rājās for help in stemming the tide of Muslim conquest from the north-west. The rājās readily responded to his appeal and despatched their contingents to swell the army which Anandpāl had mustered from all parts of his kingdom.[3] This huge host was placed under the command of Brahmanpāl,[4] son of Anandpāl, and was ordered to advance to Peshāwar.

Sulṭān Maḥmūd received news of this attack in mid-winter but disregarding the severity of the weather, he left Ghazna on 29th Rabī' ii, 399[5] (31st December, 1008), crossed the river Indus and met the invaders in the plain opposite Waihand. The Hindūs fought with great courage and towards the evening the success of the Muslims seemed to be in jeopardy, but the Sulṭān retrieved the situation by sending his personal guards to sweep round and deliver an attack

1 'Utbī, p. 212; and Gardīzī, p. 67.

2 'Unṣurī (Asiatic Society of Bengal MS) says that the Sulṭān captured 200 forts on his way to Multān, and crossed all the Punjāb rivers except Biyās and Sutlej.

3 Firishta is the only author to mention the formation of the league. He says that the Rājās of Ujjain, Gwālior, Kālinjar, Kanauj, Delhi and Ajmer joined this league, but probably Delhi was not founded at that time. Major Raverty's oral communication to Sir V. A. Smith (*Early History of India*, p. 384), fixing the date of the foundation of Delhi at A.D. 993–3 on the authority of Gardīzī, is unwarranted, as Delhi is not mentioned even by name in Gardīzī's *Zainu'l-Akhbār*.

4 'Utbī, p. 224.

5 *Ibid.*; Gardīzī, p. 69.

on the enemy's rear.[1] In effecting a partial change of front to meet the attack, the Hindū ranks fell into confusion and were utterly defeated. Valuable spoils including 30 elephants fell into the hands of the conquerors.[2]

The Sulṭān now took up the pursuit of the fugitives and followed them to the fort of Nagarkot[3] which was situated near Kāngra on the spur of a hill and was encircled by the river Bāngangā.[4] The temple in this fort was held in great veneration and was famous for the wealth that had accumulated in its vaults. The Sulṭān invested the fort, which fell after three days of heroic defence.[5] Spoils "beyond the limit of calculation" were captured by the conquerors, and consisted of 70,000,000 *dirhems* of coined money, 70,000 *manns* of gold and silver ingot and costly apparel, besides a folding house made of silver measuring 30 yards by 15 yards, a canopy of linen measuring 40 yards by 20 yards which was reared on poles of gold and silver,[6] and a richly decorated throne reputed to be that of Rājā Bhīm of the Pāndava Dynasty.[7] The Sulṭān placed the fort in charge of his officers and returned to Ghazna about the end of the year 399[8] (June 1009).

1 'Utbī, p. 224. Firishta, p. 26, makes the two armies lie facing each other for 40 days.

2 'Utbī, p. 224; Gardīzī, p. 69. It is stated in E. and D. ii, 33, note, that this expedition has been left out by all chroniclers except 'Utbī. This is perhaps due to an oversight, as it is mentioned in Ibnu'l-Athīr, *Rawḍah*, *Ḥabību's-Siyar* and elsewhere. Firishta simply shifts the scene of battle from Waihand to Peshāwar.

3 'Utbī, p. 224. Gardīzī, p. 70, further adds that the fort was reputed to have been built in the time of Rājā Bhīm of the Pāndava Dynasty.

4 'Utbī, p. 224; and 'Unṣurī, p. 84.

5 Gardīzī, p. 70.

6 'Utbī, p. 226.

7 'Unṣurī, p. 85.

8 'Utbī, p. 226. According to Gardīzī, p. 70, the Sulṭān ordered these spoils to be displayed in public in the beginning of 400 (August–September 1009).

After this victory, the Sulṭān probably annexed the whole strip of territory from the river Indus to Nagarkot but, after the departure of the Sulṭān, Anandpāl managed to re-establish his power in the Salt Range with his headquarters at Nandana. Anandpāl died some time after this and was succeeded by his son Trilochanpāl.[1]

5. CAPTURE OF NANDANA (NĀRDĪN)

The Sulṭān now resolved to crush the power of Trilochanpāl in the Salt Range. He started from Ghazna about the end of autumn 404[2] (November 1013) but he was forced to return on account of a heavy fall of snow. He started again in the following spring[3] (March 1014) and marched to Nandana[4] which, situated on the northern spur of the Salt Range, commanded the main route into the Ganges Doāb. Having learned of the Sulṭān's intention, Trilochanpāl entrusted the defence of the fort to his son Bhīmpāl the Fearless,[5] and set out for "the Kashmīr Pass"[6] to implore the assistance of Sangrāmarājā of Kashmīr.[7] Bhīmpāl entrenched himself in a strong position between two hills at the junction of which the fort was situated, and closed the entrance to the pass by a strong line of elephants. The Sulṭān advanced to the assault and, after several days of futile fighting, was at last able to draw out a detachment of Bhīmpāl into the plain and put it to the rout.[8]

1 Al-Bīrūnī, ii, 13. Sir W. Haig, p. 17, wrongly calls him Jaipāl II.

2 The Sulṭān probably marched by way of Kābul, see Baihaqī, p. 841.

3 'Utbī, p. 260.

4 It is Nārdīn of 'Utbī. Gardīzī and Baihaqī call it Nandūnah. It is situated in Lat. 32° 43′ N., Long. 73° 17′ E., at the junction of two spurs of the Salt Range. See *Punjab Dist. Gaz.* xxvii, A, 1904, pp. 46–7; *I.G.I.* xviii, 349; and *Ṭab. Nāṣ.* pp. 334–9, note.

5 He is called "Nidar" meaning Fearless by 'Utbī.

6 Gardīzī, p. 72, by which is probably meant the lower part of the Loharin valley.

7 Kalhana, Bk vii, ll. 47–53.

8 'Utbī, p. 262.

Bhīmpāl in the meantime received fresh reinforcements and leaving his entrenched position, he came out into the plain, with his rear resting on the hills and his wings protected by elephants and attacked the Sulṭān, but he was beaten back. He then ordered a charge of elephants. The Muslims assailed them with such a deadly shower of arrows on their eyes and trunks that they were forced to turn back. The Sulṭān now delivered a furious charge on Bhīmpāl which proved irresistible.[1] The Hindūs broke and fled for refuge to the fort of Nandana. The Sulṭān laid siege to it. Mines were run under the walls of the fort and the Turkomān sharpshooters poured a terrific shower of arrows on the defenders. Realising that it would be impossible to hold out long, the garrison surrendered unconditionally. The Sulṭān entered the fort and captured immense booty including a large number of elephants, and a big store of arms and other valuables.[2]

The Sulṭān now turned his attention to Trilochanpāl who, with the Kashmīr contingent, was encamped in one of the valleys to the north of Jhelum.[3] Tunga, the commander of the Kashmīr forces, was so elated with pride at an easy victory which he won over a reconnaissance party of the Sulṭān that he began to think too lightly of the strength of the invader, but on the following day, Tunga's pride received a rude shock when "the leader of the Turushka army" who was "skilled in stratagem",[4] personally led an attack on the Kashmīr

1 'Utbī's acccount ends here.

2 Gardīzī, p. 72. 'Utbī, p. 263, says that there was an idol in a temple here with an inscription indicating that it had been constructed 40,000 years ago. In E. and D. ii, 39, an incorrect translation of 'Utbī is given to imply that the temple was of "the great Budda". The word *Budd* in that passage is the Arabicised form of the Persian *But* which means an idol, see *Tāju'l-'Arūs* (Cairo ed.), ii, 295.

3 Gardīzī, p. 12; Kalhana, Bk vii, l. 53, note.

4 These epithets are used for Sulṭān Maḥmūd in Kalhana, Bk vii, l. 56. He is mentioned in l. 53 as *Hammīra* which is an

troops and put them to the rout. Tunga fled for his life.[1] Trilochanpāl rallied his forces and made a final attempt to retrieve his fortune but he was defeated.[2]

The news of this victory spread far and wide. Numerous rājās of the neighbourhood tendered their fealty to the conqueror and many of the inhabitants of these territories embraced Islam. The Sulṭān appointed teachers to instruct the converts in the rudiments of their new faith and ordered mosques to be built all over the country.[3] He then placed the fort of Nandana in charge of Sārūgh[4] and returned to Ghazna in summer 405[5] (July–August 1014).

The power of Trilochanpāl was broken and he retired to the eastern part of the Punjāb where he seems to have established himself in the Siwālik hills.[6] Trilochanpāl however did not rest in peace and carried on warfare with the neighbouring rājās, particularly Chandar Rāy of Sharwa.[7] When he heard the news of Sulṭān Maḥmūd's invasion of Kanauj in 409 (1018), he made peace with Chandar Rāy and in order to strengthen his position, secured the hand of one of his daughters for Bhīmpāl;[8] but when Bhīmpāl went to Sharwa to fetch the bride, he was detained there by Chandar Rāy.

obvious adaptation of *Amīr*, the title by which Maḥmūd was generally known. Sir Aurel Stein, Kalhana, i, 107, however, wrongly says that *Hammīra* stands for "*Amīru'l-Mu'minīn*".

1 Kalhana, Bk vii, l. 57.

2 *Ibid.* ll. 57–8; and Gardīzī, p. 72.

3 Gardīzī, p. 72.

4 *Ibid.* Sārūgh held this position till after the death of Sulṭān Maḥmūd. See Baihaqī, p. 169.

5 Gardīzī, p. 72.

6 I have drawn this inference from the events narrated below, and from 'Utbī's account of the battle on the river Ruhut.

7 'Utbī, pp. 311–13. The "Parūjaipāl", mentioned by 'Utbī in these events, is no other than Trilochanpāl of the Hindūshāhiyya Dynasty, because the other prince of this name, who was ruler of Kanauj, came to the throne long after these events. See *infra*, pp. 110 and 206.

8 Sir W. Haig, p. 20, has confused the account of these events by incorrectly making this Bhīmpāl son of a Rājā of Kanauj whom by a curious mistake he calls Jaichand.

About this time (Sha'bān 409/January 1019) the Sulṭān attacked Sharwa.[1] Chandar Rāy made preparations for resistance, but at the approach of the Sulṭān, he took to flight on the advice of Bhīmpāl who feared that in case of defeat he might fall a prisoner into the hands of the Sulṭān.[2]

6. BATTLE ON THE RIVER RUHUT (RĀHIB)

Shortly after the return of Sulṭān Maḥmūd to Ghazna from his expedition to Kanauj (close of 409/beginning of 1019), Trilochanpāl entered into an alliance with Ganda,[3] Rājā of Kālinjar, and secured from him a promise of help in winning back his ancestral kingdom from Sulṭān Maḥmūd.[4] When Sulṭān Maḥmūd received news of their alliance, he marched from Ghazna in the beginning of autumn 410[5] (October 1019), with the intention of punishing Ganda. When Trilochanpāl obtained information of this invasion, he marched south to join forces with his namesake, the ruler of Kanauj and Bārī.[6] The Sulṭān pushed forward in pursuit of Trilochanpāl[7] and overtook him on 14th Sha'bān, 410[8] (15th December, 1019) but Trilochanpāl managed to cross the river Ruhut (Rāmgangā)[9] at a place where it leaves the

1 'Utbī, p. 311, and *infra*, p. 110. 2 'Utbī, p. 311.

3 Nandā of 'Utbī and other Muslim writers. His true name is known from the Maū Chandel inscription, see *Epigraphia Indica*, i, pp. 195–207; and *JRAS*. 1909, p. 278, but Sir W. Haig, p. 21, persists in calling him Nanda.

4 Gardīzī, pp. 76–7; and Ibnu'l-Athīr, ix, 218.

5 Gardīzī, p. 76. Cf. also 'Utbī, pp. 317–18.

6 This fact is inferred from Gardīzī, p. 76. See Appendix K.

7 Farrukhī, f. 16 a, says that before he reached the river Ruhut, the Sulṭān took a fort named Sarbal which was at a distance of one day's march from the river. Sarbal may possibly be identified with Sabalgarh, 15 miles south of Hardwār, on the left bank of the Ganges. It has the ruins of a fort about 800 yards square.

8 Ibnu'l-Athīr, ix, 218.

9 The river Rāmgangā is known as Ruhut in its upper courses, see *I.G.I.* xxi, 175.

hills[1], and tried to prevent the passage of the Sulṭān. In spite of the obvious danger of crossing the river in the face of the enemy, eight intrepid warriors of the Sulṭān's body-guard threw themselves into the current on inflated skins in order to cross over to the other side.[2] Seeing this, Trilochanpāl sent a small detachment of his archers with five elephants to annihilate them before they could land. But without heeding the brisk shower of arrows that was poured on them, they plied their bows so skilfully as they swam that they safely gained the opposite bank. Encouraged by their example and by the Sulṭān's promise of "a life of repose after that day of trouble"[3] to all who would follow them, the whole army plunged into the river, some on horseback, some on inflated skins, and, without the loss of a single life, crossed over to the other side,[4] swiftly formed themselves into battle order, fell upon the Hindūs and inflicted a crushing defeat on them. Rich spoils were captured, the share of the Sulṭān alone comprising 270 elephants and two coffers full of precious stones.[5]

Trilochanpāl, though wounded in battle, managed to escape. After an unsuccessful attempt to come to terms with the Sulṭān, he marched south to solicit the help of Ganda, but he was assassinated by some of his followers in 412[6] (1021–22). His son Bhīmpāl the Fearless succeeded to the diminished dominions, or probably only the title, of his father. With his death

1 Farrukhī, f. 16 a. Probably near Afzalgarh.

2 'Utbī, p. 319; and Farrukhī, f. 16 a. Sir W. Haig, p. 21, says that "eight Muslim officers, apparently without their king's permission or knowledge, suddenly crossed the river with their contingents," but there is no authority for this.

3 'Utbī, p. 319.

4 *Ibid.*; and Farrukhī, f. 16 b.

5 Farrukhī, *ib.*; Gardīzī, p. 77; and Ibnu'l-Athīr, ix, 219. Farrukhī further adds that among the prisoners of war there were two wives and two daughters of Trilochanpāl.

6 Ibnu'l-Athīr, ix, 219; Farrukhī, f. 16 b; and al-Bīrūnī, ii, 13.

in 417[1] (1026), the Hindūs͟hāhiyya Dynasty came to an
end.[2] The rājās of this dynasty were renowned for their
love of learning, generosity and noble sentiments.[3]

B. *Relations with the Ruler of* Multān

1. CAPTURE OF MULTĀN

The province of Multān, ever since its conquest by
Muḥammad b. Qāsim, had remained an outpost of
Islam in India. Early in the fourth century A.H., the
Carmathians gained the ascendancy there and established a line of rulers who did not pay allegiance to the
Caliphs at Bag͟hdād.[4] When Subuktigīn rose into prominence, Abu'l-Fatḥ Dā'ūd b. Naṣr,[5] the Carmathian
ruler of Multān, entered into friendly relations with
him[6] and, after his death, with Sulṭān Maḥmūd.

These good relations however did not last long.
When Sulṭān Maḥmūd was returning from his expedition to Bhatinda in 395 (1005), Dā'ūd probably
resented the passage of his army through the province
of Multān.[7] With the intention of punishing him for

1 Al-Bīrūnī, ii, 13; but Sir W. Haig, p. 22, incorrectly says
that Bhīmpāl took refuge with the Rājā of Ajmer.

2 Al-Bīrūnī, ii, 13. Several members of this family took refuge
at the court of the Rājās of Kas͟hmīr and lived on the handsome
allowances that were settled on them. See Kalhana, Bk vii,
ll. 144–78, 274, 956, 1470; and Bk viii, ll. 225–27.

3 Al-Bīrūnī, ii, 13; and Kalhana, Bk vii, ll. 66–9.

4 Al-Bīrūnī, i, 116, says that Jalam b. S͟haibān was the first
Carmathian to take possession of Multān. See also Mas'ūdī,
pp. 234, 385.

5 Briggs, Firis͟hta, i, 40, says that Dā'ūd was a descendant of
"Sheikh Humeed Lody". "Lody" is an obvious error for Lawī
who, according to Mas'ūdī, pp. 234, 385, was probably one of
the ancestors of Dā'ūd. This error has misled some writers to
call Dā'ūd a Lodhī.

6 Firis͟hta, pp. 18, 24.

7 'Utbī, p. 211, says that Dā'ūd's adherence to the Carmathian
heresy was the cause of the Sulṭān's invasion of Multān.

his contumacy and reducing him to submission, Sulṭān Maḥmūd marched from Gh̲azna to Multān in the spring of 396[1] (March–April 1006) but as it was not safe to cross the river Indus lower down, he resolved to cross it near Pes̲h̲āwar. Anandpāl moved to Pes̲h̲āwar to check the advance of the Sulṭān, but he was defeated and forced to flee.[2]

The Sulṭān then marched straight across the Punjāb to Multān. Dā'ūd fled to an island in the river Indus. The garrison of Multān, however, shut the gate in the face of the Sulṭān who invested the fort, and, after a siege of seven days, carried it by assault.[3] The citizens craved protection and offered to pay a fine of 20,000,000 *dirhems*.[4] The Sulṭān accepted the offer and spared the inhabitants but he showed no mercy to the Carmathians, hundreds of whom died for their faith.[5] Even their congregational mosque suffered at the hands of the persecutor and was reduced to the humble position of a barn-floor "where bunches of Ḥinnā" were bound together.[6]

The Sulṭān now proceeded to reduce the outlying parts of the province of Multān and Bhatinda[7] but

1 'Utbī, p. 211. In *Alfī*, f. 372 a, it is incorrectly stated that the Sulṭān left Gh̲azna in the beginning of 396 (October 1005).

2 See *supra*, p. 88.

3 Gardīzī, p. 67.

4 'Utbī, p. 212; and Gardīzī, pp. 67–8; but the amount seems to be exaggerated.

5 'Utbī, p. 212; and 'Unṣurī, p. 80. In *Ādābu'l-Mulūk*, f. 80 a, it is stated that Sulṭān Maḥmūd put so many Carmathians to the sword that "a stream of blood flowed from the Lohārī gate which was on the western side of the town", and that "the hand of the Sulṭān was stuck fast to the hilt of the sword on account of congealed blood, and had to be immersed in a bath of hot water before it could be loosened".

6 Al-Bīrūnī, i, 117.

7 Ibnu'l-At̲h̲īr, ix, 132, says that after the fall of Multān, the Sulṭān advanced to Gwālior and Kālinjar, but his account of the operations against these two places is the same as that of Gardīzī and Sibṭ Ibnu'l-Jawzī under A.H. 413, which shows that Ibnu'l-At̲h̲īr has confused the two expeditions.

before long he received news of the irruption of Īlak Khān into Khurāsān and giving charge of the government of Multān to Sukhpāl, alias Nawāsa Shāh,[1] he hurried back to Ghazna to meet the danger from the north.

2. REBELLION OF SUKHPĀL

Taking advantage of the prolonged struggle between Sulṭān Maḥmūd and Īlak Khān, Sukhpāl abjured the religion of Islam and raised the standard of revolt in the winter of 398 (December 1007). The news of this rising reached the Sulṭān in Rabī' ii 398 (January 1008) while he was following the defeated army of Īlak Khān.[2] He relinquished the pursuit and, undaunted by the severity of the weather (a circumstance on which Sukhpāl seems to have counted in choosing this time for his rebellion), he hastened to India[3] and appeared before Multān. Sukhpāl offered resistance but he was defeated and forced to seek refuge, probably in the Salt Range[4] in the Punjāb where Anandpāl, his brother or cousin, still maintained his

1 *Guzīda*, p. 397; and 'Utbī, p. 223. Sir W. Haig, p. 15, however, says, without specifying his authority, that Sukhpāl was appointed governor of Ūnd, i.e. Waihand.

Sukhpāl, called Nawāsa Shāh, which means "grandson of the Shāh", was a grandson of Rājā Jaipāl of the Hindūshāhiyya Dynasty, see *Ādābu'l-Mulūk*, f. 88 a. Gardīzī, p. 69, says that he was among the prisoners of war captured from Maḥmūd by Abū 'Alī Sīmjūrī at Nīshāpūr, most probably in 385 (995), and was converted to Islam by him. Sukhpāl thus must have fallen into the hands of Subuktigīn earlier than this date, probably in 376 (986–7), when Jaipāl is said to have left some of his kinsmen as hostages with Subuktigīn.

2 Gardīzī, p. 69; and Firishta, p. 26. It is probable that Sukhpāl rebelled at the instigation of Īlak Khān.

3 'Utbī, p. 223; and Gardīzī, p. 69. Firishta incorrectly says that the Sulṭān did not advance against him in person.

4 Gardīzī, p. 69, says that Sukhpāl fled to the hills of كشنور which is probably a mistake of the copyist for كهيوره (Khewra), the name by which the Salt Range is commonly known.

authority. Sukhpāl, however, was soon captured and brought before the Sulṭān, who exacted from him a fine of 400,000 *dirhems* and placed him in confinement.[1]

3. FINAL SUBJUGATION OF MULTĀN

The Sulṭān had been forced to leave some of the outlying parts of the province of Multān unsubdued in 396 (1006) because of his sudden departure for Khurāsān to repel the invasion of Īlak Khān. He therefore again marched to Multān in the beginning of 401 (October 1010) and completed the subjugation of the province. Abu'l-Fatḥ Dā'ūd, who was probably creating some disturbance, was taken prisoner and thousands of Carmathians who had gathered strength there were put to the sword or sent as prisoners to different forts.[2] Dā'ūd was imprisoned in the fort of Ghūrak where he ended his days in peace.[3]

After this the Sulṭān returned to Ghazna.

C. *Expeditions to other parts of* India

1. CONQUEST OF BHATINDA (BHĀṬIYA)

Early in the year 395[4] (October 1004), the Sulṭān started from Ghazna to take the strong fort of Bhatinda[5]

1 Gardīzī, p. 69. In *Ādābu'l-Mulūk*, f. 76 b, it is stated that after the death of Sulṭān Mas'ūd, Nawāsa Shāh formed a confederacy of the rājās of the southern Kashmīr hill states and attacked Lahore but was defeated and slain. Cf. also Ibnu'l-Athīr's account of this attack given under A.H. 435.

2 Gardīzī, p. 70; and al-Bīrūnī, i, 116–17. But the power of the Carmathians was not broken in spite of such rigorous persecution, and they rose in rebellion under the son of Dā'ūd, shortly after the death of Sulṭān Mas'ūd. See *Ādābu'l-Mulūk*, f. 76 a; and *Ṭab. Nāṣ.* p. 491.

3 Gardīzī, p. 70. Ghūrak or Ghorak is situated about fifty miles north-west of Qandhār.

4 Ibnu'l-Athīr, ix, 130. See Appendix J.

5 "Bhāṭiya" of Muslim writers. For its identification, see Appendix J.

which guarded the passage from the north-west into the rich Ganges valley.[1] He marched by way of Ḥiṣār and Wālis͟htān in modern Balūc͟histān,[2] crossed the river Indus in the neighbourhood of Multān[3] and appeared before Bhatinda. Bajī Rāy[4] the Rājā, was so confident of his strength that instead of seeking the protection of his fort, he came out into the field to give battle to the invader. He defended his position bravely for three days against the repeated attacks of the Sulṭān.[5] This unusual tenacity of the Hindūs completely unnerved the Muslims, and on the fourth day Bajī Rāy seemed to be carrying everything before him,[6] but the Sulṭān proved equal to the occasion. He aroused the enthusiasm of his warriors by a stirring appeal and then led them in a final desperate charge on the enemy. He himself set the example and plunged into the thick of the battle, dealing hard blows on his right and left.[7] His courage and enthusiasm were soon rewarded, and before sunset the Hindū ranks were broken and shattered.

The Rājā fled for refuge to the fort which was surrounded by a deep and wide ditch, and was famous for its strength. The Sulṭān laid siege to it and ordered the ditch to be filled in with stones and trees. When Bajī Rāy saw this operation progressing satisfactorily, he despaired of standing the siege for long and, leaving the garrison to resist the invader as best they could, fled to a forest.[8] His whereabouts were however soon

1 *Gazetteer of Bīkaner* by Capt. Powlett, p. 122.

2 Gardīzī, p. 66. Wālis͟htān was the name of Sibī in Balūc͟histān, see Le Strange, p. 347. Cf. also Baihaqī, p. 72; and Ibn Funduq, f. 57 b.

3 'Utbī, p. 208.

4 Sir W. Haig, p. 14, incorrectly calls him Bajra.

5 'Utbī, p. 209.

6 'Utbī, p. 209, makes a vague reference to it. Firis͟hta, p. 24, gives many details which are not mentioned by 'Utbī or Gardīzī.

7 'Utbī, p. 209.

8 'Utbī, p. 210, also mentions some hills which might be those near Hānsī. Gardīzī, p, 67, says that he fled to the bank of "the

discovered and he was surrounded but, preferring death to the humiliation of captivity, the high-spirited Rājā stabbed himself with a sword.[1]

The death of the Rājā depressed the spirits of the garrison and the fort was taken without much further resistance. No quarter was given to the enemy and only those who embraced Islam escaped the vengeance of the conquerors. Immense booty was captured, the share of the Sulṭān alone amounting to 120 elephants besides gold, silver and arms.[2]

The Sulṭān stayed there for some time to subjugate the outlying parts of the kingdom of Bhatinda and appointed teachers to instruct the converts in the rudiments of Islam.[3] He then marched back to Ghazna but he had stayed too long at Bhatinda. The Punjāb rivers were in flood probably owing to early rains. Much of the baggage was lost and many of the warriors, who had weathered the storms of arrows, were swept away by the infuriated waters of the river Indus.[4] The sufferings of the soldiers were augmented by the hostility of the ruler of Multān, who most probably resented the Sulṭān's passage through his territories.[5]

After suffering great hardships the Sulṭān arrived in Ghazna about the middle of 395 (May–June 1005).

2. CAPTURE OF NARĀYANPŪR

In the beginning of 400[6] (October 1009), shortly after his return from Nagarkot, the Sulṭān led an

river Sāsind" which might be the old name of a branch of the river Hakra.

1 'Utbī, p. 210; Gardīzī, p. 67.

2 'Utbī, p. 210. Gardīzī, p. 67, says 280 elephants.

3 'Utbī, p. 210.

4 *Ibid.*

5 Firishta, p. 25, says that Dā'ūd had given offence to Sulṭān Maḥmūd by his unbecoming behaviour.

6 Ibnu'l-Athīr, ix, 149. 'Utbī is the only contemporary authority to mention this expedition. He omits the date but mentions it between the expeditions to Bhīmnagar and Ghūr, i.e. between A.H. 399 and 401.

expedition to Narāyanpūr,[1] probably with the object of opening up a way into the Ganges Doāb from the side of Multān and Bhatinda. The Rājā of Narāyanpūr offered resistance but he was defeated and his town was captured and given up to plunder. The Sulṭān then returned to Ghazna.[2]

Some time later, the Rājā of Narāyanpūr[3] sent a friendly embassy to the Sulṭān offering to pay annual tribute and 50 elephants, and, like other feudatory princes, to send a contingent of 2000 soldiers to serve under him, so that the Sulṭān might spare his territories from attack in future. The Sulṭān agreed to these terms. This peace is said to have given great impetus to the trade between India and Khurāsān.[4]

1 Nārāyan of 'Utbī. Cunningham, *Ancient Geography*, pp. 338–44, has identified it with Narāyanpūr in Alwar State. See also Cunningham, *Archaeological Survey of India*, ii, 242–7, and vi, 91–103.

2 'Utbī, pp. 241–2. The only other contemporary reference to this expedition occurs in a *qaṣīda* of the poet Ghaḍā'irī (as preserved in 'Unṣurī, p. 100). He says:

دو بدره زر بگرفتم بفتح ناراین
بفتح رومیه صد بدره گیرم و خرطال

"I received two purses of gold on the victory of Nārāyan,
I will get one hundred such purses and bags on the conquest of Rūmiya."

Ibn Jawzī, f. 158 a, and Sibṭ Ibnu'l-Jawzī, f. 198 b, mention that in 402 (1011–12) news was received at Baghdād of the sufferings of the army of the Sulṭān in India due to scarcity of water. It may possibly refer to this expedition as the Sulṭān might have delayed the report to Baghdād.

Sir W. Haig, p. 17, says, most probably about this expedition, that it was really intended against Delhi and that the Sulṭān fought an action at Tarāorī, near Karnāl, but there is no authority for these statements.

3 'Utbī, p. 242. 'Utbī does not mention the name of the rājā, but obviously it could be no other than the Rājā of Narāyanpūr. Mark the error in E. and D. ii, 448.

4 'Utbī, p. 242. For the commercial importance of "Nārāyan" or Narāyanpūr in the time of Sulṭān Maḥmūd, see al-Bīrūnī, i, 202–5; and Cunningham, *Ancient Geography*, pp. 338–9.

3. CAPTURE OF THĀNESAR

In autumn 405[1] (October 1014), shortly after his return from Nandana, Sulṭān Maḥmūd marched from G͟hazna[2] with the intention of taking Thānesar.[3] When Triloc͟hanpāl, son of Anandpāl, learnt the news of this attack, he offered to deliver 50 elephants if the Sulṭān spared Thānesar[4] which was held in great veneration by the Hindūs for its idol named C͟hakraswāmīn,[5] but the Sulṭān declined to alter his plans. Another Rājā named Rām,[6] ruler of Dera,[7] probably a devotee of the idol, advanced at the head of a large army to contest the passage of the river Sutlej, near the place where it debouches into the plains.[8] Rām took up a strong position along the bank of the river, with his rear resting on a hill and his front protected by a line of elephants. The Sulṭān ordered two divisions of his

1 Ibnu'l-At͟hīr, ix, 172. 'Utbī does not give the date but mentions it subsequently to the expedition against Nārdīn or Nandana. Gardīzī, p. 70, however, places it in 402 (1011–12).

2 'Utbī, p. 264, says that the Sulṭān crossed a barren tract of land where no water could be found. This may refer to the alkaline wastes of the Punjāb in the districts of Lyallpūr and S͟hāhpūr.

3 'Utbī, p. 264, says that the Sulṭān attacked Thānesar because he envied the rājā of that place the possession of a certain breed of elephants which were specially suitable for military purposes.

4 'Utbī, p. 264.

5 C͟hakraswāmīn means "the Lord of the Wheel". It was believed to have been made in the time of Rājā Bharat as a memorial of the wars connected with his name. See al-Bīrūnī, i, 117; and Gardīzī, p. 70.

6 Gardīzī, p. 71. 'Utbī gives an account of the battle but does not mention the name of the rājā. Rām is again mentioned by Gardīzī, p. 104, when he is stated to have done homage to Sulṭān Mas'ūd.

7 Gardīzī, p. 71. Dera may probably be identified with Dera Gopīpūr, District Kāngra, or with Deohra, capital of Jubbal state, Punjāb.

8 'Utbī, p. 265, but he does not mention the name of the river Sutlej. This is, however, the only river which fits in with the description of the battle.

army to cross the river at different fords and to carry out a simultaneous attack on the enemy's wings. The Hindūs fought bravely and held their ground firmly. In the evening the Sulṭān delivered an irresistible attack on the Hindūs who, leaving behind all their valuables and elephants, fled precipitately. The Sulṭān won the day but his loss on the field of battle was much heavier than that of the vanquished enemy.[1]

The Sulṭān now continued his march to Thānesar.[2] The Rājā of that place fled at his approach, leaving the idol to take care of itself. The Sulṭān entered the town unopposed and gave it up to plunder. The idol Chakraswāmīn was torn away from the place where it had received for ages the homage of countless multitudes, and was transported to Ghazna and cast into the public square.[3]

The Sulṭān returned to Ghazna in the spring of the same year (March 1015).

4. INVASIONS OF KASHMĪR

(*a*) *First Siege of Lohkot or Loharin.* In the year 406[4] (1015) the Sulṭān made preparations for an invasion of Kashmīr, probably to punish Sangrāmarājā for his assistance to Trilochanpāl. He marched to Jhelum and then, proceeding along the valley of the river Tohī, he tried to cross over to Kashmīr by the Toshmaidān Pass.[5] His progress was however checked by the hill-fort of Lohkot, modern Loharin,[6] which guarded the Pass and

1 'Utbī, p. 265; and Gardīzī, p. 71.

2 The account that follows is omitted by 'Utbī.

3 Gardīzī, p. 71; and al-Bīrūnī, i, 117.

4 Gardīzī, p. 72. 'Utbī has omitted the expedition altogether except for a casual reference on p. 304.

5 Sir Aurel Stein, Kalhana, ii, pp. 293–5, 399.

6 Gardīzī and Kalhana give it the names of Lohkot and Loharkotta respectively, both of which mean "The Iron-Fort". It is situated in Lat. 33° 48′ N., Long. 74° 23′ E. See Sir Aurel Stein's note E, Kalhana, ii, 293–300.

had the reputation of being impregnable. The Sulṭān invested the fort, but heavy falls of snow cut off his communications and after a month's fruitless endeavour he was forced to raise the siege and retire.[1]

On his return march, the Sulṭān lost his way in the hills and arrived at a place where the whole plain was covered with water.[2] Many of his troops perished and he himself escaped with difficulty.[3]

The Sulṭān spent the remaining winter months in the Punjāb and returned to Ghazna in spring[4] (March 1016).

(*b*) *Second Siege of Lohkot or Loharin.* The Sulṭān made another attempt to invade Kashmīr and in autumn 412[5] (September–October 1021) marched from Ghazna to reduce the fort of Lohkot which had formerly checked his advance. The natural defences of the fort again proved insurmountable, and for one month the besiegers made futile attempts to take it. Meanwhile severe winter set in and reduced the assailants to a pitiable condition. The Sulṭān was forced to raise the siege and finally abandon the idea of conquering Kashmīr.[6]

The Sulṭān spent the winter months in the Punjāb[7] and returned to Ghazna in the beginning of spring[8] (March–April 1022).

1 Gardīzī, p. 73. Probably it was during this expedition that some of the rājās of the south-western Kashmīr hills submitted to the Sulṭān. Cf. 'Utbī, p. 304.

2 Probably north of Mendola, a few miles south-west of Poonch, where the waters of the rivers Tausī and Swān join.

3 Ibn Jawzī, f. 162 b; Ibnu'l-Athīr, ix, 181; and *Āthāru'l-Wuzarā*, f. 98 a.

4 Gardīzī, p. 73.

5 *Ibid.* p. 79. In E. and D. ii, 464, the date is incorrectly given as 413 (1022–23).

6 Gardīzī, p. 79.

7 Gardīzī, p. 79, says that the Sulṭān returned to "Lāhūr and Tākeshar". Tākeshar was the name by which the sub-Himalayan region of the Punjāb from the Chināb westward was known. Cf. also al-Bīrūnī, i, 208; and *Ādābu'l-Mulūk*, as quoted by the author in *JRAS*. July 1927, pp. 486–91.

8 Gardīzī, p. 79. In E. and D. ii, p. 466, this expedition is mentioned as a sequel to the one against the valleys of the rivers Nūr and Qīrāt, but there is no authority for doing so.

5. INVASION OF THE GANGES DOĀB AND THE CAPTURE OF MUTTRA AND KANAUJ

The way into the Ganges Doāb, i.e. the land between the rivers Ganges and Jumna, having been cleared by recent victories, the Sulṭān resolved to lead an expedition to Kanauj. He set out from Ghazna on Saturday, 13th Jumādī i, 409[1] (27th September, 1018), with about 11,000 regulars[2] and 20,000 volunteers,[3] and marching along the sub-Himalayan range where the rivers are fordable[4] with Jānkī, son of Shāhī, son of Bamhī, Rājā of Kālanjar, in the southern Kashmīr hills,[5] as his guide, he crossed the river Jumna on 20th Rajab, 409[6] (2nd December, 1018).

The progress of the Sulṭān through the Doāb was a round of sieges, assaults and victories following each other in quick succession. The fame of his name ran on before him and made conquest easy. Shortly after crossing the Jumna he laid siege to the fort of Sirsāwa.[7] The Rājā took to flight and the garrison capitulated.

1 Ibnu'l-Jawzī, f. 166 b; Gardīzī, p. 74; and Sibṭ Ibnu'l-Jawzī, f. 149 a. Ibnu'l-Athīr incorrectly gives this expedition under A.H. 407.

2 The number of troops is inferred from Sibṭ Ibnu'l-Jawzī, f. 205 a.

3 'Utbī, p. 304.

4 *Ibid.* p. 305. Sibṭ Ibnu'l-Jawzī, f. 205 a, mentions the names of the Punjāb rivers which the Sulṭān crossed during his march.

5 'Utbī, p. 305. Baihaqī occasionally refers to this Jānkī on pp. 67, 169, 211, 664 as the ruler of Kālanjar in the Kashmīr Pass, and from what he says it is obvious that Kālanjar was not far to the north of Jhelum. Dr M. Iqbāl, Rāwandī, pp. 478–9, has failed to locate it because he started with the wrong assumption that it was near Multān. Sir Aurel Stein, Kalhana, ii, p. 433, has correctly identified it with Kotlī, Lat. 33° 33′ N., Long. 73° 58′ E. See also *Āthāru'l-Wuzarā*, f. 105 b.

6 'Utbī, p. 305.

7 Sibṭ Ibnu'l-Jawzī, f. 205 a; and 'Unṣurī, p. 141. For its antiquity, see Cunningham, *Archaeological Survey of India*, xiv, 79.

The booty consisted of 30 elephants and 1,000,000 *dirhems*.[1]

The Sulṭān then marched to Baran or Bulandshahr.[2] Hardat, Rājā of Baran, offered submission and is said to have embraced Islam with 10,000 of his followers.[3]

The Sulṭān next proceeded to the fort of Mahāban[4] which was situated on the river Jumna. Kulchand, the Rājā, drew up his army and his elephants in a thick forest and waited for an attack. He was defeated by the advance-guard of the Sulṭān and forced to flee. The fugitives threw themselves into the river to cross over to the other side but some of them were carried away by the current and the rest were taken prisoners or slain. Kulchand finding all avenues of escape closed, first slew his wife and then plunged the dagger in his own breast. Rich spoils were captured including 185 elephants.[5]

The Sulṭān now advanced to Muttra which was the reputed birthplace of the deified hero Krishna and one of the most celebrated seats of Hindū religion and learning. Muttra was well protected and was surrounded by a stone wall with two gates opening on the river Jumna,[6] but on the approach of the Sulṭān the garrison surrendered the place without offering any resistance.[7] The town was teeming with imposing temples, the glittering spires of which towered above the house-tops. The Sulṭān was so struck with their

1 Sibṭ Ibnu'l-Jawzī, f. 205 a; and Unṣurī, p. 141.

2 'Utbī, p. 305; and 'Unṣurī, p. 141. Firishta, p. 29, incorrectly reads Meerut. Baran was the old name of Bulandshahr, see *I.G.I.* vi, 428, and A. Führer, *Archaeological Survey of India*, N.W. Provinces and Oudh, p. 5.

3 'Utbī, p. 305; and 'Unṣurī, p. 141. Gardīzī, p. 75, however, says that the rājā fled.

4 Gardīzī, p. 75; and 'Unṣurī, p. 141. Mahāban is situated 6 miles south-east of Muttra, near the left bank of the river Jumna.

5 'Utbī, pp. 306–7; Gardīzī, p. 75; and 'Unṣurī, p. 142.

6 'Utbī, p. 307.

7 Gardīzī, p. 75.

massive beauty that in the letter of victory to his *amīrs* at Ghazna, he gave effusive expression to his appreciation of Hindū architecture, but this did not diminish his iconoclastic zeal, and, after they had been stripped of all their treasures, he ordered them to be burned to the ground.[1]

The booty captured included five idols of gold,[2] one of which was set with two rubies of the value of 50,000 *dīnārs*, 200 idols of silver, and a sapphire of unusually large size.[3]

Leaving the bulk of his army behind, the Sulṭān next proceeded to Kanauj, which was the seat of the government of the Pratihāra princes who were looked upon as lords paramount of northern India.[4] The Sulṭān arrived there on 8th Sha'bān, 409[5] (20th December, 1018). Hearing news of his approach, Rājyapāl, Rājā of Kanauj,[6] crossed the Ganges and fled[7] to Bārī.[8] The Sulṭān laid siege to the fort and captured all its fortifications in a single day. The town was given up to plunder and thousands of Hindūs were taken prisoners or put to the sword.[9]

1 'Utbī, p. 308; and Gardīzī, p. 75.

2 'Utbī, p. 308, says that these idols were suspended in air without any support.

3 'Utbī, p. 308, and Gardīzī, p. 76, say that this sapphire weighed 450 *mithqāls* which is an impossible weight for a precious stone.

4 'Utbī, p. 309.

5 *Ibid.* and Gardīzī, p. 76.

6 'Utbī, p. 309; and *JRAS.* 1908, p. 791. In E. and D. ii, 45, he is wrongly called "Rāī Jaipāl". Sir W. Haig, p. 19, gives him the name of Jaichand, probably in confusion with the Rāthor rājā of that name who fought with Muḥammad b. Sām, the Ghūrid.

7 'Utbī, p. 309.

8 Bārī was situated about 40 miles to the east of Kanauj but its exact situation is not known. See al-Bīrūnī, i, 200–201.

9 'Utbī, p. 309. Gardīzī's account is very much confused. Amīn Aḥmad Rāzī, *Haft Iqlīm*, f. 137 a (Bānkīpūr MS) says: "When Sulṭān Maḥmūd took Kanauj in A.H. 409 he granted Srīnagar, afterwards known as Bilgrām, as a *jāgīr* to my ancestor Muḥammad Yūsuf and appointed him his deputy at Lāhūr".

The main object of the expedition, viz., the conquest of Kanauj, was thus accomplished. The Sulṭān then started on his return march. On his way back, he passed by the fort of Munj[1] which was known as the fort of the Brahmins. He laid siege to it and captured it after some resistance. The garrison tried to escape by throwing themselves from the battlements but most of them perished in the attempt.[2]

The Sulṭān next came to the fort of Asai[3] which was surrounded by a dense jungle. The Rājā of Asai, named Chandar Pāl Bhūr,[4] fled and the Sulṭān captured his five forts. The place was then plundered and the garrison were taken prisoners or put to the sword.[5]

From Asai the Sulṭān marched straight north till he came to the fort of Sharwa.[6] The Rājā of this place named Chandar Rāy made preparations for resistance but

1 Munj is situated 14 miles north-east of Etawah. See *Dist. Gaz. U.P.* xi, 219. In E. and D. it has been identified with Manjhāwan, 10 miles south of Cawnpūr. Major Vost, *I.G.I.* xxiv, 426, suggests Ẓafarābād in District Jaunpūr and has been followed by Sir W. Haig, p. 133.

2 'Utbī, p. 310.

3 'Utbī says Āsī, which is written like Asai in Arabic script. Asai is situated on the left bank of the river Jumna, 6 miles west of Etāwah. It is said by tradition to have been one of the gates of Kanauj. See Cunningham, *Ancient Geography*, p. 339, who has discussed its locality in the light of al-Bīrūnī's itineraries. Cf. also A. Führer, *op. cit.* p. 89. In E. and D. ii, 458, Asai is identified with Asnī, 10 miles north-east from Fatḥpūr, on the river Ganges.

4 'Utbī, p. 310. Ibnu'l-Athīr, ix, 186, says Chandpāl.

5 'Utbī, p. 310.

6 I think that Sharwa was the name of the modern town Sarawa, 13 miles due south of Meerut. In E. and D. ii, 459, two places, Seunra and Sriswagarh in Bundhelkhand are suggested, but they are too far out of the way. The Rājā of Sharwa was evidently a neighbour of Trilochanpāl, son of Anandpāl, who held sway in the Siwālik hills. Gardīzī, p. 76, says that the treasure of Chandar Rāy fell into the hands of the Sulṭān during his return march from Kanauj. This statement taken together with Trilochanpāl's frequent wars with the Rājā of Sharwa (see *supra*, p. 93) clearly shows that Sharwa could not be situated as far south as Seunra or Sriswagarh.

on the approach of the Sulṭān he fled to the hills on the advice of his son-in-law Bhīmpāl, son of Trilochanpāl.[1] The Sulṭān followed him in pursuit and overtook him at a distance of about 50 miles at midnight on 25th Sha'bān[2] (6th January, 1019). The Rājā disposed his army in battle array and defended himself bravely but was defeated. His camp was plundered and rich spoils, including a large number of elephants, were captured.[3]

The Sulṭān now resumed his march to Ghazna. The total value of the booty was reckoned at about 3,000,000 *dirhems* besides 55,000 slaves and 350 elephants.[4]

6. EXPEDITION AGAINST TRILOCHANPĀL OF KANAUJ AND BĀRĪ, AND GANDA OF KĀLINJAR

Shortly after the departure of Sulṭān Maḥmūd in Sha'bān 409, Ganda the Chandel Rājā of Kālinjar, reproached Rājyapāl of Kanauj for his pusillanimous flight from Sulṭān Maḥmūd[5] and formed a league against him with the neighbouring rājās including Arjan, Rājā of Gwālior. The allied forces were placed under the command of Vidhyādhara, the Chandel crown

1 'Utbī, p. 312. See also *supra*, pp. 93–4.

2 'Utbī, p. 313. The Sulṭān must have acted with wonderful rapidity. He entered the Doāb on 20th Rajab and crossed the Jumna on his way back, probably a few days after 25th Sha'bān. The total time that he spent in achieving these numerous victories was therefore not more than about 40 days. Firishta however makes the Sulṭān stay much longer.

3 'Utbī, p. 313. Gardīzī, p. 76, says that one of the elephants of Chandar Rāy which Sulṭān Maḥmūd was willing to buy for any price or to exchange for 50 elephants, came of itself to his camp and was named Khudā-dād, or Godsend, for this reason.

4 'Utbī, p. 313; and Sibṭ Ibnu'l-Jawzī, f. 205 a.

5 'Utbī, p. 309; Gardīzī, p. 76; and Ibnu'l-Athīr, ix, 218. Niẓāmu'd-Dīn and Firishta incorrectly say that Rājyapāl had submitted to Sulṭān Maḥmūd, and they have been followed by Smith, p. 383, Sir W. Haig, p. 21, and other modern historians.

prince,[1] and sent against Rājyapāl. Rājyapāl was slain in battle[2] and Trilochanpāl, presumably a son of Rājyapāl,[3] was raised to the throne. This success considerably increased the power of Ganda, so much so that he promised to help Trilochanpāl, son of Anandpāl, in winning back his ancestral kingdom from Sulṭān Maḥmūd.[4]

On getting news of these events, the Sulṭān marched from Ghazna in the beginning of autumn 410[5] (October 1019) to crush the power of Ganda and his ally, the new Rājā of Kanauj and Bārī, and crossed the river Ganges somewhere below Hardwār.[6]

In the meantime, hearing news of the Sulṭān's advance, Trilochanpāl, son of Anandpāl, marched south to join forces with his namesake, the ruler of Kanauj and Bārī. The Sulṭān pushed forward in pursuit and overtook him near the bank of the river Ruhut or Rāmgangā but Trilochanpāl crossed over to the other side and tried to prevent the passage of the river. The Sulṭān, however, managed to cross, and after inflicting a crushing defeat on him,[7] continued his march to Bārī. On his approach, Trilochanpāl, Rājā of Bārī, and all the inhabitants of the town took to flight.[8] The Sulṭān ordered the deserted town to be levelled to the ground.[9]

The Sulṭān now turned his attention to Ganda who, with an army said to have been swelled to the huge number of 145,000 foot, 36,000 horse and 640

1 Smith, *JRAS.* 1909, p. 278.
2 Gardīzī, p. 76; and Ibnu'l-Athir, ix, 218.
3 Smith, p. 383.
4 Gardīzī, p. 76; Ibnu'l-Athīr, ix, 218; and *Ādābu'l-Mulūk* (Brit. Mus. MS Add. 16,853), f. 184 a.
5 Gardīzī, p. 76; and 'Utbī, p. 318. Ibnu'l-Athīr and Firishta wrongly place this expedition in 409 (1018–19) and 412 (1021–22) respectively.
6 Inferred from Farrukhī, f. 16 a.
7 See *supra*, pp. 94–5.
8 Gardīzī, p. 77; Farrukhī, f. 16 b; and Ibnu'l-Athīr, ix, 218.
9 Gardīzī, p. 77; and Farrukhī, f. 16 b.

elephants[1] by the contingents of his feudatories, advanced to meet the invader. The Sulṭān marshalled his army in battle array and sent an ambassador to Ganda calling upon him to accept Islam or pay tribute but Ganda indignantly rejected the proposal and prepared for battle.[2]

The Sulṭān now ascended an eminence to reconnoitre the position of the enemy, and his eyes met with a spectacle which for once shook his courage. He saw before him, as far as eye could reach, an imposing panorama of camps, pavilions and embankments and he regretted having ventured so far. In his distress, he prostrated himself in prayer to seek divine assistance, which restored his drooping spirits,[3] and in the evening a successful engagement of Abū 'Abdu'llāh Muḥammad aṭ-Ṭā'ī, commander of the advance-guard, with a detachment of Ganda, dispelled the remaining gloom.[4] The following morning Sulṭān Maḥmūd despatched his ambassador to Ganda, but he returned to report that the enemy's camp was deserted. Ganda, unaccountably stricken with panic, had fled from the field under cover of night. The sacrifice of Rājyapāl had evidently not improved the morale of his chief persecutor.[5]

The Sulṭān thanked God for this unexpected good luck and, after making sure that no ambush had been laid, he gave orders for the plundering of the camp of the enemy who had left behind all their valuables.[6] The fugitives were followed for some distance and many of them were captured or killed, but Ganda himself managed to escape.[7]

1 Gardīzī, p. 77; and Ibnu'l-Athīr, ix, 218. Farrukhī, f. 17 a, says that he had 133,000 foot, 36,000 horse, and 900 elephants.

2 Gardīzī, p. 77.

3 *Ibid.*

4 Ibnu'l-Athīr, ix, 218; and Farrukhī, f. 2 b.

5 Gardīzī, p. 77; and Ibnu'l-Athīr, ix, 218.

6 Gardīzī, p. 78; Farrukhī, f. 2 b; and Ibnu'l-Athīr, ix, 218.

7 Ibnu'l-Athīr, ix, 218.

The Sulṭān then returned to Ghazna.[1] On his way back 580 elephants of Ganda fell into his hands.[2]

7. EXPEDITION AGAINST GWĀLIOR AND KĀLINJAR

The power of Ganda had not been broken in the expedition against him in 410 (1019–20) and he still openly defied the Sulṭān. In 413[3] (1022), therefore, the Sulṭān again marched to Kālinjar to reduce him to submission. On his way thither the Sulṭān passed the fort of Gwālior, the Rājā of which, named Arjan, was a feudatory of Ganda. This fort was built on the summit of a stupendous rock and was reputed to be impregnable. The Sulṭān stormed the fort, but failed to capture it. The Rājā, despite his successful resistance, was so alarmed that after four days he sued for peace, and made a present of 35 elephants.[4]

The Sulṭān then marched to the fort of Kālinjar which was situated on the lofty crag of a precipitous rock of hard stone and was deemed impregnable. It is said that the fort provided accommodation for "500,000 men, 20,000 head of cattle and 500 elephants and contained sufficient provisions, weapons and other requirements".[5] The Sulṭān laid siege to it and closed all the

1 Faṣīḥī, f. 322 a, incorrectly prolongs the stay of the Sulṭān in India for four years.

2 Gardīzī, p. 77; and Farrukhī, f. 2 b. A long account of this battle is given in *Majma'u'l-Ansāb*, but the text is so corrupt that it is difficult to make anything out of it.

3 Gardīzī, p. 79.

4 *Ibid.* In *The Syriac Chronicle*, pp. 211–12, an account is given of the interview of the Sulṭān's ambassador with the Rājā and of the ceremony which marked the settlement of the terms of peace. A translation of this passage from the original Syriac is given in Appendix L.

5 Ibn Ẓāfir, f. 149 b; and Sibṭ Ibnu'l-Jawzī (Bodl. MS 370), under A.H. 414. Ibn Ẓāfir further adds that the Hindūs believed that the founder of this fort was the first rājā to capture and ride elephants and that other rājās followed his example.

approaches to the fort in order to starve the garrison into submission. Ganda made overtures for peace,[1] and promised to pay annual tribute and to deliver 300 elephants.[2] The Sulṭān accepted the terms and raised the siege. After this Ganda composed a verse in Hindī in praise of Sulṭān Maḥmūd, who was so pleased with it that he conferred on him the government of fifteen forts, a robe of honour and rich presents.[3]

The Sulṭān then returned to Ghazna about the close of the year 413[4] (March–April 1023).

1 Ibn Ẓāfir, f. 149 b, says that one of the ceremonies of peace among the Hindūs was that the defeated monarch had to cut off the tip of one of his fingers, which the victor kept as a trophy, and that "for this reason the Sulṭān had a number of the finger-tips of the Hindū rājās whom he had defeated". Ganda had, therefore, to cut off one of his finger-tips and give it to the Sulṭān. See also Ibnu'l-Athīr, ix, 133; and Appendix L.

2 Gardīzī, p. 80; and Ibn Ẓāfir, f. 149 b. Gardīzī, p. 80, adds that Ganda sent these elephants without riders to test the bravery of the Sulṭān's warriors, who, however, seized them and brought them to their camp; but there is no authority for a statement in E. and D. ii, 467, note 2, that these elephants had previously been intoxicated.

3 Gardīzī, p. 80; and Ibn Ẓāfir, f. 149 b. Ibnu'l-Athīr has incorrectly made this expedition a sequel to the one against Multān in 396 (1005–6); and has been followed by Ibn Khaldūn and Abu'l-Fidā. Some details of this expedition are also given in *Majma'u'l-Ansāb*, f. 234 a, but they are not corroborated by any of the earlier authorities.

4 Ibn Ẓāfir, f. 150 a, however, says that after the submission of Ganda, "when Kābakan, the Rajā of a neighbouring kingdom and master of 1000 elephants, who was commonly known as Taḥdah (or Najdah, according to the Gotha MS), learnt how well the Sulṭān had treated Ganda, he sent an ambassador to the Sulṭān and offered allegiance". He is said to have sent many presents to the Sulṭān, including two extraordinary things, namely, a bird resembling a dove, one of the qualities of which was that if it fluttered above a table on which poisonous food was laid out its eyes filled with tears, and a stone, a touch of which could heal deep wounds. These extraordinary presents are also mentioned by Ibnu'l-Athīr, ix, 234; and Sibṭ Ibnu'l-Jawzī (Bodl. MS 370) under the events of A.H. 414.

8. EXPEDITION TO SOMNĀTH

"When Yamīnu'd-Dawlah was gaining victories and demolishing temples in India, the Hindūs said that Somnāth[1] was displeased with these idols, and that if it had been satisfied with them no one could have destroyed or injured them. When Yamīnu'd-Dawlah heard this, he resolved upon making a campaign to destroy this idol",[2] and left Ghazna on the morning of Monday, 22nd Sha'bān, 416[3] (18th October, 1025) with an army of 30,000 regular cavalry and hundreds of volunteers.[4] He reached Multān about 15th Ramaḍān[5] (9th November) and halted there to enquire into the conditions of travel across the desert and to make necessary preparations for the journey.[6] Provision of water was the chief concern of the Sulṭān. Each trooper was provided with two camels to carry water for him, and the Sulṭān supplemented individual arrangements by loading his own establishment of 20,000 camels with water as a measure of precaution for the desert march.[7] He left Multān on 2nd Shawwāl[8] (26th November) and plunged into the unknown desert.

The first place of importance that fell before the

1 For the origin and sacredness of this idol, see Appendix M.
2 Ibnu'l-Athīr, ix, 241.
3 Ibn Ẓāfir, f. 150 a, and Sibṭ Ibnu'l-Jawzī, f. 215 a, but Ibnu'l-Athīr, *ib.* gives 10th Sha'bān which is probably a copyist's error.
4 Ibn Jawzī, f. 175 b; and Ibnu'l-Athīr, ix, 241. Sibṭ Ibnu'l-Jawzī, f. 215 a, adds that the Sulṭān distributed 50,000 *dīnārs* among the volunteers for their expenses.
5 Ibnu'l-Athīr, ix, 241; and Sibṭ Ibnu'l-Jawzī, f. 215 a.
6 Farrukhī, f. 18 b, describes the hardships of the journey. Sibṭ Ibnu'l-Jawzī, f. 215 a, says that the difficulties experienced on the way were beyond expectation, and that the troopers suffered immensely.
7 Ibnu'l-Athīr, ix, 241.
8 Sibṭ Ibnu'l-Jawzī, f. 215 a.

Sulṭān in the desert was the strong fort of Lodorva,[1] the capital of the Bhatī Jādons. From there he continued his march along the ridge that traverses the Jaisalmīr state and Mallānī and probably passing close to the Chiklodar Mātā hill,[2] he reached Anhalwāra in the beginning of Dhu'l-Qa'da[3] (end of December) after a march of one month across the desert. The Solankhī ruler of Anhalwāra, named Bhīmdeva, fled to the strong fort of Kanthkot[4] in Cutch, leaving the town in the hands of the Sulṭān.[5] After replenishing his stores of water and provisions, the Sulṭān continued his march southwards. At Mundher or Mudhera,[6] the Hindūs made a determined attempt to check his advance and 20,000 warriors mustered under their chiefs to try conclusions with the invader, but they were defeated and scattered.[7] The Sulṭān then marched straight to Delvāda near Ūnā, where the people, believing that the god Somnāth itself would annihilate the Muslims, did not offer any resistance, so that the place was taken without much trouble.[8]

Somnāth was at last within sight. The Sulṭān arrived there on Thursday, 14th Dhu'l-Qa'da, 416[9] (6th

1 See Appendix M. 2 *Ibid.*

3 Ibnu'l-Athīr, ix, 241.

4 Kanthkot is 16 miles south-west from Rāo and 36 miles north-east from Anjar. See J. Burgess, *Archaeological Survey of Western India*, ix, 13. It has been incorrectly identified with Gandhavī, a few miles north-east of Miyānī in the north-west of Kāthiāwār in the *Bombay Gazetteer*, viii, 280; and with Beyt Shankhodhar, at the north-western extremity of the peninsula of Kāthiāwār, by Sir W. Haig, p. 25. Cf. also E. and D. i, 445, and ii, 473, note 1.

5 Gardīzī, p. 86.

6 See Appendix M.

7 Ibnu'l-Athīr, ix, 241–2.

8 Farrukhī, f. 18 b; and Ibnu'l-Athīr, ix, 242. Sibṭ Ibnu'l-Jawzī, f. 215 a, says that at one of these places a thick fog set in and excluded the sun. The Hindūs believed that it had been caused by the idol of Somnāth in order to annihilate the Muslims.

9 Ibnu'l-Athīr, ix, 242.

January, 1026), and beheld a strong fortress[1] built on the seashore. Its ramparts were crowded with incredulous Brahmins, who mocked at the invaders and boasted that the mighty Someshwar had drawn the Muslims thither to avenge the accumulated insults against the gods of India. The commander of the fort, however, probably as sceptical of his ability to withstand the invaders as of the power of the idol to decimate them, escaped to an island and did not return till the Sulṭān had left the country.[2]

The Sulṭān laid siege to the fort of Somnāth. The garrison, assisted by the Brahmins and the devotees of the idol, defended it with the courage and desperation of fanatics, but on the following morning, Friday, 15th Dhu'l-Qa'da (7th January) the Muslims assailed them with such a deadly shower of arrows that they were forced to abandon their posts on the battlements. In the afternoon, about the time of the *Juma'* prayer, the Muslims escaladed the walls of the fort and proclaimed their success by sounding the call to prayer.[3] The Hindūs entered the temple, cast themselves before the idol, besought it for victory and, with revived hopes and courage, delivered a desperate attack on their assailants. The Muslims were staggered by the fury of the charge and before evening the Hindūs had expelled them from the position which they had captured.[4]

The next morning, Saturday, 16th Dhu'l-Qa'da[5] (8th January, 1026), the Muslims renewed the attack with greater vigour, captured the fortifications and drove the Hindūs to the gates of the shrine which became the scene of a dreadful *mêlée*. Band after band of Hindūs entered the temple, passionately invoked the assistance

1 This fortress had been built about 100 years before its capture by Sulṭān Maḥmūd. See al-Bīrūnī, ii, 105.

2 Gardīzī, p. 86.

3 *Ibid.* Ibnu'l-Athīr, ix, 242; and Sibṭ Ibnu'l-Jawzī, f. 215 b.

4 Ibnu'l-Athīr, ix, 242.

5 *Ibid.*

of the idol and then rushed upon the assailants.[1] But Hindū fanaticism was no match for Muslim valour and good generalship. The Sulṭān pushed his advantage and captured the fort. A terrible drama of bloodshed and carnage was then enacted, and no less than 50,000 devotees are said to have laid down their lives in the defence of their deity.[2] The survivors tried to escape in boats but they were followed and drowned or slain by a guard which the Sulṭān had posted along the sea-coast.[3]

The Sulṭān now entered the temple.[4] When he saw the idol, he ordered the upper part to be disfigured with pick-axes and a fire to be lighted round it so as to break it into small pieces.[5] The temple was then divested of its wealth, which is said to have amounted to 20,000,000 *dīnārs*,[6] and was burned to the ground.[7]

The Sulṭān did not stay there for more than a fortnight and started on his return march to Ghazna,[8] but

1 Ibnu'l-Athīr, ix. 242. Firishta, p. 32, gives some details which, though not improbable, are not corroborated by earlier writers. I have therefore omitted them from this account.

2 Ibn Ẓāfir, f. 151 a; and Sibṭ Ibnu'l-Jawzī, f. 216 a.

3 Ibnu'l-Athīr, ix, 242; and Firishta, p. 32.

4 For the structure of the temple and its ancient site, see Appendix M.

5 Gardīzī, p. 86; Farrukhī, ff. 20 a, 21 a; and Ibn Ẓāfir, f. 151 a. Some portions of this idol were sent to Mecca and Baghdād, and some were thrown in front of the Jāmi' Masjid at Ghazna and the palace of the Sulṭān. See al-Bīrūnī, ii, 103; and Ibn Ẓāfir, f. 151 a.

6 Ibnu'l-Athīr, ix, 242. In *Rawḍah*, p. 741, it is said that this was the value of the Sulṭān's share alone, which was one-fifth of the total spoils. As the *dīnār* of Maḥmūd was on the average 64·8 grains in weight, the approximate value of the spoils in present money would equal £10,500,000.

7 Ibn Jawzī, f. 175 b; Farrukhī, ff. 20 a, 21 a; and Ibn Ẓāfir, f. 151 a. They further add that the fire spread to the fort which was burned to the ground.

8 It is not stated by any authority that the Sulṭān left a governor at Somnāth, as mentioned in *Waṣāyā-i-Niẓāmu'l-Mulk*, *Rawḍah* and Firishta. The editor of the *Bombay Gazetteer*, viii, 607, is evidently wrong in stating in an authoritative manner that the Sulṭān left a governor.

the destruction of the idol had sent a wave of indignation among the Hindūs, and by that time the neighbouring chieftains were advancing in force under Rājā Paramdeva of Ābū[1] to block the passage of the Sulṭān across the narrow neck of land that lies between the Arāvallī hills and the Rann of Cutch. With a view to avoid a conflict, the Sulṭān resolved to take a more westerly route through Cutch and Sind[2] and marched north till he came to the shallow arm of the sea that runs like a wedge between Kāthiāwār and Cutch.[3] Not willing to be stopped by such an obstacle, the Sulṭān plunged his horse into the sea at low tide, followed by the whole army, and crossed over to the other side in safety.[4] When Bhīmdeva heard the news of the Sulṭān's approach he fled from the fort of Kanthkot where he had taken refuge. The Sulṭān took the fort, gave it up to plunder[5] and resumed his march across Cutch.[6] Here he was led astray by a devotee of Somnāth who had offered to act as a guide, but, to avenge the desecration of his deity, had intentionally brought the army to a place where water could not be procured. After a few days of hopeless wandering, the Sulṭān was able to extricate his army from this perilous situation and cross over to Sind in safety.[7]

1 Gardīzī, p. 87; and the *Bombay Gazetteer*, vol. i, pt i, p. 168.

2 Gardīzī, p. 87; and Farrukhī, f. 20 b.

3 *Ibid.*; and Ibnu'l-Athīr, ix, 242.

4 Farrukhī, f. 20 b. He further says that it took the Sulṭān two days to cross it, and that "besides soldiers, more than 200,000 horses, camels and other beasts of burden crossed this arm of the sea".

5 *Ibid.* Ibnu'l-Athīr, ix, 242, adds that this fort was at a distance of 40 *farsakh* or about 140 miles from Somnāth.

6 Firishta, p. 33, takes the Sulṭān from here again to Anhalwārā, but this is contradicted by Gardīzī, Farrukhī and Ibnu'l-Athīr.

7 Farrukhī, f. 25 a; 'Awfī, f. 179 a; *Majma'u'l-Ansāb*, f. 239 a; *Ṭab. Nāṣ.* p. 82; and *Futūḥu's-Salāṭīn*, f. 38 b. See also the *Bombay Gazetteer*, v, 14.

The Sulṭān then marched to Manṣūra.[1] Khafīf,[2] the Carmathian ruler, fled across the river and took refuge in a date-palm forest. The Sulṭān sent some of his officers after him, who surrounded his camp and put many of his followers to death.[3]

The Sulṭān then continued his march along the river Indus to Multān but owing to the barren nature of the country and the hostility of the Jāts who inhabited the surrounding country and hung upon his rear, his army suffered great hardships and many of the soldiers and beasts of burden perished.[4] After a long and weary march, the Sulṭān reached Ghazna on 10th Ṣafar, 417[5] (2nd April, 1026).

The expedition to Somnāth is one of the greatest feats of military adventure in the history of Islam. The news of this victory sent a wave of joy all over the Muslim world, and the delighted Caliph heaped titles and honours on the Sulṭān, his sons and his brother.[6] Like many other heroes, Sulṭān Maḥmūd became transformed into an almost mythical figure and generations of enthusiastic authors surrounded his name with a huge literature of fanciful stories which were intended to glorify him as a king and a warrior.[7] The

1 Manṣūra was founded on the old site of the town of Brāhmanābād, about 43 miles north-east of Haidarābād, Sind. See *Archaeological Survey of India, Annual Reports*, 1903–4, pp. 132 *et seq.*

2 Farrukhī, f. 21 a, is the only contemporary writer to mention his name. See also E. and D. i, 216.

3 *Ibid.*; and Ibnu'l-Athīr, ix, 242. It is alleged in *Tuḥfatu'l-Kirām* (E. and D. i, 482) that 'Abdu'r-Razzāq, wazīr of Sulṭān Maḥmūd, conquered Bhakkar, Siwistān and Thatta and turned the Arabs out of Sind, but there is no authority for this statement. None of the wazīrs of the Sulṭān was named 'Abdu'r-Razzāq.

4 Gardīzī, p. 87.

5 Ibnu'l-Athīr, ix, 243.

6 Gardīzī, pp. 87–8. Sulṭān Maḥmūd received the title of *Kahfu'd-Dawlah wa'l-Islām*, Mas'ūd *Shihābu'd-Dawlah wa Jamālu'l-Millah*, Muḥammad, *Jalālu'd-Dawlah wa Jamālu'l-Millah*, and Yūsuf, *'Aḍudu'd-Dawlah wa Mu'ayyidu'l-Millah*.

7 See Appendix M for some of these stories. See also *Ḥadīqah* of Ḥakīm Sanā'ī, *Kulliyyāt* of 'Aṭṭār, 'Awfī's *Jawāmi'u'l-Ḥikāyāt*, and other story books.

idol of Somnāth itself perished but it immortalised the name of Sulṭān Maḥmūd.[1]

9. A PUNITIVE EXPEDITION AGAINST THE JĀTS

In the beginning of the year 418[2] (March 1027), Sulṭān Maḥmūd set out for Multān to punish the Jāts,[3] who had harassed his army during his return march from Somnāth. He resolved to fight them on the river and ordered the construction of 1400 boats, each of which was armed with three iron spikes, projecting one from the prow and two from the sides. Each boat carried 20 archers, who, besides bows, arrows and shields, were armed with hand-grenades and naphtha-balls. This flotilla was launched on the river Indus.[4]

1 Dīwān Ranc͟hodjī Amarjī, Dīwān of Jūnāgadh State, in his work entitled *Ta'rīk͟h-i-Sorath*, J. Burgess's translation, p. 111, says that when Sulṭān Maḥmūd demolished the temple of Somnāth, "it so offended the Mahārāja Mandalika, who was a protector of his own religion, that he marched with Bhim Deva, the Rāja of Gujarāt, in pursuit.... The Muhammadans did not make a stand and fled; many of them were slain by Hindu scymitars and prostrated by Rājput war-clubs, and when the sun of the Rāja's fortune culminated, Shāh Maḥmud took to his heels in dismay and saved his life, but many of his followers of both sexes were captured...".

This account is not based on any work known to exist, and is, on the face of it, fictitious.

2 Gardīzī, p. 88. Almost all the later writers who mention this expedition place it in the year 417 (1026). Ibnu'l-At͟hīr, ix, 243, has erroneously made this expedition a sequel to the one against Somnāth.

3 According to al-Bīrūnī, ii, 104, these Jāts were the worshippers of the *linga*. In E. and D. ii, 477, they are incorrectly called the inhabitants of the Jūd hills, i.e. the Salt Range in the Punjāb. According to J. Burgess, *Archaelogical Survey of Western India*, ii, 194, they were the Bhatīs of Bhatnair who had migrated to Sind. M. Reinaud, *Mémoire sur l'Inde*, p. 272 (E. and D. ii, 477), quotes a passage from Ibnu'l-At͟hīr to the effect that these Jāts had invaded the principality of Manṣūra and had forced the Muslim ruler of that place to abjure his religion, but there is no authority for this statement in the original.

4 Gardīzī, p. 88.

The Jāts also made great preparations for the struggle and, after sending their families and effects to a distant island in the river, they are said to have brought 4000 boats[1] properly manned and equipped for the fight. The Sulṭān blocked the upper course of the river with his flotilla of boats and posted two strong detachments of cavalry supported by elephants to guard the banks of the river. The two fleets met and a desperate conflict ensued. The Jāts fought bravely but most of their boats that approached the Muslim fleet were overturned and sunk on their first impact with the projecting spikes.[2] The Sulṭān gained the day and the Jāts were beaten. Some of them tried to escape by land, but on approaching the banks of the river, they were assailed by the Turkomāns whom the Sulṭān had posted there and were driven back into the river. The victors now followed them to the places where they had deposited their valuables, killed many of them and captured large spoils.

The Sulṭān returned to Ghazna about the beginning of summer 418[4] (June–July 1027).

1 The number of boats seems to be exaggerated.

2 So in Gardīzī, p. 89, but it is difficult to understand how they could overturn the boats of the enemy without overturning their own boats.

3 Gardīzī is the only contemporary author to give an account of this expedition. Farrukhī, f. 36 a, has a passing reference to this expedition, thus:

من شکار آب مرغابی و ماهی دیده ام

تو در آب امسال شیران سیه کردی شکار

"I have seen the catching of water-fowls and fish in the river, (but) thou hast hunted black lions (the Jāts) in the river this year."

CHAPTER IX

THE CLOSING DAYS

THE strong constitution of Sulṭān Maḥmūd was weakened by the constant strain of intense fatigue and hardships to which he had been exposing himself in his numerous wars, particularly his summer campaigns in India. It appears that he contracted malaria during his expedition against the Jāts in 418[1] (1027). This became chronic and developed into consumption accompanied by diarrhoea.[2] For two years he suffered from this malady,[3] but he would not yield to it and endeavoured to conceal his ill-health from his people. In spite of the warning of physicians who advised complete rest, he persisted in carrying on his daily routine. He held court as usual, and gave audience twice a day.[4] He chased the Seljuks out of Khurāsān, proceeded against Raiy, and by swift marches repressed the insubordination of Mīnūchihr. He did not miss even his annual tour in the empire, and spent the summer of 420 (1029) in Khurāsān and the following winter at Balkh.[5] The climate of Balkh, however, did not agree with him and he returned to Ghazna. He arrived there about the middle of Rabīʿ ii 421[6] (about 22nd April, 1030), but the change of climate did not effect any improvement in his condition, and after a week of

1 Sibṭ Ibnu'l-Jawzī, f. 220 a, says that he contracted his last illness during one of his expeditions to India.

2 *Ibid.* Gardīzī, p. 92, says that the Sulṭān had consumption (دق). It is probable that his malaria developed into tuberculosis of the intestines.

3 Ibnu'l-Athīr, ix, 281.

4 *Ibid.*; Gardīzī, p. 92; and Farrukhī, f. 41 b.

5 Gardīzī, p. 92.

6 *Ibid.*

suffering, he passed away at 5 o'clock in the afternoon, on Thursday, 23rd Rabī' ii, 421[1] (30th April, 1030), at the age of fifty-nine years.[2] He was buried the same evening at the time of the *'ashā* prayer in the Fīrūzī garden, which was his favourite pleasure-resort.[3]

During his long illness, the Sulṭān showed marvellous powers of endurance, and refused to lie in bed like a sick man. He sat day and night propped up with pillows, and breathed his last in this posture.[4]

The end of Sulṭān Maḥmūd was in harmony with his life—a monument of self-reliance, personal intrepidity, contempt of danger and defiance of obstacles. He died as he had lived. He defied even Death.

A short time before his death, the Sulṭān ordered the royal jewels and precious stones to be displayed in his presence. He saw before him seventy *raṭls* of them

1 Baihaqī, p. 12; Gardīzī, p. 92; and Sibṭ Ibnu'l-Jawzī, f. 220 a. This date is inscribed on the sarcophagus of Sulṭān Maḥmūd. See *Syria*, vi, 61–90; and *JASB*. xii, 76–7.

2 Sixty-one years, according to lunar reckoning.

3 Baihaqī, p. 12; and Sibṭ Ibnu'l-Jawzī, f. 220 a.

Sulṭān Mas'ūd erected a magnificent mausoleum over the tomb of his father and settled rich endowments on it. See Baihaqī, p. 310. The memory of the Sulṭān was cherished with great reverence, and even 'Alā'u'd-Dīn, "the world-incendiary", spared his tomb from the indiscriminate devastation with which he visited Ghazna in the following century. His tomb has, however, suffered from the ravages of his Muslim admirers, who for ages have resorted to it for the purpose of seeking divine grace and have carried away to their homes fragments of wood or handfuls of earth as keepsakes; from the sacrilege of the savage hordes of Hulāgū Khān; and, in more recent times, from the misguided enthusiasm of Lord Ellenborough, who, believing that its gates were those of the temple of Somnāth which the Sulṭān was supposed to have carried away, ordered them to be removed and brought back to India. The dilapidated ruins of what was once a grand edifice stand out on the plain, about one mile from the town of Ghazna, and bear silent testimony to the mutability of human greatness.

4 Gardīzī, p. 92; Ibnu'l-Athīr, ix, 281; and Sibṭ Ibnu'l-Jawzī, f. 220 a.

(about as many pounds avoirdupois) arranged in glittering rows;[1] and, possibly the terrible drama of a lifetime—the burning towns, the ruined castles, the fields of battle seething with blood, the yells of frightened fugitives and the groans of dying wretches mingled with the clatter of victorious arms—all rose in a ghastly vision before his troubled soul. A pang of remorse shot through his heart; tears trickled down his cheeks; and he wept bitterly.[2]

His dying moments must have been rendered more painful by a presentiment that the huge empire, built up at the cost of so much suffering and bloodshed, was tottering to its fall. On the distant horizon, his keen eye could discern a dark cloud, the harbinger of a threatening storm: for the Seljuks, whom in a moment of weakness he had permitted to settle in Khurāsān,[3] were gathering force with ominous rapidity. The stupendous achievement of a life of vigorous warfare appeared to be crumbling away as the great Sulṭān lay on his death-bed.

1 Sibṭ Ibnu'l-Jawzī, f. 220 a.

2 Sibṭ Ibnu'l Jawzī, f. 220 a, citing aṣ-Ṣābī's *Dhail*, says that when the Sulṭān saw the precious stones he wept bitterly. Later writers, like Mīr-Khwānd, attribute this weeping to the pangs of sorrow which they suppose the Sulṭān felt at the prospect of leaving all these treasures behind and accuse him of a sordid love of mammon for not having given away a portion of these precious stones to the poor; but as the Sulṭān was well-known among his contemporaries for his generosity, my interpretation of his grief is more probable because it is more consistent with the facts of his life.

3 *Ṭab. Nāṣ.* p. 119.

Part Three

CHAPTER X

THE ADMINISTRATIVE SYSTEM OF SULṬĀN MAḤMŪD

THE key-note of the new social and political order that Islam created was the principle which affirmed the indefeasible equality of man and man. This principle was maintained in practice by the immediate successors of the Prophet Muḥammad, but, with the extension of the boundaries of Islam, it underwent a sad metamorphosis by the interaction of the political theories of the conquered races, so that eventually the democratic government of the early days of Islam was superseded by an absolute and hereditary monarchy based on the model of the one which the Arab arms had overthrown in Persia; and although a mockery of an election was still held when a new Caliph ascended the throne, Muslim government henceforth became synonymous with autocracy and despotism.

THE SULṬĀN

Sulṭān Maḥmūd, like his former overlords, the Sāmānids of Bukhārā, was an autocrat of the most absolute kind: "the Shadow of God on Earth". He was the supreme legislative, judicial and executive authority in the empire and had the power of life and death over his subjects.[1]

The position of the Sulṭān was no sinecure since the

1 'Utbī, p. 5. For the powers of a king see Baihaqī, pp. 108–120; 'Utbī, p. 5; ath-Tha'ālibī, *Arba' Rasā'il*, p. 160; Ibn Qutaiba, *'Uyūnu'l-Akhbār*, p. 3; and *Siyāsat Nāmah*, p. 110.

stability and efficient working of a medieval state depended to a great extent on the personality of the autocrat at its head. The whole life of Sulṭān Maḥmūd was an untiring application to hard work, and although the wazīr was officially responsible for the smooth running of the machinery of the state, the Sulṭān nevertheless personally supervised every department of government,[1] and was, by his extraordinary ability, able to control and check the laxity in administration which was habitual to his officers. Whenever any act of tyranny, peculation or extortion was brought to his notice, he inflicted punishment on the offenders. His frequent marches across the length and breadth of his empire continually reminded his distant provincial officers of their vigilant master at G͟hazna. The Sulṭān kept a watchful eye on the doings of the high dignitaries of the empire, particularly his military commanders; and being only too familiar with what ambition could dictate to a warrior who had at his command the revenue of a province and the mercenary valour of Turkistān, he did not allow them to hatch dubious designs in the isolation of their distant provinces. It was thus only by means of ceaseless energy that the Sulṭān could maintain peace and order in his vast empire and keep under control his haughty and restless nobility, in an age when, by the frequency of its occurrence and the success which had usually attended it, rebellion had acquired the sanctity of a well-established custom.

The Sulṭān was his own commander-in-chief and either personally led all the campaigns or directed them from the capital. He constituted the highest court of appeal for his empire and dealt out impartial justice to high and low alike.[2] He exercised a general supervision over the working of an efficient and well-organised system of spies and news-writers who kept

1 'Utbī, p. 304. 2 Baihaqī, p. 182.

him informed of the doings of the state officials and provincial governors. The Sulṭān personally directed foreign policy and himself dictated all important correspondence. He himself made all the higher appointments and consulted the ministers only as an additional source of information regarding the candidates. He was a keen judge of merit in men as is shown by the subsequent career of numerous officers of his choice.

The Sulṭān was also a judge of literary merit, and, surrounded by a host of poets and men of letters, he distributed money unstintingly among them in proportion to their worth. He was, in short, the centre round which revolved all the activities of the state.

THE COUNCIL

The Sulṭān was not bound to consult his ministers in state affairs,[1] but in practice he followed the divine commandment which bids Muslims consult each other in all matters.[2] Whenever he was confronted with a serious situation, he called a council of all the important civil and military officers to hear their opinion and advice. The proceedings of the council which he called to consider the situation created by the assassination of his brother-in-law, Abu'l-'Abbās, the Khwārizmshāh, have been preserved and furnish an excellent specimen of the arbitrary ways of the Sulṭān. When all the important civil and military officers were assembled, the Sulṭān addressed them thus:

"What should be done in regard to Khwārizm, the people of which have behaved outrageously by assassinating my brother-in-law, their king? Unless the regicides are apprehended and punished, I cannot escape the reproaches of the neighbouring monarchs, who will cease to put any faith in my friendship. To declare war on the regicides is to run great risks, as they have a

1 Baihaqī, p. 266. 2 *Siyāsat Nāmah*, p. 84.

large and well-equipped army, and the chances of battle might go against us. On the other hand, if Khwārizm is conquered, it will have to be placed under a trustworthy officer, as it is a vast country and is contiguous to the territory of our enemies; but in that case the meagre revenue of Khwārizm will not suffice for the expenses of administration. I am unable to decide in this dilemma: what say you?"[1]

The wazīr was expected to speak first but being afraid of declaring his mind before the Sulṭān, he endeavoured to shift the responsibility to the commanders of the army on the plea of their better knowledge of military affairs. They in their turn waived the responsibility by contending that their duty was "to do and die" in the service of their lord, the Sulṭān. Thus cornered, the wazīr tried to evade the question. The Sulṭān was furious and unceremoniously dismissed his counsellors, thus: "Avaunt, you cowards. It is not your desire that my kingdom should expand. I will myself decide upon the best course of action".[1]

The Sulṭān was prepared to hear only that advice which was acceptable to him,[2] while his counsellors, afraid of provoking his anger if their advice proved disastrous, spoke in a guarded manner. Thus the council was nothing more than a deliberative and consultative body at best, and the Sulṭān was not bound either to ask or accept its advice.[3] The prerogative of an Eastern prince was "not circumscribed, either in right or in fact, by the power of the nobles, the freedom of the commons, the privileges of the church,...or the memory of a free constitution".

1 *Athāru'l-Wuzarā*, ff. 95 b–99 a.

2 Baihaqī, p. 330. In *Chahār Maqāla*, p. 58, kings are compared to children, and it is laid down as a condition of service under them that one should speak according to their wish.

3 Baihaqī, p. 266.

THE FIVE MINISTERS

The kingdom of Ghazna, being a dependency of Bukhārā in its earlier days, was administered as a part of the Sāmānid empire. Sulṭān Maḥmūd adopted and continued the system of administration which was already in operation, without making any appreciable alterations or improvements in it. He had five important ministers,[1] who were in charge of (*a*) Dīwān-i-Wizārat or Finance Department, (*b*) Dīwān-i-'Arḍ or War Department, (*c*) Dīwān-i-Risālat or Correspondence Department, (*d*) Dīwān-i-Shughl-i-Ishrāf-i-Mamlukat or Secret Service Department, and (*e*) Dīwān-i-Wikālat or Household Department.[2]

METHOD OF THEIR APPOINTMENT

Every appointment in the state was a matter of contract, and before assuming charge of his office an officer had to enter into a *muwāḍa'a*, or covenant, with his royal master.[3] The terms of the covenant differed with the nature and importance of the office. On his appointment as wazīr in 422 (1031) Aḥmad b. Ḥasan al-Maimandī prepared the draft of his *muwāḍa'a*,[4]

1 Narshakhī, p. 24, gives a list of some of the Dīwāns under the Sāmānids, e.g. the Dīwāns of 'Amīdu'l-Mulk, Ṣāḥib-i-Shurṭa, Mamluka-i-Khāṣ, Muḥtasib, etc., but Dīwān-i-'Arḍ is omitted from this list.

2 See *Ṣubḥu'l-A'shā*, ii. 455–92, iv, 14–67, for the constitution of the different Dīwāns in the Muslim states of a later period.

3 Baihaqī, p. 326.

4 This *muwāḍa'a* contained the following important conditions: (*a*) That the Sulṭān would overlook Aḥmad's bona-fide errors of judgment in the execution of his duties, (*b*) that the Sulṭān would not give credence to evil reports against him, (*c*) that the War and the Household Departments would work under his general supervision, (*d*) that the Sulṭān would not allow the deputies of princes and provincial governors to extort money from his subjects, and (*e*) that the Sulṭān would leave to Aḥmad the appointment of the deputies of the chief Secret Agents and

in which he specified his own rights as against the Sulṭān and other ministers and high officials, and tried to secure a promise from Sulṭān Mas'ūd to allow him a free hand in the administration of the country. After this he submitted it to Sulṭān Mas'ūd, who appended a note of approval to each clause and promised to support him in all administrative measures. Aḥmad then wrote at the bottom of this document an elaborate oath of loyalty to Sulṭān Mas'ūd and handed it over to the Dawāt-Dār (Record Keeper) for safe custody. After this formal ceremony Mas'ūd invested Aḥmad with the robes of his office and declared him his deputy in all matters.[1] Other ministers were appointed in the same manner in consultation with the wazīr, after careful consideration of the relative merits of the candidates.[2]

The important offices in the state were not the monopoly of any particular class and were open to any one who had the necessary qualifications.[3] The Sulṭān did not maintain the distinction which Niẓāmu'l-Mulk later advised, of never giving an office to Nadīms (boon-companions),[4] some of whom rose to the highest positions in the state. A regular hierarchy of officials was thus established and a man who entered the service as a clerk might rise to the position of a wazīr in the course of time.[5]

the Masters of the Post. See *Āthāru'l-Wuzarā*, ff. 107 a–111 a; and Faṣīḥī, ff. 340 b–344 b. Cf. also Baihaqī, pp. 820–1, for another *muwāḍa'a* between Sulṭān Mas'ūd and his wazīr Aḥmad b. 'Abdu'ṣ-Ṣamad.

1 Baihaqī, pp. 177–8.

2 *Ibid.* pp. 416, 453, 504.

3 As a matter of fact, however, the Persians had complete control of the civil administration of the empire, which sometimes annoyed the Sulṭān (*Āthāru'l-Wuzarā*, f. 101 a), but neither the fiery Arab nor the illiterate Turkomān was a serious rival to the diligent and obsequious Persian. Consequently all the wazīrs and heads of different Dīwāns were of that nationality.

4 *Siyāsat Nāmah*, p. 82.

5 Baihaqī, p. 166.

THE WAZĪR: HIS QUALIFICATIONS

The qualifications requisite for a wazīr were a fertile brain and a facile pen, coupled with *kifāyat*, i.e. competency to deal with a situation as it arose, and vast experience of administrative work.[1] Aḥmad b. Ḥasan al-Maimandī, the famous wazīr of Sulṭān Maḥmūd, was at different times Tax-collector, Head of the Correspondence Department, Accountant General, and Head of the War Department, before his elevation to this important office.[2]

DUTIES OF THE WAZĪR

The wazīr was directly in charge of the Dīwān-i-Wizārat or Finance Department.[3] He usually appointed the 'Āmils for different provinces[4] who collected the state revenue with the help of a large staff of officials and deposited it in the provincial treasury without making any deductions from it for salary, etc.[5] The revenue for each province and its sub-divisions was assessed beforehand and when the 'Āmils had paid their collections, the balance, if any, was debited to them. After the payment of the salary of the local army and of any cheques issued by the Sulṭān or the wazīr, the surplus in the local treasury was transferred by the Ṣāḥib-i-Dīwān, who was the chief civil officer in the province, into the central treasury at Ghazna, and a copy of the balance-sheet was kept in the Dār-i-Istīfā[6] or Account Office. The Mustawfī-i-Mamālik, or the Accountant General, was responsible to the wazīr and kept an account of all the items of income and expenditure.

1 *Ādābu'l-Mulūk*, f. 36 b.
2 'Utbī, p. 271; and *Āthāru'l-Wuzarā*, f. 88 a.
3 Baihaqī, p. 663; and *Ādābu'l-Mulūk*, f. 36 a.
4 *Āthāru'l-Wuzarā*, f. 89 a.
5 *Siyāsat Nāmah*, p. 206.
6 Baihaqī, p. 145; and *Āthāru'l-Wuzarā*, f. 114 b.

The revenue was usually collected in cash but payments in kind were also permitted. The huge quantities of grain and large numbers of sheep which were thus collected[1] were stocked for the use of the Sulṭān when he travelled through the empire,[2] or were distributed among the sufferers in times of famine.[3]

All revenue due to the state was considered to be the first charge on the property of every individual concerned in its collection or payment, and no measure was regarded as too severe when the balance had to be recovered from a defaulting 'Āmil or a fraudulent Ṣāḥib-i-Dīwān. As the ultimate responsibility for the collection of the revenue rested with the wazīr, he exacted the government dues in case of defalcation by torture or by the sale of the defaulter's property.[4] If the wazīr himself incurred the displeasure of the Sulṭān, all such arrears were recovered from him in a similar manner.[5]

The chief permanent sources of income were the land revenue, the *zakāt* or 2½ per cent. tax on property,[6] tribute and presents from the feudatory princes, the produce of the gold[7] and silver mines[8] and the duties

1 Baihaqī, pp. 144–5.

2 *Ibid.* p. 146.

3 'Utbī, p. 247.

4 Baihaqī, p. 146. Farrukhī, f. 185 a, in a *qaṣīda* in praise of Ḥasanak, wazīr of Sulṭān Maḥmūd, says: "Tomorrow when he (the wazīr) demands an account from the Sulṭān's 'Āmils, their extortions will become manifest. The money which they have embezzled, he will recover from them to the last *dāng*, and will send them to prison". The defaulting 'Āmils were lashed, placed on the rack, or had their hands and feet amputated, and sometimes soldiers were ordered to recover the arrears from them. The only justification for such harsh and even brutal measures was that, in those days of slow communication, it would have otherwise been impossible for the government to make itself feared by dishonest officials in remote parts of the empire.

5 *Āthāru'l-Wuzarā*, f. 89 a.

6 *Siyāsat Nāmah*, p. 20.

7 There was a gold mine in Sīstān (*Guzīda*, p. 395), to which there is also a reference in *Shāhnāmah*.

8 There were some silver mines in the vicinity of Panjhīr.

on the huge amount of trade that passed between China, Turkistān and India, and Khurāsān, 'Irāq and Syria.[1] This income, which could have barely sufficed for the expenses of government and the magnificent court of the Sulṭān, was supplemented by the rich spoils captured in successful wars, especially the expeditions to India.

In times of drought or when a province was harried by the enemy, the wazīr usually remitted the land revenue[2] and issued loans to the cultivators to enable them to buy seed and cattle.[3]

As the deputy of the Sulṭān, the wazīr exercised a general supervision over all the departments of government and the administration of justice.[4] He held court daily, till the time of the afternoon prayer, for the redress of grievances[5] and constituted the court of first instance in all cases involving important fiscal questions.[6]

THE POSITION OF THE WAZĪR

Sulṭān Maḥmūd is credited with the statement that wazīrs are the enemies of kings;[7] and, if a wazīr was not an enemy, he soon came to be regarded as such by reason of the jealousy and suspicion which a domineering monarch naturally felt for an ambitious minister.[8] The position of the wazīr was precarious

1 Most of the articles of luxury used by the Sulṭān and his noblemen were imported from abroad. Al-Maqdisī gives a list of the chief imports and exports of the Islamic countries. The vastness of the empire itself gave great impetus to trade, because there were fewer rulers to whom the merchants passing through their territories had to pay duties on merchandise.

2 *Chahār Maqāla*, pp. 18–19.

3 'Utbī, p. 321; and *Siyāsat Nāmah*, p. 18.

4 *Ādābu'l-Mulūk*, f. 36 b.

5 Baihaqī, pp. 181, 297.

6 *Chahār Maqāla*, pp. 18–19.

7 *Āthāru'l-Wuzarā*, f. 94 a.

8 *Ādābu'l-Mulūk*, f. 39 a.

and beset with danger. He was invariably the scape-goat of the Sulṭān's wrath at the failure of any of his schemes. He was a buffer between the Sulṭān and his people, and had to bear the caprices of the one and the hatred of the other. A competent wazīr was particularly disliked by the nobility of the empire because he exercised a check on their ambition, and consequently they availed themselves of every opportunity to bring him into disgrace with the Sulṭān. The unpopularity of the wazīr was thus usually in direct proportion to his efficiency and enthusiasm in safeguarding the interests of his master.

THE WAZĪRS OF THE SULṬĀN

Abu'l-'Abbās Faḍl b. Aḥmad, the first wazīr of Sulṭān Maḥmūd, was the Ṣāḥib-Barīd of Marv under the Sāmānids. At the request of Subuktigīn, Amīr Nūḥ sent him to Nīs͟hāpūr in 385 (995) as wazīr of Maḥmūd, who at that time was in command of the troops of K͟hurāsān. Faḍl managed the affairs of the expanding empire of Sulṭān Maḥmūd with great tact and ability. He was not, however, a great scholar, and during his wazīrate all official correspondence was carried on in Persian.[1] About 404 (1013) he was charged with extortion, but instead of answering the charge he voluntarily went to prison, in spite of the remonstrances of his friends. The Sulṭān was so annoyed at this that he let him remain there. He died the same year during the absence of the Sulṭān on the expedition to Nandana.[2]

S͟hamsu'l-Kufāt Abu'l-Qāsim Aḥmad b. Ḥasan al-Maimandī, the successor of Abu'l-'Abbās Faḍl, was a man of great scholarship and vast experience in the work of administration. He was a foster-brother of Sulṭān Maḥmūd and had been brought up with him.[3]

1 'Utbī, p. 273; and *Āt͟hāru'l-Wuzarā*, ff. 88 a, 90 a.
2 'Utbī, pp. 265–71; and *Āt͟hāru'l-Wuzarā*, ff. 88 a–89 b.
3 *Āt͟hāru'l-Wuzarā*, f. 89 b.

Before his elevation to the wazīrate in 405 (1014), he had occupied at different times the important posts of Ṣāḥib-i-Dīwān-i-Khurāsān, Mustawfī-i-Mamālik and 'Āmil of the provinces of Bust and Rukhkhaj. Shortly after taking office he ordered Persian to be replaced by Arabic in all official correspondence.[1] He was a strict disciplinarian and did not tolerate any evasion of duty or departure from the usual official procedure.[2] He was very exacting in his dealings with the dignitaries of the empire,[3] with the result that many of them became his enemies and intrigued to bring about his fall. In 416 (1025) he was dismissed and sent as a prisoner to the fort of Kālanjar in southern Kashmīr hills.[4] After the death of Sulṭān Maḥmūd, Mas'ūd again appointed him wazīr in 422 (1031). He died in Muḥarram 424[5] (December 1032).

Aḥmad was a scholar of great reputation and some of his official endorsements have passed into proverbs for their terseness.[6]

Aḥmad was succeeded in office by Abū 'Alī Ḥasan b. Muḥammad b. 'Abbās, commonly known as Ḥasanak. He had been in the service of Sulṭān Maḥmūd since his childhood and had gradually risen to the position of *ra'īs* of Nīshāpūr.[7] In 414 (1023) he went on a pilgrimage to Mecca[8] and while returning received a *khil'at* from the Fāṭimid Caliph al-Ẓāhir, which so offended al-Qādir Bi'llāh the 'Abbāsid Caliph that he denounced him as a Carmathian and demanded his execution, but the Sulṭān appeased the Caliph by

1 'Utbī, pp. 272–3; and *Āthāru'l-Wuzarā*, ff. 88 a–89 b.

2 *Siyāsat Nāmah*, p. 206.

3 *Ibid.*

4 Baihaqī, p. 211; *Āthāru'l-Wuzarā*, f. 105 b.

5 Baihaqī, pp. 447–51; and Ibnu'l-Athīr, ix, 294.

6 *Chahār Maqāla*, p. 19. For an account of his life, see my article "Al-Maimandī" in *Ency. of Islam*.

7 'Utbī, pp. 329–33.

8 Baihaqī, pp. 209–12; Ibnu'l-Athīr, ix, 239; and Ibn Jawzī, f. 172 a. Cf. *infra*, p. 165.

sending the *khil'at* to Baghdād to be burnt. In 416[1] (1025) the Sulṭān appointed him wazīr in place of Aḥmad. The Sulṭān was well-disposed towards him,[2] and so great was his power that he occasionally offended and sometimes even insulted prince Mas'ūd with impunity.[3] When Mas'ūd ascended the throne Ḥasanak was tried on the old charge of being a Carmathian and was put to death in 422[4] (1031).

THE 'ĀRIḌ: HIS QUALIFICATIONS

The next important minister of the Sulṭān was the 'Āriḍ or Ṣāḥib-i-Dīwān-i-'Arḍ,[5] who was the head of the Military Department. He was generally an officer of distinction and proved merit. The qualifications requisite for this post were those of a civilian rather than a general, viz. capacity for organisation and executive work and general familarity with military affairs.

PEACE-TIME DUTIES OF THE 'ĀRIḌ

Besides the wazīr, the 'Āriḍ was the chief adviser of the Sulṭān in military matters.[6] His main duty was to look after the welfare of the soldiers and to see that the army was maintained at a high standard of efficiency. He annually reviewed the army in the plain of Shābahār in the vicinity of Ghazna,[7] when all the cavalry in full armour, the infantry under its commanders and the elephants in their rich trappings, passed in a line before him.[8] The Sulṭān himself occasionally attended these reviews to satisfy himself that the army was properly looked after.[9] The 'Āriḍ or his

1 Baihaqī, pp. 210–11.
2 *Āthāru'l-Wuzarā*, f. 111 a.
3 Baihaqī, pp. 208, 210.
4 *Ibid.* pp. 208–10.
5 In E. and D. ii, 73, *Shughl-i-'Arḍ* is incorrectly translated "the business of reporting matters".
6 Baihaqī, p. 100.
7 *Ibid.* pp. 329–30, 625.
8 Farrukhī, f. 41 b.
9 Gardīzī, p. 80.

assistant, the Nā'ib-i-'Arḍ, paid the *bīstgānī*, i.e. quarterly salary, to the troops from the provincial treasury and submitted the accounts to the wazīr through the Dār-i-Istīfā.[1] The 'Ārīḍ kept a muster-roll of the soldiers showing all losses by illness, retirement or war.[2] A copy of the muster-roll was deposited in the Correspondence Department for ready reference.[3] The 'Āriḍ was further required to see that when the Sulṭān travelled through the empire his camp was well supplied with provisions, fodder and other requirements of the journey.[4]

WAR-TIME DUTIES OF THE 'ĀRIḌ

In times of war, the 'Ārīḍ acted as the Quartermaster-General of the army. At different halting stations he provided facilities to enable soldiers to make necessary arrangements for provisions and transport. After a victory, the 'Āriḍ supervised the collection of the booty which was divided in the presence of the Sulṭān.[5] Articles of different kinds were brought in lots, valued by experts and distributed among officers and soldiers in proportion to their ranks,[6] but precious stones, gold and silver, arms and elephants to the value of one-fifth of the total spoils, were set apart for the Sulṭān in accordance with the Muslim Law.[7]

1 Gardīzī, pp. 23–4; Baihaqī, pp. 402, 484, 619, 644, 685, 818; and *Siyāsat Nāmah*, pp. 92–3. The *bīstgānī* was paid in cash every quarter, and sometimes annually.

2 Baihaqī, p. 532.

3 *Ibid.* p. 332.

4 Usually traders accompanied the army and catered for the soldiers. See 'Awfī, f. 166 b; and *Siyāsat Nāmah*, p. 91.

5 Farrukhī, f. 26 b.

6 *Ibid.* In *Ādābu'l-Mulūk*, f. 113 a, it is stated that the share of a foot-soldier was half of that of a mounted soldier.

7 Farrukhī, f. 16 b.

THE ARMY

The army of the Sulṭān consisted of cavalry, a majority of which were two-horse troopers,[1] infantry, the number of which was small because it was not so swift and mobile, the body-guard of the Sulṭān, and elephants.

The body-guard of the Sulṭān consisted chiefly of slaves,[2] who, from the nature of their position, were considered to be more devoted to their master than any other class of soldiers. They were under the personal supervision of the Sulṭān and had their own separate commanders and administrative officers.[3] Their banner had the distinctive device of a lion and spears.[4]

The elephants, too, were under the direct control of the Sulṭān.[5] The elephant-drivers were mostly Hindūs and their commander was called Muqaddam-i-Pīl-bānān.[6] The Sulṭān personally reviewed the elephants every year and ordered lean and thin ones to be sent to India to recover their weight and strength.[7] Almost all the elephants had either been captured in Indian wars or received as tribute from Hindū rājās.[8]

NUMERICAL STRENGTH OF THE ARMY

For lack of proper records it is impossible to ascertain exactly the numerical strength of the Sulṭān's

1 Baihaqī, p. 313; *Siyāsat Nāmah*, p. 106; and *Āt͟hāru'l-Wuzarā*, f. 100 a.

2 The slaves formed a pampered class in the state. They had many opportunities of coming under the notice of the Sulṭān and of giving proof of their merit. Whenever any important appointment had to be made they were the first to be considered. Most of the commanders in the service of the Sulṭān, like Altūntās͟h, Arslān Jād͟hib and Qarātigīn-i-Dawātī, were either his own slaves or those of his father.

3 Baihaqī, p. 488. 4 *Ibid.* p. 329. 5 *Ibid.* p. 488.

6 *Ibid.* pp. 29, 709. 7 Farruk͟hī, ff. 41 b, 97 b.

8 Baihaqī, p. 709, gives 100,000 *dirhems* as the price of an elephant.

army. In 389 (999), when Maḥmūd defeated 'Abdu'l-Malik b. Nūḥ, the Sāmānid, at Marv, he was in command of at least 32,000 horse.[1] In 406 (1015–16) he advanced to Balkh at the head of an army said to have numbered 100,000 soldiers,[2] while in 414 (1023), when he reviewed his army in the plain of Shābahār, "it was 54,000 in number, besides the garrisons in the outposts of the empire" to guard the long frontier. The strength of his army, therefore, in times of peace can be placed roughly at 100,000, including both the cavalry and infantry.[3] In times of war, however, the number was greatly swelled by the contingents supplied by feudatory princes, fresh recruits, volunteers and local militia.[4]

The total number of the slaves was about 4000,[5] but it is not known how many of these formed the bodyguard of the Sulṭān. The number of elephants in his army was approximately 1700.[6]

The army was mainly recruited from Transoxiana, but as the preponderance of any one element would have been fraught with danger, Arabs, Afghāns, Dailamites, Khurāsānīs, Ghūrīs and Indians were also enlisted.[7] This not only acted as a check on the insubordination of any one of the different sections but also served to create a spirit of emulation among them to

1 See *supra*, p. 44.
2 Baihaqī, p. 846.
3 Sibṭ Ibnu'l-Jawzī, f. 219 b, on the authority of aṣ-Ṣābī.
4 Baihaqī, p. 332; and *Āthāru'l-Wuzarā*, f. 99 b.
5 Baihaqī, p. 652; *Ṭab. Nāṣ.* p. 83; and *Futūḥu's-Salāṭīn*, f. 35 b.
6 Farrukhī, f. 3 b. Gardīzī, p. 80, says that their number in 414 (1023) was 1300. *Futūḥu's-Salāṭīn*, f. 35 b, says 2000. Farrukhī, f. 7 a, also gives the names of some of the important elephants of the Sulṭān.

Every horse and camel in state service was branded to prevent fraudulent musters. See Baihaqī, p. 752; and *Chahār Maqāla*, p. 36.

7 There was a large number of Hindūs in the Sulṭān's army and they lived in a separate quarter of Ghazna. Al-Ma'arrī, *Risālatu'l-Ghufrān*, p. 153, describes the scene of a Hindū woman's *satī* in Ghazna.

excel each other in courage and valour on the field of battle.[1]

ORGANISATION AND ADMINISTRATION OF THE ARMY

The military service under the Sulṭān was highly organised. The Sulṭān was his own commander-in-chief. The next highest office under him was that of the Commander of the troops of Khurāsān, which was held throughout his reign by his brothers Naṣr and Yūsuf successively. Besides this every province had a commander of the local troops, who was usually a Turkomān. His duties were chiefly military but if the province happened to be on the frontier, he was also required to collect the tribute from the neighbouring feudatory rulers.[2] The 'Āriḍ was appointed in the same manner as the wazīr, but as an additional precaution he was required to leave a son as a hostage at the court of the Sulṭān before he was invested with the insignia of his office.[3]

Every provincial army had its own 'Āriḍ[4] whose duties were on a small scale similar to those of the Ṣāḥib-i-Dīwān-i-'Arḍ. He had an assistant called Nā'ib-i-'Arḍ and a Kat-khudā,[5] i.e. Quarter-master, to help him in the administration of the army. The 'Āriḍ or his assistant drew money from the local treasury to disburse *bīstgānī* to the troops.[6] There was a Ṣāḥib-Barīd, or Master of the Post, attached to every army and his duty was to report to the Sulṭān all matters of importance that occurred within his knowledge.[7]

Service in the army was graded. The lowest officer was the Khail-tāsh, who was probably the commander

1 *Siyāsat Nāmah*, p. 92; and *Qābūs Nāmah*, p. 176.
2 Baihaqī, p. 325.
3 *Ibid.* pp. 328–9.
4 *Ibid.* pp. 145, 619.
5 *Ibid.* p. 421.
6 *Ibid.* pp. 619, 818.
7 *Ibid.* pp. 332, 423.

of ten horse. Above him were the Qā'id, who commanded a *khail*, probably of one-hundred horse, the Sarhang, who was the commander of five-hundred horse, and the Ḥājib, who was the officer commanding the *jaish* or army,[1] while all the troops in a province were, as already stated, under the command of the provincial Sipāh-Sālār. Promotion was given on the strict principle of merit and efficiency, and even a trooper could rise to the position of a commander in course of time.

When proceeding on an expedition, every soldier was required to make his own commissariat arrangements[2] and received his salary in advance for the purpose, but if the expedition was directed to a distant country, the Sulṭān, as a measure of precaution, made additional arrangements for the requirements of the journey.[3]

Every army had a separate magazine and armoury[4], and arms were distributed among the soldiery shortly before the battle.[5]

THE CORRESPONDENCE DEPARTMENT

The Dīwān-i-Risālat or Correspondence Department, which has been called "the repository of secrets",[6] was placed under the charge of a tried and trusted servant

1 The grades in the army are not given by any contemporary writer. I have taken these details from occasional hints in Baihaqī, pp. 23, 24, 36, 149, 332, 345, 353, 396, 397, 420, etc.; *Siyāsat Nāmah*; and as-Subkī, *Kitāb Mu'īdu'n-Ni'am*, pp. 57 *et seq.*

2 Baihaqī, pp. 629, 808; and Farrukhī, f. 111 b.

3 Ibnu'l-Athīr, ix, 241.

4 Baihaqī, p. 6. It is implied from Gardīzī, p. 82, that at the time of battle a separate armoury was placed behind each wing.

5 Baihaqī, p. 130. Farrukhī, f. 41 b, seems to suggest that the soldiers were supplied with a uniform at the expense of the state.

6 Jurbādhqānī, p. 30; and *Āthāru'l-Wuzarā*, f. 88 a.

of advanced age and ripe experience.[1] He was usually a man of high literary attainments and great diplomacy and tact. The nature of his duties was such as to make him many enemies but he was invariably able to win the regard of his fellow-officers by civility and complacent behaviour.[2]

The chief duty of the Ṣāḥib-i-Dīwān-i-Risālat, or head of the Correspondence Department, was to write the Sulṭān's letters to the Caliph, foreign princes, local governors and other state dignitaries. Important correspondence was dictated by the Sulṭān himself, but in ordinary matters he gave oral instructions to the head of the Correspondence Department who communicated them to the officers concerned. The confidential reports of the governors, commanders, Mushrifs and Ṣāḥib-Barīds were deciphered by the Ṣāḥib-i-Dīwān-i-Risālat and submitted to the Sulṭān.[3]

The Ṣāḥib-i-Dīwān-i-Risālat had an assistant and a numerous staff of Dabīrs or clerks who received handsome salaries.[4] The sons of Dabīrs and Mustawfīs were usually taken into the office as unpaid probationers.[5] Service in this department was graded and vacancies were filled by promotions from lower ranks.[6]

The usual office hours were from 9 or 10 o'clock in the morning to about 3 in the afternoon.[7] Tuesday and

1 Abu'l-Faḍl Baihaqī, the author of *Ta'rīkh-i-Mas'ūdī*, was considered too young for this post at the age of forty-five. See Baihaqī, p. 753.

2 See *Chahār Maqāla*, pp. 12–13, for the qualifications of a secretary.

3 Before proceeding to his post, every important officer was supplied with a code language by the Ṣāḥib-i-Dīwān-i-Risālat. See Baihaqī, pp. 541, 821.

4 Baihaqī, p. 166.

5 *Ibid.*

6 Abu'l-Faḍl Baihaqī entered the office as a Dabīr and rose to the position of Ṣāḥib-i-Dīwān-i-Risālat in course of time.

7 Baihaqī, p. 297.

Friday were observed as holidays.[1] One clerk, however, always remained on duty to deal with cases of emergency.[2] Even when the Sulṭān went out on a pleasure trip, a clerk from the Correspondence Department was in attendance on him.[3]

THE DEPARTMENT OF SECRET INTELLIGENCE

The Dīwān-i-Shughl-i-Ishrāf-i-Mamlukat, or Department of Secret Intelligence,[4] was another important branch of administration.[5] The head of this department had numerous agents, called Mushrifs, all over the country. He was invariably able, by lavish grants of money and promise of future favours, to induce the trusted slaves and servants of important officers and foreign princes to spy on their own lords.[6] Persons of both sexes served as spies and travelled to foreign lands in disguise to collect useful information for the Sulṭān.[7] Sometimes an officer who had incurred the displeasure of the Sulṭān and had taken refuge at a foreign court was received back into favour if he consented to act as spy on the confiding prince.[8]

A large number of Mushrifs, called Mushrifān-i-Dargāh, were attached to the court and their duty was to

1 Baihaqī, pp. 186, 581; and 'Awfī, f. 356 a, who calls Tuesday "the navel of the week".

2 Baihaqī, p. 191.

3 *Ibid.*

4 In E. and D. ii, 74, *Shughl-i-Ishrāf-i-Mamlukat* is incorrectly translated "the duty of controlling the financial affairs", and Mushrif, "an accountant". The term *ishrāf* literally means "observation from an eminence".

5 Baihaqī, p. 416, says that it was more important than Dīwān-i-'Arḍ. In *Siyāsat Nāmah*, p. 57, and *Ādābu'l-Mulūk*, f. 40 b, honesty and clear judgment are given as the qualifications requisite for a Mushrif. See also Barthold, p. 231.

6 Baihaqī, p. 846, says that the spies of Sulṭān Maḥmūd "counted the very breaths of the Khāns of Turkistān".

7 *Ibid.* pp. 493, 522; and *Siyāsat Nāmah*, p. 68.

8 Baihaqī, p. 609.

keep a sharp look-out on the doings of ministers and courtiers.[1] Even the sons of the Sulṭān did not escape this secret surveillance and their most trusted slaves and servants were usually in the pay of this department,[2] but sometimes the Sulṭān was outwitted by the princes who also had their secret agents among the confidential servants of their father.[3] There were numerous spies in the household of the Sulṭān and their reports were taken down by special Mushrifs.[4]

This system of spying played some part in the daily court-life. When the Sulṭān wanted to communicate a verbal order to an officer, he usually sent two men, one of them being a *mushrif* on the other, to guarantee that the message and its reply were correctly delivered.[5]

The Mushrifs were appointed by the Sulṭān in consultation with the Ṣāḥib-i-Dīwān-i-Ishrāf-i-Mamlukat, while their assistants were nominated by the wazīr from among those in whose loyalty and integrity he had full confidence.[6] They were paid handsome salaries to preclude the danger of their being tempted to accept the gold of the officers whose indiscretions they were expected to report.[7]

THE POSTAL SYSTEM AND OFFICIAL NEWS-WRITERS

To assist in the transmission of news and reports of spies, there was a regular official postal service throughout the empire. The Ṣāḥib-Barīd or Master of the Post

1 *Āthāru'l-Wuzarā*, f. 96 b. The Sulṭān used to receive information of even the private meetings of his ministers.

2 Baihaqī, p. 135.

3 *Ibid.* pp. 135–8, 164–5.

4 *Ibid.* p. 331.

5 *Ibid.* p. 812. In *Ādābu'l-Mulūk*, f. 41 a, it is stated that there used to be Mushrifs whose duty was to see that provisions were not stolen from the royal kitchen.

6 *Āthāru'l-Wuzarā*, f. 110 a.

7 *Siyāsat Nāmah*, p. 57.

at the headquarters of every province[1] was the official news-writer and his duty was to keep the Sulṭān in touch with everything of importance that happened in the province, particularly the doings of the local officers and commanders.[2] It was a position of great trust and responsibility and some of the wazīrs, like Abu'l-'Abbās Faḍl b. Aḥmad and Abū 'Alī Ḥasan b. Muḥammad, had held this post before their elevation to the wazīrate.[3] Like the Mushrifs, and for the same reasons, the Ṣāḥib-Barīd and his assistants were paid handsome salaries in cash.[4] The Ṣāḥib-Barīd submitted his reports in a cipher which he had previously arranged with the Ṣāḥib-i-Dīwān-i-Risālat.[5]

All official correspondence, including the reports of the Barīds and Mushrifs, was conveyed by Askudārs or mounted couriers,[6] but important communications were conveyed by special messengers[7] who were usually Arab horsemen. But this postal arrangement failed when a local commander defied the central authority. In order to gain time, the rebel either forced the local Ṣāḥib-Barīd to send false reports or waylaid the official courier and destroyed implicating documents.[8] In such circumstances, the Ṣāḥib-Barīd managed to send information through secret agents who, disguised as travellers, traders, Ṣūfīs or apothecaries, carried the news-letter sewn into the saddle-cloth, or hidden in the soles of their shoes or the handles of implements of daily use specially made hollow for this purpose.[9]

1 Baihaqī, pp. 165, 423, 627.

2 *Ibid.* p. 346; *Siyāsat Nāmah*, pp. 57, 58, 65; and 'Awfī, f. 319 a.

3 Baihaqī, p. 166; and Jurbādhqānī, p. 356.

4 *Siyāsat Nāmah*, pp. 57–8.

5 Baihaqī, pp. 541, 821.

6 *Ibid.* pp. 425, 494. The important officers enjoyed the privilege of using this service for their private communications.

7 Baihaqī, p. 139. These couriers were paid for each journey in addition to their usual salary.

8 *Ibid.* p. 854.

9 *Ibid.* pp. 27, 493, 522, 523; and *Siyāsat Nāmah*, p. 68.

THE COMPTROLLER OF THE HOUSEHOLD

The Ṣāḥib-i-Dīwān-i-Wikālat, or the Comptroller of the Household,[1] was a man of established reputation for honesty and integrity.[2] Very little is mentioned about him by the contemporary authors,[3] probably because the nature of his duties did not bring him much in contact with the court and courtiers of the Sulṭān. The Wakīl, as he was sometimes called, exercised supervision over the Master of the Revels, the Royal Kitchen, the Royal Stables and the numerous staff attached to the Sulṭān's palace.[4] The Wakīl was also in charge of the private treasury of the Sulṭān, and distributed rations and salaries to his personal staff and his body-guard.[5] Sometimes the Wakīl also administered the private estate of the Sulṭān (*ḍiyā'-i-khāṣ*) which was usually under a separate officer.[6]

ADMINISTRATION OF JUSTICE

In an Islamic state the administration of justice was theoretically the duty of the Caliph as the successor of the Prophet. The Caliph was supposed to have delegated his powers to the rulers of different states who, in their turn, appointed Qāḍīs to assist them in this work by their expert knowledge of Muslim Law.[7] Justice was thus administered on similar lines all over the Muslim world. There was a Qāḍī for every town and a Qāḍī'l-Quḍāt or Chief Qāḍī for every province.[8] As there are four important schools of jurisconsults

1 Baihaqī, p. 620; and Farrukhī, ff. 171 b, 192 b.

2 *Āthāru'l-Wuzarā*, f. 109 a; *Siyāsat Nāmah*, p. 81; and *Ādābu'l-Mulūk*, f. 42 b.

3 For his qualifications and duties, see *Ādābu'l-Mulūk*, f. 42 b; and *Inshā*, f. 10 a, as given in Barthold, *Texts*, p. 23.

4 Baihaqī, p. 173; *Siyāsat Nāmah*, p. 81.

5 Farrukhī, f. 171 b.

6 Baihaqī, p. 308.

7 *Siyāsat Nāmah*, p. 54.

8 Baihaqī, p. 246.

among "the followers of the Sunna", sometimes, when their number justified such a course, additional Qāḍīs representing each school were appointed to adjudicate disputes between the followers of their particular school of law.

The position of a Qāḍī was of particular importance in the state. He was said to have power over "the life and property of the Muslims".[1] The Qāḍīs were paid handsome salaries[2] and were not removed from office except for misconduct in the discharge of their duties. The Qāḍī's sentence was executed by officers of the local governor and disobedience to his summons was severely punished.[3]

The procedure at the court of a Qāḍī was very simple. There were no pleaders or lawyers, and the Qāḍī himself was the judge of the fact as well as of the law. The parties to a case and their witnesses made their statements, and the Qāḍī formulated his judgment after careful consideration of the question. If the law was not clear on the point at issue, the Qāḍī was guided by equity, commonsense and precedents.

Sulṭān Maḥmūd took great interest in the administration of justice in his empire[4], and chose his Qāḍīs from among Muftīs and Faqīhs of established reputation for learning and probity of character. When a Qāḍī was suspected of malpractices or partiality, the Sulṭān personally investigated the matter and, if the charge was proved, immediately dismissed the offender.[5]

Besides the Qāḍīs, almost all the princes, wazīrs, commanders of the provincial armies and other high officials[6] decided cases which were either connected with their own departments or did not involve any

1 *Siyāsat Nāmah*, p. 38. 2 *Ibid.*

3 *Ibid.* p. 40. For the numerous duties of a Qāḍī, besides the administration of justice, see *Sulūku'l-Mulūk*, f. 42 a.

4 *Siyāsat Nāmah*, p. 65. 5 *Ibid.* p. 77.

6 Baihaqī, pp. 40, 181.

intricate questions requiring expert knowledge of the law. The Sulṭān himself held court daily and dealt out impartial justice to all alike without distinction of rank or position. He was accessible on such occasions even to the humblest of his subjects and did all he could to redress their grievances.

PROVINCIAL GOVERNMENT

The details of the provincial government are given very sparingly, and all that can be gleaned from the contemporary writers has been mentioned in the preceding pages. Generally speaking, the provincial government was based on the model of the central administration.

There were three important branches of administration in a province: civil, military, and judicial. The chief civil officer was called Ṣāḥib-i-Dīwān.[1] He was in charge of the collection of revenue and was directly responsible to the wazīr.[2] Under him were numerous 'Āmils whose duty was to collect revenue from the subdivisions of the province.[3]

The highest military officer in the province was the commander of the provincial army.[4] His duties and functions have already been mentioned. The provincial commander and the Ṣāḥib-i-Dīwān worked independently of each other but in case of need one was required to help the other.[5]

The highest judicial officer in a province was the Qāḍī'l-Quḍāt, who besides his duties as a judge supervised the administration of justice within his jurisdiction and saw that the Qāḍīs in the outlying towns carried out their judicial functions satisfactorily.[6]

1 Baihaqī, pp. 447, 559. 2 *Siyāsat Nāmah*, p. 150.

3 Baihaqī, pp. 352, 488; Farrukhī, f. 41 a; and *Siyāsat Nāmah*, pp. 18, 149.

4 Baihaqī, p. 496. 5 *Ibid.* pp. 325, 327.

6 *Ibid.* p. 246. Besides their judicial duties, the Qāḍīs acted as trustees of the property of orphans and of persons going abroad on travels. See *Siyāsat Nāmah*, pp. 77–8.

ADMINISTRATION OF THE TOWNS

Very little is known about the village institutions and the government of the towns in the time of Sulṭān Maḥmūd. Every town was protected by a fort, and the commander of the fort, called Kotwāl, was the chief military officer in the locality.[1] The chief civil officer in a town was the Muḥtasib or S͟hiḥna who, in addition to keeping peace and order within his jurisdiction, was required to see that the foodstuffs were not adulterated, that weights and measures were correct according to the legal standard, that the artisans carried on their trades without molestation, and that the Muslim Law regarding public morality was not violated.[2] Offenders were apprehended and sent to the Amīr-i-Ḥaras,[3] or the Chief Jailor, for safe custody till they could be brought for trial before a competent authority. There was a paid K͟haṭīb whose duty was to lead the Muslims in prayer and to read the *k͟huṭba* in the name of the Sulṭān.[4] Although municipal government was not known in those times, there is evidence to show that the officials and notables of the town were consulted in all matters of importance concerning the town.[5]

The religious and educational endowments in each town were administered by a separate office called Is͟hrāf-i-Awqāf.[6] The head of this office supervised the collection and expenditure of the income from endowments.

1 Baihaqī, pp. 4, 5, 8, 288.
2 *Ibid.* p. 664; 'Utbī, p. 332; and *Siyāsat Nāmah*, p. 41.
3 Baihaqī, pp. 189, 197, 271, 538; and *Siyāsat Nāmah*, p. 121.
4 Baihaqī, pp. 4, 5.
5 *Ibid.* p. 19.
6 *Ibid.* p. 308.

CHAPTER XI

SULṬĀN MAḤMŪD AND HIS WORK

SULṬĀN MAḤMŪD, like other great men in history, has his admirers as well as his detractors. Muslim writers have attempted to elevate him to the position of a saint and have even gone the length of attributing miraculous powers to him, while some modern historians, who had a very superficial knowledge of his career, have tried to depict him in such lurid colours as to give him the character of a brigand chief who took delight in plunder and bloodshed. Maḥmūd was neither the one nor the other. He was endowed with remarkable qualities and an extraordinary military genius.

Sulṭān Maḥmūd was a man of medium height, and of a powerful and symmetrical build. He had a fine complexion, handsome face, small eyes and a firm, round chin which was covered with a scanty beard.[1]

The Sulṭān was affectionate by nature as is shown by the care that he bestowed on the education and proper training of his sons, and the generosity with which he treated his brothers. In spite of his inflexible sternness, he was very considerate to his officers; and after his death they spoke of him in terms of affection.[2] Those who incurred his displeasure, and even rebels, were treated kindly and were not punished with anything worse than imprisonment.[3] But his kind nature never betrayed him into favouritism, and there is nothing on record to suggest that he ever chose his ministers for any other reason but their abilities.

1 Ibnu'l-Athīr, ix, 284; and Sibṭ Ibnu'l-Jawzī, f. 220 a, who gives it as a quotation from aṣ-Ṣābī. There is thus no truth in the story about the ugly looks of the Sulṭān as given in *Siyāsat Nāmah*, p. 44; and *Guzīda*, p. 395.

2 Baihaqī, pp. 69, 99.

3 *Ibid.* p. 84.

Sulṭān Maḥmūd was very kind to his relatives. Ismā'īl, his brother and rival to the throne, enjoyed every consideration consistent with his position till he was found to have been concerned in a plot against the life of the Sulṭān; and then he was only sent away from Ghazna to Jūzjānān where he ended his days in peace. His second brother Abu'l-Muẓaffar Naṣr was given the highest military office in the empire, viz. the command of the troops of Khurāsān, and the governorship of the province of Sīstān, both of which he held till his death in 412[1] (1021–22). His third brother Abū Ya'qūb Yūsuf, who was still a child at the death of Subuktigīn, was brought up and educated with Mas'ūd and Muḥammad[2] and, after the death of Naṣr, was elevated to his rank and position.[3] In 417 (1026) the Caliph conferred on Yūsuf, probably at the instance of the Sulṭān, the title of *'Aḍudu'd-Dawlah wa Mu'ayyidu'l-Millah*.[4]

Sulṭān Maḥmūd had seven sons, namely Abū Sa'īd Mas'ūd, Abū Aḥmad Muḥammad, Sulaimān, Ismā'īl, Naṣr, Ibrāhīm and Abū Manṣūr 'Abdu'r-Rashīd,[5] and at least three daughters, one of whom was given in marriage to Mīnūchihr, ruler of Ṭabaristān,[6] another named Zainab to Yaghāntigīn, son of Qadir Khān of Kāshghar,[7] and the third to 'Unṣuru'l-Ma'ālī Kaikā'ūs b. Dārā b. Qābūs, the author of the *Qābūs Nāmah*.[8]

The Sulṭān bestowed great care on the proper training of his sons and exercised strict supervision over their private life. His secret agents reported to him their youthful peccadilloes, for which they were severely reprimanded.[9] Besides the usual literary education, they were trained in the military arts of the times, and, to give them experience of administrative work, they were

1 Gardīzī, p. 79.
2 Baihaqī, pp. 123–4.
3 Farrukhī, f. 119 a; and Gardīzī, p. 93.
4 Gardīzī, p. 88.
5 *Ṭab. Nāṣ.* p. 88. 'Abdu'r-Rashīd was the ruler of Ghazna from 441 to 444 (1049–52).
6 'Utbī, p. 279; and Baihaqī, p. 245.
7 Baihaqī, p. 655.
8 *Qābūs Nāmah*, p. 4.
9 Baihaqī, pp. 134–7.

placed in charge of important provinces with capable men as their wazīrs. In 408 (1017–18) Mas'ūd was appointed governor of Herāt[1] and in 420 (1029) was placed in charge of the newly conquered province of Raiy.[2] Muḥammad was appointed governor of Jūzjānān after the death of Abū Naṣr Muḥammad, the ruler of that province,[3] and in 409 (1018) was entrusted with the administration of the empire during the Sulṭān's absence on the expedition to Kanauj.[4]

Very little is known about the private life of Sulṭān Maḥmūd, but it can be stated with certainty that he was not tainted with the licentious sensuality which often disgraced the life of Oriental despots. He lived more or less in accordance with the Muslim code of morality. He does not seem to have exceeded the prescribed limit with regard to the number of wives.[5] He, however, indulged in wine-drinking as a pastime and not as a besotting habit. His drinking bouts were limited to a select circle, and the merry winebibbers had to walk out sober for fear of being apprehended and punished by the Muḥtasib.[6] The proverbial attachment of the Sulṭān to his handsome Turkomān slave Abu'n-Najm Ayāz b. Ūymāq was due to the extraordinary devotion of Ayāz rather than to his good looks. This point has been clearly brought out by Farrukhī in one of his *qaṣīdas*,[7] and by Niẓāmī Samarqandī and Shaikh Farīdu'd-Dīn 'Aṭṭār in the stories in which they have mentioned this affair.[8] The existence of such a tender sentiment between a king and his slave soon captured the fancy of poets and story-tellers who developed it into an exciting love-romance.[9]

1 Gardīzī, p. 74; and Baihaqī, p. 256.
2 Baihaqī, pp. 258, 359.
3 See Appendix C.
4 'Awfī, *Lubāb*, pt i, pp. 25–6.
5 *Mujmal*, f. 262 b; and Ibnu'l-Athīr, ix, 262.
6 *Siyāsat Nāmah*, pp. 41–2.
7 Farrukhī, ff. 148 b–149 b.
8 *Chahār Maqāla*, pp. 34–6; and *Kulliyyāt-i-'Aṭṭār*.
9 See e.g. Zulālī's *Maḥmūd wa Ayāz*.

The Sulṭān was self-willed, stubborn and impatient of contradiction[1]—the usual defects of great conquerors. He could not brook opposition to his will even when he was conscious of his error, but it is to his credit that, after some show of petulance, he had usually the grace to acknowledge his mistakes.[2] He is never stated to have let momentary anger get the better of his reason. Ḥāfiẓ Abrū quotes, from the lost portion of Baihaqī's *Mujalladāt*, a characteristic story[3] of a splendid garden made by the orders of Sulṭān Maḥmūd at Balkh, the upkeep of which had been made obligatory on the people of Balkh, who groaned under this unnecessary burden. Abū Naṣr-i- Mushkānī brought this matter to the notice of the Sulṭān, who was so angered that he did not speak to him for some days, but he soon realised his mistake and issued an order releasing the inhabitants of Balkh from the obligation of maintaining the garden.

That the Sulṭān was physically brave is shown by his fearless bearing in war. He fought in the front ranks of his army and usually plunged into the thickest part of the battle.[4] He is said to have received seventy-two cuts and wounds during his numerous wars.[5] At the siege of Multān he killed so many of the enemy that his hand was stuck fast to the hilt of his sword with congealed blood and had to be immersed in a bath of hot water before it could be loosened.[6] It was the Sulṭān's personal valour and fearlessness of danger which inspired his soldiers with confidence and enthusiasm even in moments of extreme despair.

1 Baihaqī, p. 495.
2 *Ibid.*
3 Ḥāfiẓ Abrū, f. 184 a; and 'Awfī, f. 173 a.
4 'Utbī, p. 129; and Farrukhī, f. 8 b.
5 *Majma'u'l-Ansāb*, f. 246 a. It is stated in *Ādābu'l-Mulūk*, f. 80 a, that the sword was the favourite weapon of the Sulṭān and that he was skilled in the use of the bow and arrow.
6 *Ādābu'l-Mulūk*, f. 80 a.

Sulṭān Maḥmūd was endowed with a genius for war. He was a scientific general, skilful in planning and thorough in executing. His brilliant victories equal the exploits of Alexander the Great in the East. His field of action extended from 'Irāq to the Ganges Doāb, and from Khwārizm to Kāthiāwār; and within this wide arena, he moved and fought for thirty-three years with matchless energy and success, sometimes fighting against the whole might of Turkistān and sometimes bidding defiance to the united prowess of northern India. Sulṭān Maḥmūd is not said to have invented anything, neither a new formation nor a new principle of attack and defence. He accepted what he found ready to his hands, viz. the tactics of the old royal armies of the Sāmānids in which he had served his apprenticeship, but he infused into the old system a new life with his energy. His armies, consisting of such heterogeneous elements as Arabs, Khaljīs, Afghāns, Turkomāns, Dailamites and Hindūs, were, under his iron discipline, welded together into one invincible whole.

Inglorious ease was little to the warrior's taste. He exposed his body to all the fatigues of marching, bivouacking and skirmishing on the borderland of his extensive empire. His summers were usually occupied with campaigns in Central Asia, while his winters were frequently spent on the plains of India. Neither heat nor cold, nor even the natural barriers could prevent him from waging a desperate war. The inaccessible mountains of Ghūr, the snow-clad hill-passes of Kashmīr, the foaming rivers and the torrential rains of India, the alkaline wastes of the Punjāb, the parched desert of Rājpūtāna—nothing stood in the way of his indomitable will. His rapid marches surprised his enemies. He thundered at the gates of Multān while the rebel Sukhpāl was slumbering in security, and he surrounded the town of Quṣdār before its ruler was well aware of his approach. Even when he was in the grip of his fatal malady, the swiftness of his movements surprised Mīnūchihr and forced the Seljuks to clear out of Khurāsān.

Sulṭān Maḥmūd was strict in the administration of justice.[1] He enforced respect for law by all the means at his disposal and within his empire nobody could plead rank or birth as an excuse for leniency or exceptional treatment. When sued for debts by a merchant of Ghazna, prince Mas'ūd could escape being summoned before a Qāḍī only by an immediate settlement of the claim;[2] and 'Alī Nūshtigīn, a high military officer, was arrested and lashed in public for open defiance of the Muslim Law.[3]

The story-tellers and other Muslim writers credit Sulṭān Maḥmūd with a strong sense of responsibility towards his subjects and would make us believe that he did his best to protect their life and property. It is said that at the complaint of a woman who had been robbed by a gang of highwaymen in a remote part of the empire, the Sulṭān took effectual measures for their extermination,[4] and that at the appeal of another woman the 'Āmil of Nīshāpūr, who had seized her property, was flogged and dismissed.[5] When there was a serious famine in Khurāsān in 401 (1010–11) owing to early frost, the Sulṭān tried his best to alleviate distress and ordered money and corn to be distributed among the sufferers all over the affected area.[6]

Sulṭān Maḥmūd was a poet and scholar of some reputation.[7] He is said to have been the author of a book named *Tafrīdu'l-Furū'* which was regarded as a

1 *Siyāsat Nāmah*, p. 44.
2 *Ibid.* p. 208.
3 *Ibid.* p. 41.
4 *Ibid.* p. 58.
5 *Ibid.* p. 66.
6 'Utbī, p. 247; and Ibn Funduq, f. 102 a.
7 'Awfī, *Lubāb*, pt i, p. 24, where a few specimens of his poetical compositions are also given.

standard work on Fiqh.[1] He took part in the religious and literary discussions of the scholars at his court, not with the morbid scepticism of Akbar, the Great Mogul, but with the healthy interest of a learned Muslim.[2]

The Sulṭān was a great patron of learning and his court was the rendezvous of scholars from all parts of the Muslim world.[3] Crowds of poets sang his praises,[4] and he is said to have spent on them 400,000 *dīnārs* annually.[5] The most celebrated of them were Abu'l-

1 Ḥājjī Khalīfa, ii, 327, on the authority of Imām Mas'ūd b. Shaibān.

In a *qaṣīda* of 'Asjadī, in praise of the Sulṭān (quoted in full in a MS in the 'Alīgarh Muslim University, named the *Ḥikāyātu's-Salāṭīn*), it is stated that

بر دادن صلات کتابی بکرد شاه

چونانکه بو حنیفه کتاب صلات کرد

"The Shāh (Maḥmūd) wrote a book on the giving of rewards,
Like Bū Ḥanīfa who wrote the Book of Prayers."

In the introduction of *Majmū'a-i-Sulṭānī* (I.O. MS No. 508), which is a work on Fiqh, it is stated that it was composed at the desire of Sulṭān Maḥmūd by eminent jurisconsults; but this statement does not seem to be true. There are references to Delhi as the capital of a Muslim empire, on ff. 96 a, 96 b, and to the famous sixth-century work named *Hidāya*, on f. 99 a. It was not, however, unusual for the Sulṭān to ask scholars to compose books. See *Tarjuma-i-Faḍā'il-i-Balkh* (f. 198 a) by Abū Bakr 'Abdu'llāh b. 'Umar b. Muḥammad b. Dā'ūd al-Wā'iẓ.

2 *Minhāju's-Salāṭīn*, f. 112 b.

3 Barthold, p. 289, says that Sulṭān Maḥmūd's patronage of poets and scholars was due to an ostentatious desire to make his court the centre of all brilliance and distinction and not to sincere love of enlightenment. The Sulṭān may have been influenced by the former motive, but being himself a poet and scholar, it cannot be denied that in his encouragement of learning he must also have been actuated by love of enlightenment. In any case the great services which he rendered to Persian literature by his patronage of learning ought not to be ignored.

4 Dawlat Shāh, p. 44, says that there were 400 poets at his court. For an account of some of these, see ath-Tha'ālibī, *Yatīma*; 'Awfī, *Lubāb*; and Browne, vols. i and ii. 'Utbī also mentions the names of several poets who wrote in praise of the Sulṭān.

5 *Guzīda*, p. 395.

Qāsim Firdawsī, Abu'l-Qāsim Ḥasan b. Aḥmad 'Unṣurī, Farruk̲h̲ī, 'Asjadī and G̲h̲aḍā'irī. Firdawsī composed a large portion of his immortal S̲h̲āhnāmah at his court, and probably at his request, but his merit did not receive proper recognition because 'Unṣurī, the poet-laureate, being jealous of his genius, used his influence in order to bring him into disgrace with the Sulṭān.[1] Maḥmūd had a great passion for collecting scholars at G̲h̲azna, and any man or woman of remarkable intellectual gifts was at once sent for to adorn his court.[2] He founded a university at G̲h̲azna containing a vast collection of valuable books on all branches of literature, and when a town was captured all rare volumes found in its libraries were transported to G̲h̲azna to enrich the store of learning already accumulated there.[3]

The Sulṭān was very generous to scholars and his liberality in this respect has rarely been surpassed. His meanest rewards were calculated in thousands of dīnārs,[4] and the later generations of poets cherished his memory chiefly as a giver of "elephant-loads" of gold and silver.[5] His treatment of Firdawsī and al-Bīrūnī does

1 Majmaʿuʾl-Ansāb, ff. 246 b–247 b. The subject of Firdawsī and his relations with Sulṭān Maḥmūd, together with many other matters of literary and historical interest, has been dealt with exhaustively in a series of scholarly articles by Professor Maḥmūd K̲h̲ān S̲h̲īrānī in the quarterly journal Urdū, 1921–3. Professor S̲h̲īrānī has conclusively proved that the reputed satire of Firdawsī is a cento made up of verses which occur elsewhere in the S̲h̲āhnāmah.

2 Baihaqī, pp. 232–3, 245, 247; and Ibn Balk̲h̲ī, p. 118. The famous story that the Sulṭān demanded al-Bīrūnī, Bū 'Alī Sīnā and other scholars from Abu'l-'Abbās K̲h̲wārizmshāh, is unfounded, as shown by Mīrzā Muḥammad, C̲h̲ahār Maqāla, pp. 193–7, 243.

3 Ibn Jawzī, f. 178 a; Ibnu'l-Athīr, ix, 262; and supra, p. 83.

4 C̲h̲ahār Maqāla, pp. 35, 37, where it is stated that as a reward for a few verses composed by the poet 'Unṣurī, Sulṭān Maḥmūd ordered his mouth to be filled thrice with precious stones. See also Dawlat S̲h̲āh, p. 33.

5 Taʾrīk̲h̲ Fak̲h̲ruʾd-Dīn Mubāraks̲h̲āh, p. 52, and the lexicon Bahār-i 'Ajam, under the word Pīlwār.

not accord with his habitual generosity, but as he may have been influenced by their jealous rivals, it is doubtful whether the whole blame should be put on him alone.[1]

The Sulṭān was respectful to genuine piety.[2] He undertook a long journey to visit the famous saint Abu'l-Ḥasan Kharaqānī;[3] and he used to advance and welcome another saint Abū Sa'īd 'Abdu'l-Malik b. Abū 'Uthmān Muḥammad b. Ibrāhīm al-Khargūshī whenever he came to his court.[4]

Sulṭān Maḥmūd was a follower of the Ḥanafite school of law, but shortly after his accession to the throne he showed an inclination towards the Karrāmite sect which ascribed "substantiality" to God,[5] and he ultimately changed over to the Shāfi'ite school of law.[6] These frequent changes of belief in matters of religious detail go to show that he was imbued with a spirit of enquiry in religion.[7]

The Sulṭān was punctilious in the performance of his religious duties. He offered the usual prayers regularly and read the *Qur'ān* daily.[8] In the month of Ramaḍān he set apart the *zakāt* or 2½ per cent. tax on property, which usually amounted to a large sum, and spent it in alleviating distress. In addition to this, he daily distributed alms among the poor and settled handsome allowances on scholars and disabled persons in the empire.[9] He usually gave monetary help to the volunteers who accompanied him on his Indian expeditions.[10]

1 See *supra*, p. 158.
2 Baihaqī, p. 233.
3 As-Sam'ānī, f. 194 b; and 'Aṭṭār, *Tadhkiratu'l-Awliyā*, pt ii, p. 209.
4 Ibnu'l-Athīr, ix, 247; and as-Sam'ānī, f. 195 b.
5 'Utbī, pp. 324–33.
6 *Mughīthu'l-Khalq*, f. 14 b.
7 *Siyāsat Nāmah*, p. 44.
8 Farrukhī, ff. 22 a, 23 a.
9 Baihaqī, p. 330; *Majma'u'l-Ansāb*, f. 246 a; and *Rabī'u'l-Abrār*, f. 195 a.
10 Sibṭ Ibnu'l-Jawzī, f. 215 a.

Even in the din and bustle of battle, he found time to implore divine assistance. He wished to perform the pilgrimage to Mecca[1] but could not do so on account of political reasons. He, however, tried his best to provide facilities for the pilgrims and offered liberal subsidies to the Beduins of the desert if they allowed their caravans to pass unmolested.[2]

The Sulṭān did not tolerate any deviation from belief in the orthodox Sunnī sect. He instituted a censorship of the religious beliefs of his Muslim subjects, and appointed an officer to punish those accused of moral delinquency or heresy.[3] The followers of the Carmathian and Bāṭinī sects were rigorously persecuted everywhere in the empire. They were captured, imprisoned and, if they did not recant, were sometimes brutally murdered and burnt. Even the literature dealing with their doctrines did not escape the fury of the persecutor. When the town of Raiy was taken, Maḥmūd ordered all the books on Carmathian doctrines, or those in any way savouring of heresy, to be cast into the flames. An invaluable store of learning, which the liberal policy and scholarly zeal of the Buwaihids had accumulated in the course of years, was thus consumed in an instant to satisfy the enthusiasm of the puritan warrior.[4]

But the Sulṭān was not a fanatic.[5] He believed in the religious unity of the state,[6] and severely punished all dissenters. His hostility to the Carmathians was accentuated by the intolerant attitude of the Caliph of Baghdād

1 Farrukhī, f. 34 b.

2 Ibnu'l-Athīr, ix, 229.

3 Farrukhī, f. 165 a; and *Majma'u'l-Ansāb*, f. 245 b.

4 Ibn Jawzī, f. 178 a; Ibnu'l-Athīr, ix, 262; and *Mujmal*, f. 262 b.

5 Sachau, al-Bīrūnī, ii, 268–9. Barthold, p. 287, however, accuses him of fanaticism, apparently on inadequate grounds.

6 'Utbī, p. 5; and al-Bīrūnī, i, 99.

towards them. In the third century A.H. the Fāṭimids, who claimed descent from Fāṭima, the daughter of the Prophet and the spouse of ʻAlī, had established themselves in the north of Africa. About the middle of the following century they extended their power to Egypt, and, not contented with the influence which they commanded in the West, they initiated a long and bitter struggle with the ʻAbbāsids of Baghdād for the allegiance of "the Faithful" in the East. They despatched their emissaries to different countries to induce the rulers to recognise their claims to the overlordship of the Muslim world. The ʻAbbāsids took up the struggle in right earnest and Sulṭān Maḥmūd, being their most powerful vassal, was naturally drawn into it.

The secular power of the ʻAbbāsids had declined with the establishment of the Ṭāhirid Dynasty in Khurāsān, but the religious character of their office became more prominent as their political power decreased. The Caliph was regarded as the successor of the Prophet, and, although he himself occupied a precarious throne, he was supposed to possess the right to bestow any part of the Muslim world on whomsoever he pleased, while sovereigns who had trampled powerful monarchies under their feet quailed before his hollow majesty. The Caliph was thus a useful ally for a warrior who was burning with a desire for expansion; and, to maintain and strengthen the alliance with him, the Sulṭān placed the resources of his empire at the service of the Caliph in his war against the Carmathians.

The political colour which the rivalry between the Caliphs of Baghdād and Cairo lends to the Sulṭān's persecution of the Carmathians, takes much of the fanatic out of him. When his mind was not biassed by any such considerations, he showed a laudable spirit of toleration for religious differences. In India, for example, he is not said to have forced any Hindū to abjure his religion[1], or to have put any person to death for the sake of his conscience. He had, however, the missionary spirit in him, and the preacher invariably followed in the wake of his victorious army. Mosques were erected all over the conquered country and preachers were appointed to instruct the Hindūs in the simple faith of their conquerors.[2] Some Hindū rājās are said to have embraced Islam, but they did so most probably as a political shift to escape the fury of the conqueror and returned to their faith as soon as his back was turned on them. Some critics hold that "a burning hatred" for Islam was created in the Hindū mind because Islam was presented "in the guise of plundering armies".[3] This view, however, is not convincing. The Hindūs rejected Islam as their national religion because of the fundamental and irreconcilable differences between Islam and Hindūism.[4] Islam, with its definite articles of faith, could not appeal to the average Hindū to whom religion had never meant any specified set of doctrines. To regard an idol as a helpless piece of stone, instead of a source of life and death, and to believe in one Omnipotent God, instead of myriads of deities one of which could be played off against the other, was diametrically opposed to Hindū ways of thinking. To this fundamental difference was added the hostility of the Brahmin, whose keen eye must have foreseen that the propagation of the democratic principles of Islam would undoubtedly bring about a social revolution and breakdown of the caste

1 On one occasion the Sulṭān is stated to have offered the alternatives of Islam, tribute or the sword to a Hindū rājā (*supra*, p. 112), but this does not imply that he forced the rājā to accept Islam.

2 Gardīzī, p. 72.

3 Mawlavī Dhakā'u'llāh Khān, *Ta'rīkh-i-Hindūstān*, p. 304. His argument has been adopted and amplified by Professor M. Ḥabīb in his *Sultan Mahmud of Ghaznin*, p. 81.

4 Al-Bīrūnī, i, 100.

system on which depended his own exclusive privileges. The Brahmins therefore as a class must have thrown the whole weight of their position against the spread of Islam. Besides this, hatred of change inherent in the Hindū mind would in any case have offered strong though passive resistance to the onward march of Islam. In spite of this, Islam did make some headway in the Punjāb, but the time was not yet ripe for missionary work, which requires settled government. The period of Sulṭān Maḥmūd was essentially a period of conquest.

The Hindūs enjoyed toleration under the Sulṭān. They were given separate quarters in Ghazna and were permitted free observance of their religious ceremonies.[1] The critics who accuse the Sulṭān of wanton bloodshed and reckless spoliation of Hindū temples, forget that these so-called barbarities were committed in the course of legitimate warfare, when such acts are sanctioned by the practice of all the great conquerors of the world. Spoils captured from a defeated enemy have always been considered the lawful property of the victorious army. In India, however, wealth was accumulated, not only in the coffers of the kings, as in other countries, but also in the vaults of the temples which were consecrated to the service of various deities. The consequence was that, while elsewhere the capture of the defeated monarch's treasury usually gratified the conqueror's lust for mammon, in India temples were also ransacked to secure the piles of gold and precious stones in them. The Sulṭān is never said to have demolished a temple in times of peace. If he harassed the Hindū rājās of India, he did not spare the Muslim sovereigns of Īrān and Transoxiana. The drama of plunder and bloodshed that was enacted in the sacred Ganges Doāb was

1 Al-Ma'arrī, *Risālatu'l-Ghufrān*, p. 153.

repeated with no less virulence on the slopes of the Mount Damāwand and the banks of the river Oxus. Religious considerations rarely carry weight with a conqueror, and the Sulṭān does not appear to have been influenced by them in his schemes of conquest.

In his relations with the Caliph al-Qādir Bi'llāh, Sulṭān Maḥmūd was guided by religious as well as political motives.[1] When the Caliph aṭ-Ṭā'ī was deposed in 381 (991), the Sāmānid Amīr Nūḥ b. Manṣūr did not recognise his successor al-Qādir and continued to read the *khuṭba* in the name of the deposed Caliph. Maḥmūd defeated 'Abdu'l-Malik, the Sāmānid, at Marv in 389 (999), conquered Khurāsān and ordered the *khuṭba* to be read in the name of al-Qādir,[2] who promptly granted to him the patent of the sovereignty of Khurāsān and bestowed on him the honorific title of *Yamīnu'd-Dawlah wa Amīnu'l-Millah*.[3] Maḥmūd henceforth maintained a very respectful attitude towards al-Qādir. About 391 (1001) Wāthiqī, who was a descendant of the Caliph Wāthiq (227–32/842–7), claimed the Caliphate and secured the assistance of the Khāns of Turkistān, but when he came to Khurāsān, Maḥmūd had him arrested and sent to a fort where he remained till his death.[4] In 403 (1012–13) al-Ḥākim, the Fāṭimid Caliph of Cairo, sent a letter to Sulṭān Maḥmūd, probably with a view to securing his allegiance, but the Sulṭān forwarded it to Baghdād where it was burnt in public.[5] A little later in the same year al-Ḥākim despatched an emissary, called Tāhartī, with the same object, but the Sulṭān, in compliance with a religious injunction of eminent theologians, ordered him to be put to death.[6] On such evidence of devotion, al-Qādir further honoured the Sulṭān by bestowing on

1 'Utbī, pp. 296–7.
2 *Tajārib*, iii, 341.
3 'Utbī, p. 133.
4 *Tajārib*, iii, 393.
5 Ibn Jawzī, f. 159 a.
6 'Utbī, p. 299; and Gardīzī, p. 71.

him the title of *Niẓāmu'd-Dīn*. But as time passed, and the name of the Sulṭān was surrounded by a halo of glory, the moral support of the Caliph became less important. The Sulṭān became less obsequious towards him and sometimes months passed before Baghdād was officially informed of his victories.[1] In 414 (1023), however, a serious rupture occurred in their relations. Abū 'Alī Ḥasan, known as Ḥasanak, afterwards the wazīr of the Sulṭān, while returning from his pilgrimage to Mecca, received a *khil'at* from the Fāṭimid Caliph aẓ-Ẓāhir. Suspecting that he had done so at the command of the Sulṭān, al-Qādir addressed a strongly worded letter to him in which he charged Ḥasanak with belief in the Carmathian doctrines and demanded his execution. The Sulṭān was at first enraged with the Caliph, but he soon adopted his usual reverential attitude and despatched the offending *khil'at* to Baghdād, where it was burnt in the public square.[2] This satisfied the Caliph, who, in Shawwāl 417 (November–December 1026), expressed his appreciation of the Sulṭān's victory of Somnāth by bestowing on him the title of *Kahfu'd-Dawlah wa'l-Islām*, and other titles on his sons Mas'ūd and Muḥammad and his brother Yūsuf.[3]

About the close of his reign, the Sulṭān appears to have resolved to bring the Caliph under his sway. When he left Mas'ūd at Raiy in 420 (1029), he instructed him to conquer Iṣfahān and to release the Caliph from the bondage of the Buwaihids, but he died before his plans could materialise.[4]

1 Cf. the Sulṭān's letters to the Caliph, preserved in *Tajārib*, iii, 341–4, and Sibṭ Ibnu'l-Jawzī, f. 204 b. The tone and the form of address of these letters indicate that, during the last years of his reign, the Sulṭān's attitude towards the Caliph had considerably changed.

2 Baihaqī, pp. 211–12; Ibn Jawzī, f. 172 a; and Ibnu'l-Athīr, ix, 239.

3 Gardīzī, pp. 87–8.

4 Baihaqī, pp. 83, 359.

The Sulṭān had a great fondness for architecture. The wealth accumulated by successful wars was spent in beautifying the capital and provincial towns. Before proceeding on his expedition to Kanauj in 409 (1018), he ordered the construction of a magnificent mosque at Ghazna, of marble and granite and of exquisite design and workmanship. Attached to this mosque was a splendid library which was enriched by works of rare value collected from all parts of the empire, and a university on which rich endowments were settled for current expenses and for salaries and stipends to professors and students. The nobles were not slow in following the lead of the Sulṭān, and vied with each other in the magnificence of their private and public buildings.[1] The result was that, within a short time, Ghazna and the provincial capitals were ornamented with palaces, mosques, porches, gardens, reservoirs and aqueducts.[2]

Very little is known about the public works of the Sulṭān. A market at Balkh,[3] a bridge over the river Oxus,[4] and the Band-i-Sulṭān (the Sulṭān's Dam) across the river Nawar,[5] about 18 miles to the north of Ghazna,[6] are almost all that have been mentioned by historians. Of these only the Band-i-Sulṭān has survived and, though much out of repair, is still in use. It was constructed to supply water for irrigation purposes, during dry seasons, to the district round Ghazna. The mouth of the narrow gorge, through which the river Nawar debouches into the plains, was closed with a dam of rough stone-work, about 200

1 'Utbī, pp. 314–17. 2 *Ibid.* p. 333. 3 Baihaqī, p. 688.

4 Sibṭ Ibnu'l-Jawzī, f. 219 b, says that it was constructed at the cost of 2,000,000 *dīnārs*, which appears to be a highly exaggerated figure.

5 It is commonly called the Ghazna river.

6 Bābur's *Memoirs*, ii, 219; and Vigne, pp. 138, 202. This dam was destroyed by 'Alā'u'd-Dīn, the world-incendiary, in 550 (1155), and was repaired by order of Bābur in 932 (1525–6).

yards in length and 25 feet above the sheet of water formed by it. There were two flood-gates, one at the top of the dam and the other at the foot, to regulate the flow of the stream.[1]

The only architectural remains of the time of the Sulṭān are, firstly, his mausoleum which is situated in a little village named Rawḍa-i-Sulṭān (the Sulṭān's Tomb) about two miles to the north of the present town of Ghazna. The tomb is in a dilapidated condition and stands in a rude chamber with a dome of clay. The sarcophagus is a triangular prism of white marble, standing on a plinth of the same material and bearing a Cufic inscription praying the mercy of God on the Sulṭān and recording his glorious titles.[2] Secondly, two minarets, about 400 yards apart and each 144 feet in height, which mark the site of the ancient town of Ghazna. They are exquisite specimens of brick-work. The section of the lower part of each minaret, for about one-third of its height, is a star with eight points. The upper part is round like the third and fourth storeys of the Quṭb Mīnār at Delhi. They are hollow, and a winding stair, which is much damaged, leads to the top. Beautiful ornaments and Cufic inscriptions are placed in different parts of the minarets. The northern minaret was constructed by Sulṭān Maḥmūd and the southern by his son Mas'ūd.[3]

The settlement of the succession early occupied the attention of the Sulṭān. In 406 (1015–16) he nominated his eldest son Mas'ūd as his heir-apparent and made all the noblemen take an oath of loyalty to him.[4] In 408 (1017–18) he appointed him governor of the province of Herāt with Abū Sahl Muḥammad b. Ḥusain az-

1 Vigne, pp. 138, 202.
2 *Syria*, vi, 61–90; and *JASB*. xii, 76–7.
3 Vigne, p. 129; and Fergusson, *History of Indian and Eastern Architecture*, ii, 194.
4 Baihaqī, p. 256.

Zawzanī as his wazīr.[1] The stubborn nature and haughty temperament of Mas'ūd, however, soon brought him into disgrace with his father. He was exiled to Multān in 412 (1021),[2] but a little later he was recalled and restored to his post. In the meantime, Prince Muḥammad, governor of Jūzjānān, won his way into the favour of the Sulṭān who, on his departure for Kanauj in 409 (1018), left him as his deputy in Ghazna,[3] and asked the Caliph to give precedence to his name over that of Mas'ūd in official correspondence.[4] The rivalry between the brothers led to the formation of parties at the court which carried on bitter propaganda against each other.

The Ghaznawid empire, which was by far the largest empire established after the dissolution of the 'Abbāsid Caliphate, attained to its greatest extent under Sulṭān Maḥmūd. When Maḥmūd ascended the throne in 388 (998), he was the ruler of the provinces of Ghazna, Bust and Balkh, which he held as a vassal of the Sāmānids of Bukhārā. Before the end of the following year, he conquered the province of Khurāsān from his overlord Amīr 'Abdu'l-Malik, threw off the allegiance which he had hitherto paid to him, and, like other independent sovereigns, established direct relations with "the Commander of the Faithful". After this, he gradually added the provinces of Sīstān, Ghūr, Gharshistān, Khwārizm, Kāfiristān, Raiy, Jibāl and Iṣfahān to his kingdom, and was recognised as suzerain by the rulers of Quṣdār, Mukrān, Ṭabaristān and Jurjān, Khutlān, Ṣaghāniyān and Qubādiyān. Besides this, he conquered the Hindū-shāhiyya kingdom, which extended from Lamaghān to the river Biyās, and the provinces of Multān and Bhatinda, and received the allegiance of the rājās of the southern Kāshmīr hill states, Narāyanpūr, Kanauj, Gwālior, Kālinjar, and of many other petty states in the

1 Baihaqī, p. 256; and Gardīzī, p. 74. 2 Ibnu'l-Athīr, ix, 283.
3 See *supra*, p. 153, note 4.
4 Baihaqī, p. 258; and *Ṭab. Nāṣ.* p. 91.

Ganges Doāb. Thus the empire of Sulṭān Maḥmūd, at the height of his power, included the vast territories from 'Irāq and the Caspian Sea to the river Ganges, and from the Aral Sea and Transoxiana to the Indian Ocean, Sind and the Rājpūtāna desert. Its greatest length from east to west was about 2000 miles and its greatest width from north to south was about 1400 miles.

The Sulṭān realised that it would be almost impossible for his successor to control the unwieldy empire from Ghazna. He therefore divided it between his sons Mas'ūd and Muḥammad, giving the well-established provinces of Khurāsān, Ghazna, Balkh and Northern India to Muḥammad, and the recently conquered and more or less disturbed kingdom of Raiy to Mas'ūd.[1] This unequal division naturally annoyed Mas'ūd and accentuated the differences between the rival parties at court, so much so that some of the Sulṭān's slaves formed a plot to take him prisoner and raise Mas'ūd to the throne. Mas'ūd emphatically refused in words which are a fitting tribute to the greatness of the Sulṭān: "Beware of the consequences of your action," he said to the conspirators; "I will not be a party to any vile plots against my father. I cannot bear to see him come to grief. His reprimands are agreeable to me. He is a king whose peer you will not find in the whole world".[2] The bitterness of the Sulṭān towards Mas'ūd, however, increased, and shortly before his death the Sulṭān disinherited him and left the whole empire to Muḥammad.[3]

In his settlement of the succession, the Sulṭān cannot escape the blame of short-sightedness and imprudence. The division of the empire was a wise step in itself but its value was considerably diminished by the inequality of the shares of the two brothers. The nomina-

1 Baihaqī, p. 258. Baiḍāwī, *Niẓāmu't-Tawārīkh* (E. and D. ii, 256), however, says that Mas'ūd was given Raiy, 'Irāq and Khurāsān, and Muḥammad the rest of the empire.

2 Baihaqī, p. 151. 3 *Ibid.* pp. 27–8.

tion of Muḥammad as successor was a serious mistake because Mas'ūd, even in the opinion of Sulṭān Maḥmūd himself,[1] was more fit to govern in the troubled times that were approaching. A fierce fratricidal war, which would have been the consequence of this ill-advised measure, was averted only by the desertion of Muḥammad's army when Mas'ūd approached Ghazna to contest the throne with him.

This is a brief sketch of the private life and public career of Sulṭān Maḥmūd. As a man, he was affectionate, just, pure, kind, generous, devout and religious—a truly great and admirable character. As a conqueror, he stands conspicuous among the greatest warriors of the world; for, throughout the long period of thirty-three years of active warfare, he never was beaten. As an encourager of learning, he deserves the fulsome praises which Oriental writers have lavished on him, for he did more than any other sovereign before him towards forming and developing a national Persian literature. As an administrator, he deserves to be mentioned with respect, for even during his long and frequent absences on distant expeditions, he was able to keep good order in his vast empire. As the founder of a dynasty, however, he failed, because he extended the area of his empire beyond the capacity of one person to control and keep intact. But in spite of his shortcomings he deserves to be ranked among the greatest rulers and conquerors of the world. In the words of his son Mas'ūd:[2]

> Peace be on him! No mother shall give
> birth to another one like Maḥmūd.

1 *Ṭab. Nāṣ.* pp. 91–3.
2 Baihaqī, p. 28.

PARALLEL passages from some Oriental historians are given below to show the extent of their indebtedness to each other.

(1)

ذکر غزو مولتان

ابو الفتح والی مولتان بر
دحس اعتقاد و قبح الحاد
موصوف بود و اهل خطهٔ مولتان
را برای و هوای خویش
دعوت می کرد و خلایق‌را در
مزلهٔ ضلالت و مهلکهٔ جهالت می
انداخت حال او بسلطان انها
کردند حمیت اسلام و غیرت
دین اورا بر کفایت و حسم مادهٔ
معرت او باعث و محرض شد
در مهم این کار استخارت کرد و
همت بر این کار دینی گماشت
و آمادهٔ کار شد و لشکری بسیار
جرار جمع کرد . چون نقاش
ربیع نقشهای بدیع باطراف
کوه و هامون نگاشت آهنگ
ناحیت مولتان جزم کرد و
باندبال بادشاه هند کس فرستاد
تادر و اسطهٔ مملکت خویش راه
دهد تا لشکر اسلام بگذرد او
دست رد بر روی التماس سلطان

ذکر غزوهٔ مولتان

ابو الفتوح والی مولتان
بخبث نحلت و فساد دخلت و
دحس اعتقاد و قبح الحاد
موصوف و معروف بود و اهل
خطهٔ مولتانرا برای و هوای
خویش دعوت میکرد و خلق را در
مزلهٔ ضلالت و مهلکهٔ جهالت
می انداخت — حال او بسلطان
انها کردند حمیت اسلام و
غیرت دین اورا بر کفایت
مضرت و حسم مادهٔ معرت او
باعث و محرض شد و در این
باب استخاره کرد و همت بر
این مهم دینی گماشت و آمادهٔ
کار شد و از اولیای دین و
مطوعهٔ اسلام حشمی بسیار و
لشکری جرار فراهم آورد و چون
نقاش ربیع نقشهای بدیع بر
اطراف کوه و هامون نگاشت
.... آهنگ ناحیت مولتان کرد
و بحکم آنکه ..... راه ممتنع و

نهاد و راه تمرد پیش گرفت
سلطان ازین سبب در خشم شد
و نیت غزو مثنی کرد و در یك
پرده دو نوا آغاز کرد و جازم شد
که بیضهٔ ملك و آشیانهٔ دولت
او بصرصر قهر برباد دهد
بفرمود . . . .

Jāmi'u't-Tawārīkh, f. 228 a.

متعذر شده باندبال که شاه
هند بود کس فرستاد تادر
واسطهٔ مملکت خویش راه دهد تا
لشکر اسلام بگذرد و او دست رد
بر روی التماس سلطان گذاشت
و راه تمرد پیش گرفت و سلطان
ازین سبب در خشم شد و نیت
غزو مثنی کرد و در یك پرده دو
نوا آغاز نهاد و جازم شد که
اول . . . . . . بیضهٔ ملك و آشیانهٔ
دولت او بصرصر قهر بر باد دهد
بفرمود . . . . . .

Jurbā<u>dh</u>qānī, pp. 289–90.

(2)

تا بدان رسید که نطاق
اسمعیل از اعتناق آن بتنگ آمد
و از ضعف طبعیت بشرایط
سیادت و سیاست قیام نتوانست
نمود چون سیف الدولة از واقعهٔ
پدر خبر یافت مراسم عزا
بجای آورد و ببرادر تعزیت نامه
نوشت و ابو الحسن حمولی را
برسالت نزد او فرستاد و پیغام
داد که امیر ناصر الدین افاض
الله علیه شآبیب الغفران که
جنهٔ نوائب و عمدهٔ ظهور
حوادث بود رحلت نمود و مرا
امروز در همهٔ جهان گرامی‌تر

و او خزائن جهان بر ایشان
تفرقه کرد و نطاق او از اعتناق
آن منصب تنگ آمد و ضعف
منت و خور طبعیت او ظاهر شد
و بشرائط سیادت و سیاست
قیام نتوانست نمود . . . . . . چون
سیف الدولة از حادثهٔ پدر خبر
یافت بشرائط عزا قیام نمود و
ببرادر تعزیت نامه نوشت و ابو
الحسن حمولی‌را بسفارت بدو
فرستاد و پیغام داد که پدر که
جنهٔ نوائب و عمدهٔ حوادث
بود رفت و مرا امروز در همه
جهان از تو گرامی‌تر کس

از تو کس نیست از جان شیرین و از روشنائی چشم عزیز تری هر آنچه متمنی تو باشد از حکم و فرمان و خزائن و ممالك و ساز و لشکر دریغ نیست اما کبر سن و تجربهٔ ایام و وقوف بر دقائق سرداری و معرفت مقادیر حشم در ثبات ملك و دوام دولت اصل مبین و حبل متین است.

Rawḍatu'ṣ-Ṣafā, p. 734.

نیست و از جان شیرین و روشنائی چشم عزیزتری هر آنچه بمراد و تمنای تست بتو باز خواهد گشت از حکم و فرمان و خزائن و ممالك و ساز و لشکر دریغ نیست اما کبر سن و تجارب ایام و قدرت بر دقائق سرداری و معرفت بر مقادیر حشم و ارتیاض بآداب جهانبانی در استثبات ملك و استدامت دولت اصلی مبین و حبلی متین است.

Jurbā<u>dh</u>qānī, pp. 187–9.

(3)

در اوائل این سال عزیمت تسخیر ملتان نمود چه از والئ آن مملکت که ابو الفتح نام داشت حرکات ناپسندیده بسمع سلطان رسانیده بودند چون ایام بهار بود و بواسطهٔ کثرت میاه گذشتن از بعضی راهها متعذر بود سلطان به جیپال که پادشاه معظم بلاد هندوستان بود کس فرستاد که از میان مملکت خویش راه دهد تا لشکر اسلام بگذرد جیپال دست رد بر سینهٔ ملتمس سلطان نهاده طریقهٔ تمرد و عصیان پیش گرفت

چون سلطان ازان غزا فارغ شد عزیمت ملتان نمود چه از والئ آن مملکت که ابو الفتح نام داشت حرکات نا مناسب بسمع سلطان رسانیده بودند چون ایام بهار بود و اعبار از بعضی طرق بواسطهٔ کثرت میاه متعذر می نمود سلطان بجیپال که بادشاه معظم ممالك هند بود کس فرستاد و التماس کرد که در واسطهٔ مملکت خویش راه دهد تا لشکر اسلام بگذرد جیپال دست رد بر سینهٔ ملتمس سلطان نهاده تمرد پیش

يمين الدولة محمود ازين معنى
در خشم شد و فرمود تا سپاه او
دست بقتل و غارت بلاد ملك
جيپال دراز كرده دمار از روزگار
ايشان بر آوردند و جيپال خود
را به نواحئ كشمير انداخته از
صدمات قهر سلطان محمود
خلاص شد و چون ابو الفتح
والئ ملتان مشاهده نمود كه
مقدم ملوك هند را چه پيش آمد
خزائن و دفائن ......

Ta'rīkh-i-Alfī, f. 372 a.

گرفت سيف الدولة محمود
ازينصورت درخشم شد و نيت غزو
مثنى كرده در يك پرده دو
نوا آغاز نهاد فرمانداد تا دست
نهب و ارهاق و هدم و احتراق
بر ديار و امصار دراز كردند و
جيپال را از مضيقى بمضيقى مى
انداختند تا به نواحئ كشمير
افتاد و ابو الفتح والئ ملتان
چون مشاهده نمود كه معظم
ملوك هند را چه پيش آمد خزائن
و دفائن .....

Rawḍatu'ṣ-Ṣafā, p. 735.

APPENDIX B

CHRONOLOGY OF THE PREDECESSORS OF SUBUKTIGĪN

MOST historians do not mention the predecessors of Subuktigīn even by name. Gardīzī gives some details about Alptigīn and his rise to power, but he has ignored Abū Isḥāq Ibrāhīm, Bilkātigīn, Pirītigīn and even Subuktigīn. 'Utbī has omitted them except for a very vague reference. *Siyāsat Nāmah* contains numerous details about Alptigīn but they are not trustworthy. The brief notice of these rulers in *Ṭabaqāt-i-Nāṣirī* is valuable as it is a quotation from the lost portion of Baihaqī's *Mujalladāt*. *Majma'u'l-Ansāb* contains a brief account of these rulers, but unfortunately the reign of Bilkātigīn is left blank in the only manuscript in which the chapter on the G͟haznawids has been preserved. Besides these, some works of the tenth and eleventh centuries A.H. like *Jahān Ārā*, *Zīnatu'l-Majālis*, *Ṣubḥ-i-Ṣādiq* and *Jannātu'l-Firdaws* give an account of these rulers in varying degrees of detail, but their authorities are not specified.

I have been able to determine the precise dates of the predecessors of Subuktigīn by a critical comparison of the authorities. It is stated in Ibnu'l-At͟hīr, viii, 404, and *Tajāribu'l-Umam*, ii, 192, that Alptigīn defeated the forces of Amīr Manṣūr in the middle of Rabī' i 351 (23rd April, 962). After this he turned his attention to G͟hazna and conquered it in four months, i.e. about the close of the year 351 and probably in D͟hu'l-Ḥajja (January 963), as stated in *Jahān Ārā* and elsewhere.[1] Alptigīn died on 20th S͟ha'bān, 352 (13th September,

1 See *supra*, p. 25, note 6.

963), after a reign of eight months[1] and was succeeded by his son Abū Isḥāq Ibrāhīm.

The date of the death of Ibrāhīm or of the accession of Bilkātigīn is determined by the statement in *Ṭabaqāt-i-Nāṣirī*, p. 76, that Sulṭān Maḥmūd was born in the seventh year of the reign of Bilkātigīn. As the Sulṭān was born in Muḥarram 361 (November 971), Bilkātigīn must have ascended the throne in 355 (966) on the death of Ibrāhīm, whose rule therefore lasted from 352 to 355 (963–66). Bilkātigīn ruled for ten years[2] and died in 364 (974–5). His successor Pirītigīn ruled from 364 (974–5) to the accession of Subuktigīn in Sha'bān 366 (April 977).

1 Not "eight years" as given in Raverty's translation of *Ṭabaqāt-i-Nāṣirī*. If eight years is taken to be the period of Alptigīn's reign, either Alptigīn himself or Ibrāhīm would have been the ruler of Ghazna in 359 (969–70), which is the date on one of the coins of Bilkātigīn (*JRAS.* xvii, pp. 142–3). The words *sāl*, meaning "year", and *māh*, meaning "month", are very easily interchangeable if written carelessly in Arabic script.

2 Not "two" as given in Raverty's translation of *Ṭabaqāt-i-Nāṣirī*. A very old MS of *Ṭabaqāt-i-Nāṣirī* (Brit. Mus. Add. 26,189, f. 97 b) gives ten years. Moreover, Sulṭān Maḥmūd's birth could not have fallen within the reign of Bilkātigīn, as stated above, if Bilkātigīn had reigned only for two years. The words *dū*, meaning "two", and *dah*, meaning "ten", are easily confused in Arabic script.

APPENDIX C

THE FARĪGHŪNIDS

THE Farīghūnids were the hereditary rulers of Jūzjānān[1] under the overlordship of the Sāmānids. The first ruler of this dynasty mentioned by Muslim historians was Aḥmad b. Farīghūn, who about 285 (898) is said to have done homage to Ismā'īl b. Aḥmad the Sāmānid.[2] In 365 (975–6) Nūḥ b. Manṣūr, the Sāmānid, entered into a matrimonial alliance with Abu'l-Ḥārith Muḥammad b. Aḥmad b. Farīghūn, ruler of Jūzjānān.[3] In 372 (982–3) a geographical treatise entitled *Ḥudūdu'l-'Ālam* was written for him by an unknown author.[4] Some time after this, Muḥammad was succeeded by his son Abu'l-Ḥārith Aḥmad who, in 380 (990–1) and again in 384 (994), helped his suzerain Amīr Nūḥ b. Manṣūr to crush the power of his rebellious noblemen, Abū 'Alī Sīmjūrī and Fā'iq. Aḥmad was on terms of friendship with Subuktigīn, and in 385 (995) assisted him in turning out Abū 'Alī Sīmjūrī from Khurāsān.[5] A little later, these relations were strengthened by a matrimonial alliance. Aḥmad gave one of his daughters in marriage to Maḥmūd, son of Subuktigīn, and Subuktigīn gave one of his to Abū Naṣr Muḥammad, son of Aḥmad.[6]

In the struggle for the throne that followed the death of Subuktigīn, Aḥmad took up the cause of his son-in-law Maḥmūd against Ismā'īl and, after the overthrow of the Sāmānid power, recognised him as his overlord.[7]

Aḥmad died some time between 390 and 398 (1000–

1 Jūzjānān is written Gūzgānān in Persian works.
2 Narshakhī, p. 85.
3 Gardīzī, p. 48.
4 Barthold, p. 13.
5 'Utbī, pp. 69, 78, 88.
6 *Ibid.* p. 227.
7 *Ibid.* p. 116.

1008), and was succeeded by his son Abū Naṣr Muḥammad, who accompanied the Sulṭān on some of his expeditions to India and elsewhere.[1] He gave one of his daughters in marriage to prince Abū Aḥmad Muḥammad, son of Sulṭān Maḥmūd.[2] Abū Naṣr Muḥammad died in 401 (1010–11),[3] leaving a son named Ḥasan,[4] who being probably too young to succeed to the throne the province of Jūzjānān was placed under the governorship of Abū Aḥmad Muḥammad.[5]

The Farīghūnids were well-known for their noble character and love of learning, and their court was the resort of poets and scholars.[6]

1 'Utbī, pp. 218, 225.
2 *Ibid.* p. 295; and 'Awfī, *Lubāb*, pt i, p. 25.
3 'Utbī, p. 227; and Ibnu'l-Athīr, ix, 159.
4 Baihaqī, p. 125.
5 'Utbī, p. 295; and 'Awfī, *Lubāb*, pt i, pp. 25–6.
6 'Utbī, p. 228; and Ibnu'l-Athīr, ix, 159.

APPENDIX D

MAḤMŪD'S TITLE TO THE THRONE

Maḥmūd's repeated attempts at reconciliation with his brother Ismā'īl have been misinterpreted by Elphinstone (*History of India*, p. 316), to signify the "consciousness of a weak title" to the throne. Maḥmūd seems to have been the heir-apparent, and although there is no direct reference to this, it is borne out by sufficient circumstantial evidence. From his childhood—when Subuktigīn is said to have left him as his deputy at Ghazna and given him charge of the province of Zamīn Dāwar—on to his youth—when he showed conspicuous skill and energy in the contests with Rājā Jaipāl and Abū 'Alī Sīmjūrī—he had always been associated with his father in the administration of the country and the conduct of the wars, so that when Amīr Nūḥ recognised the services of Subuktigīn, Maḥmūd too received a title and the command of the troops of Khurāsān which was the highest office in the empire; while the name of Ismā'īl is not mentioned in any connection whatsoever. It is highly improbable that Ismā'īl would have been kept so much in the background if he had been the heir-apparent. Moreover, Subuktigīn showed his eagerness to advance the interests of Maḥmūd by securing for him the hand of a princess of the Farīghūnid house which was connected by marriage with the Sāmānids.

Thus it appears that Maḥmūd had tacitly enjoyed the honours due to a heir-apparent, and Ismā'īl's nomination to the succession was probably only a freak of the dying man's capricious temperament. Maḥmūd's repeated attempts at reconciliation were not therefore due to any weakness of his title to the throne but to a genuine desire, as stated by 'Utbī, p. 115, to avoid a fratricidal war.

APPENDIX E

THE SĀMĀNIDS

SĀMĀN-I-KHUDĀT, the founder of the Sāmānid Dynasty, was a Zoroastrian nobleman of Balkh who traced his descent from Bahrām Chūbīn.[1] Sāmān embraced Islam at the hands of al-Ma'mūn, son of the Caliph Hārūnu'r-Rashīd, who was at that time governor of Khurāsān under his brother al-Amīn.[2] Asad, the eldest son of Sāmān, had four sons, named Abū Muḥammad Nūḥ, Abū Naṣr Aḥmad, Abu'l-'Abbās Yaḥyā, and Abu'l-Faḍl Ilyās. They won the admiration of al-Ma'mūn,[3] who, after his accession to the Caliphate, commanded Ghassān b. 'Abbād, governor of Khurāsān, to appoint each of the brothers to the government of a province. Accordingly in 204[4] (819–20) Ghassān gave Samarqand to Nūḥ, Farghāna to Aḥmad, Shāsh and Ushrūsana[5] to Yaḥyā; and Herāt to Ilyās.[6]

After the death of Nūḥ, Aḥmad became the master of Samarqand, and within a few years added Kāshghar to his kingdom.[7] Aḥmad died in 249[8] (863–4), and was succeeded by his son Abu'l-Ḥasan Naṣr, who acquired

1 Gardīzī, p. 19, traces his genealogy to Gayūmarth. See also *Mujmal*, f. 251 a; and *Guzīda*, p. 379.

2 Gardīzī, pp. 19–20. Narshakhī, pp. 57, 74, however, gives quite a different version which seems to be incorrect.

3 Gardīzī, p. 20. Narshakhī, p. 74, says that they had won his favour by assisting him in quelling the rebellion of Rāfi' b. Laith.

4 Gardīzī, p. 20. Narshakhī, p. 75, incorrectly says 292 (905). See also Gardīzī (King's College MS), f. 81 a.

5 Modern Tāshkand and Ura Tipa, see Le Strange, pp. 474, 481.

6 Gardīzī, p. 20. According to as-Sam'ānī, f. 286 b, Nūḥ died in 227 (842), Yaḥyā in 241 (855–6), Ilyās in 242 (856–7), and Aḥmad in 250 (864).

7 *Ṭab. Nāṣ.* p. 29.

8 Narshakhī, p. 76; but *Mujmal*, f. 241 b, and *Ṭab. Nāṣ.* p. 29, seem to suggest 261 (874–5).

Bukhārā in 260 (873–4) and placed it in charge of his brother Abū Ibrāhīm Ismā'īl.[1] In the following year, the Caliph al-Mu'tamid granted to him the patent of the sovereignty of Transoxiana. In 275 (888–9), owing to some disagreement with his brother Ismā'īl, Naṣr attacked Bukhārā but was defeated and taken prisoner. Ismā'īl, however, treated him with respect and allowed him to return to his capital at Samarqand.[2]

Naṣr died in 279 (892–3) and was succeeded by his brother Abū Ibrāhīm Ismā'īl, who was already in charge of Bukhārā. Ismā'īl defeated 'Amr b. Laith at Balkh on 15th Rabī' i, 287 (20th March, 900), sent him a prisoner to Baghdād and annexed Khurāsān.[3] He then marched against Muḥammad b. Zaid, the 'Alid ruler of Ṭabaristān and Jurjān, inflicted a crushing defeat on him and took possession of his kingdom.[4]

Ismā'īl died on 14th Ṣafar, 295 (24th November, 907), and was succeeded by his son Abū Naṣr Aḥmad, who, during his short rule, added Sīstān to his empire. Owing to his savage cruelty, he was put to death by his slaves on 23rd Jumādī ii, 301 (24th January, 914), and his son Abu'l-Ḥasan Naṣr, who was only eight years of age, was raised to the throne. The governors of distant provinces frequently rose in rebellion against him, but he was usually successful in reducing them to obedience. After his death on 27th Rajab, 331 (6th April, 943), the Sāmānid empire went the inevitable round of decay and downfall. Disastrous wars with the Buwaihid sovereigns sapped the energy of his son and successor Abū Muḥammad Nūḥ, and Raiy, Ṭabaristān and Jurjān fell off one by one from the empire. Nūḥ died on 19th Rabī' ii, 343 (22nd August, 954), and was succeeded by his son Abu'l-Fawāris 'Abdu'l-Malik,[5]

1 Narshakhī, p. 77.
2 Gardīzī, p. 20.
3 Ṭabarī, iii, 2194.
4 Gardīzī, p. 21.
5 In *Siyāsat Nāmah* his name is altogether omitted, but see 'Utbī, p. 149; and Narshakhī, p. 24.

who tried in vain to restore his influence in the West. He died of a fall from his horse while playing *chawgān* on 11th Shawwāl, 350 (23rd November, 961).

'Abdu'l-Malik was succeeded by his brother Abū Ṣāliḥ Manṣūr.[1] During his reign the provinces of Ghazna and Bust became independent under Alptigīn, formerly commander of the troops of Khurāsān.

Manṣūr died on 11th Shawwāl, 365 (12th June, 976), and was succeeded by his son Abu'l-Qāsim Nūḥ, whose reign was marked by the mutual jealousies of a multitude of rebellious nobles. The most ambitious of them, Fā'iq and Abū 'Alī Sīmjūrī, intrigued with Bughrā Khān of Kāshghar and invited him to attack Bukhārā. The Khān accepted the invitation and advanced on the city. Amīr Nūḥ fled at his approach, and Bughrā Khān entered Bukhārā in triumph in Rabī' i 382[2] (May–June 992). The climate, however, did not agree with him and he returned to Kāshghar in Jumādī i of the same year (July 992), leaving behind 'Abdu'l-'Azīz b. Nūḥ b. Naṣr as his deputy. Amīr Nūḥ hurried back, defeated 'Abdu'l-'Azīz and occupied Bukhārā on the 15th of Jumādī ii[3] (18th August, 992).

Amīr Nūḥ died on 13th Rajab, 387 (22nd July, 997). The whole period of his reign was an unending succession of intrigues, revolts, murders and civil wars. He had managed to maintain himself on the throne by a clever scheme of plots and counter-plots, by sowing dissension among the rebels, and by setting one rebel against another. Of all his vassals, Subuktigīn alone

1 According to Maqdisī, p. 338, Naṣr, son of 'Abdu'l-Malik, was recognised Amīr for one day.

2 Al-Bīrūnī, *The Chronology of Ancient Nations*, p. 131; Gardīzī, p. 53; and Baihaqī, p. 233. Ibnu'l-Athīr, ix, 70; Faṣīḥī, f. 305 a; Lane-Poole, *The Mohammadan Dynasties*, p. 132; Sir H. H. Howorth, *JRAS*. 1898, p. 470; and Mīrzā Muḥammad of Qazwīn, *Chahār Maqāla*, p. 185, have made wrong statements with regard to the date of this event.

3 Gardīzī, pp. 53–4; and Baihaqī, p. 234.

remained steadfast in his loyalty, and his devoted service brought for a short time a spark of life to the sinking house of Sāmān.

Nūḥ was succeeded by his son Abu'l-Ḥārith Manṣūr. He lacked the capacity of his father for intrigue and was a mere puppet in the hands of his noblemen Fā'iq and Begtūzūn who at first tried to embroil him with Maḥmūd and then thought it more convenient to put him aside. Consequently they deposed and blinded him on 12th Ṣafar, 389 (2nd February, 999), and raised his brother 'Abdu'l-Malik to the throne.[1] But 'Abdu'l-Malik did not enjoy the honours of sovereignty for long. Īlak Khān, the successor of Bughrā Khān, invaded Bukhārā. 'Abdu'l-Malik, with a view to organising a national resistance, made an appeal to the people. It was read from the pulpit of the Friday Mosque in Bukhārā but the congregation listened to it in sullen silence. The jurists of Bukhārā voiced the popular opinion by declaring it unlawful to bear arms against the invader on the ground of his being one of "the Faithful".[2] Īlak Khān entered Bukhārā unopposed on 10th Dhu'l-Qa'da, 389 (23rd October, 999). 'Abdu'l-Malik was taken prisoner and sent to Ūzgand for safe custody.[3]

But one of the princes, Abū Ibrāhīm Ismā'īl b. Nūḥ, known as al-Muntaṣir, managed to escaped the vigilance of his guards, and for a period of six years, made spasmodic efforts to regain his lost inheritance. His wanderings from Raiy to Samarqand, sometimes at the head of a victorious army and sometimes in hasty flight before a triumphant rival or a treacherous ally, form a thrilling chapter in the history of those times. The unfortunate prince was murdered in Rabī' i 395 (December 1004) by Ibn Buhaij, chief of the Arabs in the Ghuzz desert, with whom he had taken refuge.

1 'Utbī, p. 124; and Baihaqī, p. 804.

2 *Tajārib*, iii, 373–4, but Īlak Khān has been confused with Bughrā Khān.

3 'Utbī, p. 135; and Gardīzī, p. 61.

APPENDIX F

CHRONOLOGY OF THE MA'MŪNIDS

VERY little is known about the history of the Ma'mūnid Dynasty. Some Oriental historians like Ḥamdu'llāh Mustawfī,[1] Aḥmad Ghaffārī, and Faṣīḥī, and in modern times, Major Raverty[2] and his followers, have confused them with the Farīghūnids who were the rulers of Jūzjānān.[3]

Abū 'Alī Ma'mūn b. Muḥammad is the first ruler of this dynasty mentioned by the Muslim writers. He is first mentioned by 'Utbī in *Kitābu'l-Yamīnī* in 382 (991–2).[4] He was assassinated in 387 (997),[5] and was succeeded by his son Abu'l-Ḥasan 'Alī. The date of his death and of the accession of his brother and successor, Abu'l-'Abbās Ma'mūn, is not mentioned. 'Utbī, p. 216, refers to him as the ruler of Khwārizm in 397 (1006–7); while in Baihaqī, p. 838, it is implied that Abu'l-'Abbās had ruled for at least seven years before his assassination in 407 (1017), that is at least from 400 (1010). Thus Abu'l-Ḥasan 'Alī died between 397 and 400 (1006–10). Again, Baihaqī, p. 838, says that Abu'l-'Abbās sent al-Bīrūnī (who according to Baihaqī, p. 838, had arrived at his court about 400) to meet half-way the messenger bringing a *khil'at* and a title which the Caliph had bestowed upon him. As titles and *khil'ats* were usually bestowed on the accession of a sovereign, and as al-Bīrūnī could not have been sent on this business before 400 (1009–10), the probable conclusion is that Abu'l-'Abbās had ascended the throne about the

1 *Guzīda*, p. 400.
2 *Ṭab. Nāṣ*. p. 232, note.
3 See the note of Mīrzā Muḥammad, *Chahār Maqāla*, p. 243.
4 'Utbī, p. 77; and Gardīzī, p. 53.
5 *Ibid.* pp. 106, 110.

year 399 (1008–9), that is, a short time before the *khil'at* and the title were bestowed on him.[1]

This date is corroborated by some of the later writers. In *Jannātu'l-Firdaws* it is mentioned that Abu'l-Ḥasan 'Alī ruled for thirteen years, that is, from 387 to 399 (997–1009). In *Zīnatu'l-Majālis* the date of his death is given as 400 (1009–10).

Abu'l-'Abbās was assassinated on 15th Shawwāl, 407 (17th March, 1017), and one of his sons was raised to the throne. He ruled for four months till the conquest of Khwārizm in Ṣafar 408 (July 1017), when the dynasty came to an end.[2]

1 Faṣīḥī, f. 310 b, places his death in 390 (1000) which is incorrect. Barthold, p. 147, note 4, mentions an inscription on a minaret in old Gurgānj or Jurjāniyyah, dated 401 (1010–11), which was erected by Abu'l-'Abbās Ma'mūn.

2 See also Barthold, pp. 147, 275–8.

APPENDIX G

THE ṢAFFĀRIDS

YA'QŪB B. LAITH B. MU'ADDAL, a resident of Qarnīn[1] in Sīstān, left his native village and adopted the profession of a *ṣaffār* or brazier; but his high spirits revolted at this peaceful occupation and he soon took to highway robbery.[2] By a freak of fortune, he was promoted in 237 (851–2) from the leadership of a band of outlaws to the government of Bust, by Ṣāliḥ b. Naḍr, the Ṭāhirid governor of Sīstān.[3] Ya'qūb consolidated his power, defeated Ṣāliḥ, took possession of Sīstān, conquered Ghazna, Zābulistān and Gardīz, and in 253 (867), added the provinces of Herāt, Balkh and Bāmiyān to his empire. He then defeated Muḥammad, the last of the Ṭāhirids, in 259[4] (872–3), and became the master of Khurāsān. In the following year, he conquered Ṭabaristān from its 'Alid ruler and then marched on Baghdād.[5] Here his victorious arms received a check. He was defeated and forced to retire. He refused, however, to be reconciled to the Caliph[6] and marched again on Baghdād, but he died on the way on 14th Shawwāl, 265 (9th June, 879).[7]

'Amr, brother of Ya'qūb,[8] succeeded to the throne. He reconciled the Caliph but the latter, being afraid of

1 Gardīzī, p. 10. According to Yāqūt, iv, 73, it was a village in the district of Neshak in Sīstān.

2 Gardīzī, p. 11. *Guzīda*, p. 373, says that it was Laith who took to highway robbery.

3 Ibnu'l-Athīr, viii, 43; and *Ta'rīkh-i-Sīstān* as quoted in *Kāvah* (Berlin), vol. ii, No. 2, p. 14.

4 Ṭabarī, iii, 1880.

5 *Ibid.* 1883.

6 *Guzīda*, p. 434, says that the Ṣaffārids were Shī'as.

7 Ṭabarī, iii, 1883.

8 *Ibid.* iii, 1931; not son, as said by Muir, *The Caliphate*, p. 544.

his power, induced Ismā'īl b. Aḥmad, the ruler of Transoxiana, to attack him. 'Amr was defeated near Balkh in Rabī' i 287 (March 900) and was sent a prisoner to Baghdād, where he died two years later.[1]

The army then raised his grandson Ṭāhir b. Muḥammad b. 'Amr to the throne. His sway did not extend beyond Sīstān. In 293 (905–6) Subkarī,[2] a slave of 'Amr b. Laith, revolted against him, took him prisoner, and sent him to Baghdād. He was succeeded by Mu'addal b. 'Alī b. Laith. Aḥmad b. Ismā'īl, the Sāmānid, defeated him in Rajab 298[3] (March 911), sent him a prisoner to Baghdād and annexed Sīstān. The people, however, rebelled against him, took his governor, Manṣūr b. Isḥāq, prisoner and raised 'Amr, a great-grandson of 'Amr b. Laith, to the throne. 'Amr was defeated in Dhu'l-Ḥajja 300 (July 913), and sent as a prisoner to Bukhārā. Sīstān henceforth became a part of the Sāmānid empire and was placed under the command of Sīmjūr-i-Dawātī.[4]

Some years after this,[5] the glories of the Ṣaffārid house were to some extent revived in the person of Abū Ja'far Aḥmad b. Muḥammad, a grandson of Ṭāhir b. Muḥammad b. 'Amr, who had taken to the profession of a labourer to earn his living. His noble bearing attracted the notice of Amīr Naṣr b. Aḥmad the Sāmānid, who was so moved to pity at his misfortune that he appointed him governor of Sīstān and married him to a princess of his own house.[6]

Aḥmad died about the year 353 (964) and was suc-

1 Ṭabarī, iii, 2208.

2 Gardīzī, p. 28. Major Raverty, *Ṭab. Nāṣ.* p. 184, note, thinks that it is "Sigizī", meaning the inhabitant of a range of hills in Zābulistān, known as Sigiz.

3 *Tajārib*, i, 19; and Ibnu'l-Athīr, viii, 45.

4 Gardīzī, p. 24.

5 In *Zubdatu't-Tawārīkh* it is mentioned in the year 309 (921–22).

6 *Guzīda*, p. 382.

ceeded by his son Abū Aḥmad K̲h̲alaf.[1] In 354 (965), K̲h̲alaf went on a pilgrimage to Mecca, and during his absence Ṭāhir b. Ḥusain won over the army and usurped the kingdom. K̲h̲alaf defeated Ṭāhir with the help of Amīr Manṣūr b. Nūḥ the Sāmānid, but shortly after that Ṭāhir again invaded Sīstān and forced K̲h̲alaf to take refuge at Buk̲h̲ārā. The Amīr received him kindly and sent him back with the necessary reinforcements. Ṭāhir having died in the meantime, his son Ḥusain took up the defence. After some resistance, Ḥusain offered submission to the Amīr, delivered Sīstān to K̲h̲alaf and retired to Buk̲h̲ārā. After some time, K̲h̲alaf himself revolted against the Amīr, who now sent his old rival Ḥusain against him. K̲h̲alaf took refuge in the strong fortress of Ūk, and for seven years defied all the attempts of the besiegers to reduce him. In 371 (981–2), however, he evacuated the fortress at the request of his friend Abu'l-Ḥasan Sīmjūrī, and the province of Sīstān was placed in charge of Ḥusain b. Ṭāhir; but K̲h̲alaf soon managed to oust Ḥusain and make himself master of the province.[2]

Shortly after this, K̲h̲alaf came into conflict with Subuktigīn. He occupied Bust during the absence of Subuktigīn on his expedition against Jaipāl in 376 (986–7). Subuktigīn drove out the officers of K̲h̲alaf and made preparations for a counter-attack on Sīstān, but K̲h̲alaf appeased Subuktigīn by making profuse apologies for his conduct and surrendering the amount of the taxes that he had collected from Bust.[3]

K̲h̲alaf now turned his attention to Kirmān and sent his son ʿAmr to conquer it. ʿAmr was defeated in Muḥarram 382 (March 992) near Sīrjān and forced to

---

[1] According to ad̲h̲-D̲h̲ahabī, f. 181 a; and *Jannātuʾl-Firdaws*, f. 36 a, K̲h̲alaf was born in 326 (937–8), and came to the throne in 353 (964). See also *Cat. of Coins in the Brit. Mus.* by S. Lane-Poole, iii, 16; and Zambaur, pp. 200–1.

[2] ʿUtbī, pp. 31–5.   [3] *Ibid.* pp. 151–2.

return to Sīstān. Khalaf became so furious at the failure of 'Amr that he had him arrested and put to death. He now devised a vile stratagem to create public enthusiasm for his enterprise against Kirmān. He pretended to make peace with the governor of Kirmān, and sent Qāḍī Abū Yūsuf, who was greatly respected by the people, to settle the terms, but he secretly arranged his murder in such a manner that the crime could be imputed to the governor of Kirmān. This was carried out; and, as expected, the people of Sīstān were infuriated at the enormity of the outrage. Khalaf now despatched his son Ṭāhir to avenge the alleged crime, but he was defeated and forced to fall back on Sīstān.[1]

After the failure of his plans of conquest, Khalaf established friendly relations with Subuktigīn, and assisted him in his struggle with Abū 'Alī Sīmjūrī in 385 (995).[2] Soon after this, however, Khalaf turned against Subuktigīn and when Īlak Khān threatened Bukhārā in 386 (996), he invited him to attack Ghazna. Subuktigīn now made preparations to invade Sīstān, but Khalaf propitiated him by professing friendship and denying the reports against him.[3] When Subuktigīn died in 387 (997), Khalaf offended Maḥmūd by publicly rejoicing at his bereavement.[4] Again, while Maḥmūd was engaged in his struggle for the throne with his brother, Khalaf took the province of Fūshanj which formed part of the kingdom of Ghazna. This brought him into conflict with Maḥmūd and led to the conquest of Sīstān.[5]

1 *Tajārib*, iii, 190–7.
2 'Utbī, pp. 88, 152.
3 *Ibid.* pp. 152–3.
4 *Ibid.* p. 154.
5 For the details of the relations of Khalaf with Sulṭān Maḥmūd, see *supra*, pp. 67–70.

APPENDIX H

THE BUWAIHIDS

ABŪ SHUJĀʿ BUWAIH, the ancestor of the Buwaihid sovereigns of Persia, was a resident of Kayā-Kālish[1] in the neighbourhood of Qazwīn and claimed descent from the Sāsānid monarch Bahrām Gūr.[2] When Mākān b. Kākī conquered Ṭabaristān, Abū Shujāʿ, with his three sons, ʿAlī, Ḥasan and Aḥmad, took up service under him. In 315 (927–8), however, Mākān, was overthrown by Asfār b. Shīrawaih and forced to take refuge in Khurāsān. During his exile, Mardāwīj b. Ziyār put Asfār to death,[3] and proclaimed himself ruler of Ṭabaristān. The three sons of Buwaih now went over to the side of Mardāwīj, who appointed ʿAlī, the eldest, to the governorship of Karaj,[4] where his brothers also accompanied him.[5] They now embarked on a career of conquest. ʿAlī conquered Fārs, and Ḥasan and Aḥmad occupied Raiy and ʿIrāq respectively. At the death of Mardāwīj in 323[6] (934–5), ʿAlī assumed independence, seized Iṣfahān and appointed his brothers Ḥasan and Aḥmad to the governorship of the provinces which they had already conquered. In a short time, Aḥmad extended his sway to Ahwāz and Wāsiṭ, and in 334 (945–6) obtained effective control of Baghdād itself.[7] The Caliph al-Mustakfī conferred the titles of *ʿImādu'd-Dawlah* on ʿAlī, *Ruknu'd-Dawlah* on Ḥasan and *Muʿizzu'd-Dawlah* on Aḥmad.[8]

1 *Guzīda*, p. 414.

2 Al-Bīrūnī, *The Chronology of Ancient Nations*, p. 45, does not admit the genuineness of this claim.

3 *Tajārib*, i, 161, 275.

4 Karaj was situated near Hamadān, see Le Strange, p. 197.

5 *Tajārib*, i, 275; and *Guzīda*, p. 414.

6 *Tajārib*, i, 310; and Ibnu'l-Athīr, viii, 222.

7 *Tajārib*, ii, 85.

8 *Ibid.*

'Imādu'd-Dawlah died in Jumādī ii 338 (December 949) and left his kingdom to Fannākhusraw, son of Ruknu'd-Dawlah. In Rabī' ii 356 (March 967) Mu'izzu'd-Dawlah died and was succeeded by his son 'Izzu'd-Dawlah Bakhtiyār, who recognised his uncle Ruknu'd-Dawlah as his suzerain. 'Izzu'd-Dawlah was beheaded in Shawwāl 367 (May 978), and his kingdom passed on to 'Aḍudu'd-Dawlah. The sons of 'Izzu'd-Dawlah were taken prisoners and were beheaded in 383 (993–4) by the order of Ṣamṣāmu'd-Dawlah.[1]

Shortly before his death in Muḥarram 366 (September 976), Ruknu'd-Dawlah appointed his eldest son 'Aḍudu'd-Dawlah his successor, and left to his other two sons Mu'ayyidu'd-Dawlah and Fakhru'd-Dawlah the provinces of Iṣfahān, and Hamadān and Jibāl respectively.[2] In the following year 'Aḍudu'd-Dawlah conquered 'Irāq from 'Izzu'd-Dawlah. The three brothers soon began to quarrel among themselves. Fakhru'd-Dawlah refused to do homage to 'Aḍudu'd-Dawlah, who attacked Fakhru'd-Dawlah in 370 (980–1), and forced him to leave Hamadān and take refuge with his father-in-law Qābūs, ruler of Jurjān and Ṭabaristān. As Qābūs refused to surrender Fakhru'd-Dawlah, 'Aḍudu'd-Dawlah sent against him his brother Mu'ayyidu'd-Dawlah who inflicted a defeat on Qābūs at Astarābād in Jumādī i 371 (November 981) and forced him and his *protégé* Fakhru'd-Dawlah to flee to Khurāsān.[3] When Mu'ayyidu'd-Dawlah died in Sha'bān 373 (January 984), Fakhru'd-Dawlah returned to Jurjān at the invitation of the Ṣāḥib b. 'Abbād, wazīr of the late sovereign,[4] and within a few years extended his sway to Raiy and Hamadān. Fakhru'd-Dawlah died in Sha'bān 387[5] (August 997) and was succeeded by his

1 *Tajārib*, iii, 248.
2 *Ibid.* ii, 362–3.
3 'Utbī, pp. 36–7; but cf. *Tajārib*, iii, 15–17.
4 'Utbī, pp. 49–50; and *Tajārib*, iii, 93.
5 'Utbī, p. 108; but Banākathī, f. 77 b, incorrectly says A.H. 413.

son Majdu'd-Dawlah, who was about nine years of age. About this time Qābūs returned from Khurāsān and took possession of Jurjān and Ṭabaristān. Majdu'd-Dawlah ruled till Jumādī i 420[1] (May 1029), when he was taken prisoner by Sulṭān Maḥmūd, and his kingdom was annexed to the Ghaznawid empire.[2]

'Aḍudu'd-Dawlah died in Ramaḍān[3] 372 (February–March 983). His kingdom was divided between his sons Ṣamṣāmu'd-Dawlah, who got the province of 'Irāq, and Sharafu'd-Dawlah, who received Kirmān and Fārs. The brothers soon began to quarrel between themselves, and in 376 (986–7) Sharafu'd-Dawlah defeated Ṣamṣāmu'd-Dawlah, took him prisoner and annexed his kingdom. On the death of Sharafu'd-Dawlah in Jumādī ii 379 (September 989), Ṣamṣāmu'd-Dawlah regained his freedom and took the province of Fārs. He was put to death in Dhu'l-Ḥajja 388 (December 998). Sharafu'd-Dawlah was succeeded by his brother Bahā'u'd-Dawlah,[4] who strengthened his position by entering into an alliance with Sulṭān Maḥmūd.[5]

Bahā'u'd-Dawlah died in Jumādī ii 403 (December 1012) and was succeeded by his son Sulṭānu'd-Dawlah.[6] In 407[7] (1016–17) Qawāmu'd-Dawlah, governor of Kirmān, rebelled against his brother Sulṭānu'd-Dawlah, fled to Bust and implored the assistance of Sulṭān Maḥmūd. The Sulṭān sent Abū Sa'd aṭ-Ṭā'ī at the head of a large army to reinstate him in Kirmān, but when the Ghaznawid troops retired, Sulṭānu'd-Dawlah returned and forced him to flee.[8] Later on, however, the

1 Gardīzī, p. 91; but Banākathī, f. 77 b, incorrectly says A.H. 414.

2 See *supra*, pp. 80–2.

3 'Utbī, p. 235. Ibnu'l-Athīr, however, says Shawwāl 372 (March–April 983).

4 Ibnu'l-Athīr, ix, 13, 33, 42.

5 'Utbī, pp. 240–1; and *Guzīda*, p. 430.

6 Ibnu'l-Athīr, ix, 169.

7 *Ibid.* p. 207. 'Utbī, pp. 283–4, 290–1, seems to corroborate this date, but Gardīzī, p. 71, says that these events took place in 403 (1012–13).

8 'Utbī, pp. 289–90; and Ibnu'l-Athīr, ix, 207.

brothers were reconciled and Sulṭānu'd-Dawlah restored the province of Kirmān to Qawāmu'd-Dawlah.[1] In Dhu'l-Ḥajja 411 (March–April 1021) Musharrafu'd-Dawlah, son of Bahā'u'd-Dawlah, deprived Sulṭānu'd-Dawlah of 'Irāq. Musharrafu'd-Dawlah died in Rabī' i 416 (May 1025) and was succeeded by his son Jalālu'd-Dawlah. On his death in Sha'bān 435 (March 1044), the kingdom of 'Irāq was conquered by Abū Kālinjār, son of Sulṭānu'd-Dawlah.[2]

Sulṭānu'd-Dawlah died in Shawwāl 415 (December 1024) and was succeeded by his son Abū Kālinjār, who took Kirmān on the death of Qawāmu'd-Dawlah in Dhu'l-Qa'da 419 (November–December 1028), and 'Irāq in Sha'bān 435 (March 1044) on the death of Jalālu'd-Dawlah. Abū Kālinjār died in Jumādī i 440 (October 1048) and was succeeded by his son al-Maliku'r-Raḥīm. He was defeated and taken prisoner by Sulṭān Ṭughrilbek the Seljuk, in Ramaḍān 447 (December 1055).[3]

1 Ibnu'-Athīr, ix, 208.
2 *Ibid.* pp. 224, 243, 352, 353.
3 *Ibid.* pp. 236, 259, 373, 420.

APPENDIX I

THE HINDŪSHĀHIYYA DYNASTY OF WAIHAND

In the tenth century A.D., a dynasty of Hindū princes, with their capital at Waihand,[1] ruled the territory from Lamaghān to the river Chināb[2] and from the southern Kashmīr hills to the frontier of the kingdom of Multān. Lalliya,[3] the founder of this dynasty, was the wazīr of the last sovereign of the Turkīshāhiyya Dynasty,[4] named Lagatūrmān.[5] In the last quarter of the ninth century A.D.,[6] Lalliya deposed Lagatūrmān and usurped the throne, but on the death of Lalliya, a representative of the late Turkīshāhiyya Dynasty named Sāmantdeva,[7] regained the throne. About A.D. 903 he was, however, defeated and deposed by Gopālvarman, Rājā of Kashmīr, who raised Tormāna Kamaluka, son of Lalliya, to the throne.[8] Kamaluka was succeeded by Bhīm, possibly his son, who was the grandfather of the famous queen Diddā, wife of Rājā Kshemgupta and ruler of Kashmīr from A.D. 980

1 Udabhānda of Kalhana, and modern Hund.

2 See my article in *JRAS.* (1927), pp. 485–6, and note the error of V. A. Smith, *The Early History of India*, p. 396.

3 Kalhana, ii, 336–9, Note J, in which Sir Aurel Stein has given a learned discussion of the various disputed points regarding the early history of this dynasty. Sir E. C. Bayley has made numerous misstatements in the *Numismatic Chronicle*, 3rd Series, ii (1882), 128–65. According to al-Bīrūnī, ii, 13, the rulers of this dynasty were Brahmins, but in *Ādābu'l-Mulūk*, f. 92 b, it is implied that Jaipāl and his descendants were Bhatīs.

4 They boasted descent from Rājā Kānishka of the Kushan Dynasty.

5 Al-Bīrūnī, ii, 13. Cunningham, *Coins of Medieval India*, p. 55, prefers Kitormān.

6 Kalhana, ii, 336–9.

7 *Ibid.*

8 *Ibid.*

to 1003.[1] Bhīm was succeeded by Jaipāl[2] about A.D. 960.[3] Jaipāl soon came into conflict with the rulers of the neighbouring kingdom of Ghazna, one of whom, Subuktigīn, defeated him in two pitched battles and annexed the whole territory up to Lamaghān.[4]

But Jaīpal made up his losses in the west by territorial acquisitions in the east. About A.D. 991, Bharat, Rājā of Lahore, invaded the kingdom of Jaipāl, with a view to conquering the districts of Nandana and Jhelum, and, at the head of a formidable force, crossed the river Chināb which marked the boundary between the two kingdoms. Jaipāl sent his son Anandpāl, who scattered the army of Bharat and entered Lahore in triumph. The notables of the town, however, interceded on behalf of Bharat, and, on his promising to pay tribute, Anandpāl reinstated him in his kingdom.[5]

Shortly after the retirement of Anandpāl, Bharat was deposed by his son Chandardat, who adopted a hostile attitude towards Jaipāl. In 389 (999) Jaipāl again sent Anandpāl to punish him. Chandardat made great preparations for defence and advanced from Lahore to meet the invader, but one day, while he was hunting, he ventured too far out of his camp and was surprised and taken prisoner by an ambush which Anandpāl had laid in a jungle close by. The sons of Chandardat escaped and took refuge with the Rājā of Jālandhar.[5]

Jaipāl annexed the kingdom of Chandardat which

1 Kalhana, i, 105.

2 Al-Bīrūnī, ii, 13, mentions the name of Jaipāl after that of Bhīm in the list of the Hindūshāhiyya Rājās, which implies that Jaipāl was the successor of Bhīm, and most probably his son; but Firishta, p. 19, says that Jaipāl was the son of Ishtpāl.

3 As Jaipāl is said to have died at an advanced age ('Utbī, p. 158), this date is not too early for his accession to the throne.

4 For details of these battles, see *supra*, pp. 29–30.

5 *Ādābu'l-Mulūk*, as quoted by the author in *JRAS.* (1927), pp. 486–93.

probably extended on the east to the river Biyās, and placed it under the governorship of Anandpāl.[1]

A little before this, in A.D. 997, Subuktigīn died and was succeeded by his son Maḥmūd, who in A.D. 999 resolved to lead every year an expedition to India. The brunt of his invasions was borne by Jaipāl and his descendants till the whole of the Hindūshāhiyya kingdom was gradually conquered and annexed to the Ghaznawid empire.[2]

1 *Ādābu'l-Mulūk*, as quoted by the author in *JRAS*. (1927), pp. 486–93. 'Utbī, p. 158, also makes a reference to this fact.

2 See *supra*, pp. 86–96, for details of their relations with Sulṭān Maḥmūd.

Al-Bīrūnī, ii, 13, pays a glowing tribute to the rulers of this dynasty for their noble sentiments. Kalhana, Bk vii, ll. 66–9, refers in a pathetic manner to the vanished glory of this house.

APPENDIX J

1. *Identification of* "Bhāṭiya"

"BHĀṬIYA", to which Sulṭān Maḥmūd led an expedition in 395 (1004–5), has been variously identified with Bhera,[1] Lat. 32° 28′ N., Long. 72° 56′ E., in the Punjāb; with Uchh,[2] Lat. 29° 15′ N., Long. 71° 6′ E.; and with Bhatnair,[3] Lat. 20° 35′ N., Long. 74° 20′ E., in the Bīkānīr state. Contemporary historians and geographers say very little about its position. 'Utbī, pp. 208–9, says that on his way to "Bhāṭiya" Sulṭān Maḥmūd crossed the river Indus in the neighbourhood of Multān, that the fort of "Bhāṭiya" was high and was surrounded by a deep and wide ditch, and that there was a jungle close to it in the direction of the mountains.

'Unṣurī, the panegyrist of Sulṭān Maḥmūd, in one of his *qaṣīdas*, says:

ور از بهاطیه[4] سویم عجب فرومانی
که شاه ایران آنجا چگونه شد بسفر
رهی که خاک درستش چو تودهای خسك
بسان عالم و منزلگه اندرو کشور (?)

1 E. and D. ii, pp. 439–40. One of the reasons given in support of the identification of "Bhāṭiya" with Bhera is that *Khulāṣatu't-Tawārīkh* and *Akhbār-i-Maḥabbat*, composed about 1107 and 1190 (1695 and 1776) respectively, read Bhera. Both Elliot and Dowson failed to note that if "Bhāṭiya" were taken to stand for Bhera, the whole account of the expedition as given by 'Utbī and Firishta would become a tangled mass of confusion.

2 Raverty, *The Mihrān of Sind*, in *JASB.* (1892), p. 247; and Sir W. Haig, p. 14.

3 J. Bird, in his translation of *Mir'āt-i-Aḥmadī*, p. 21.

4 Other possible variants of Bhāṭiya that would suit the metre of the verse are Mahāṭila, Hayāṭila, Mahāṭiyah, Hayāṭiyah, etc.

اگرش گرگ بدرد بریزدش چنگال
ورش عقاب گذارد بیفگنند همه پر
نباتهاش تو گفتی که کژدمانندی
گره گره شده و خارها برو نشتر
برون گذشته برو شاه شهریار چو باد
بزور دین و بآزار مذهب آذر
گرفت ملك بجیرا و گنج خانهٔ او
زخون لشکر او کرد دشت خشك شمر
چنانش کرد خداوند خسروان زمین
که نام او بجهان گم شداست طول و قصر[1]

And if I should speak of Bhāṭiya, you would be astounded
(To know) how the king of Īrān (Maḥmūd) journeyed thither.

The way to this place where it was smoothest, was like scattered heaps of thorns,
....(?)

The wolf would lacerate its paws if it were to traverse that road,
And (on account of the heat) the eagle would drop its pinions were it to soar above that tract.

Its (xerophytic) plants, you would say, are scorpions,
Coiled and curled with thorns for stings.

The king of kings (Maḥmūd) crossed it like unto a blast of wind,
By the strength of his faith, and to the detriment of idolatry.

He subdued the country of Bajī Rāy and acquired his treasures,
And with the blood of the enemy's warriors he irrigated the arid tract.

The lord of the kings of the earth (Maḥmūd) reduced the place so completely,
That its very name has been forgotten.

'Unṣurī thus implies that "Bhāṭiya" was situated in a barren country, and that on his way to it the Sulṭān crossed a sandy desert overgrown with thorny bushes.

1 I have followed the text of the MS in the Asiatic Society of Bengal.

Al-Bīrūnī, on p. 100 of his famous work named *Taḥqīq mā li'l-Hind...*,[1] says that Bhātī (or Bhāṭiya) lay between Nārāyan[2] (Narāyanpūr in Alwar state) and Multān; and between Nārāyan and Aror or Rohrī; and, on p. 82, that a particular alphabet called Ardhanāgarī was common both to "Bhāṭiya" and Sind. Again, in *Qānūnu'l-Mas'ūdī*, f. 90 a, al-Bīrūnī places "Bhāṭiya" in Lat. 29° 40′ N., the same as he gives for Multān. Thus, according to al-Bīrūnī, "Bhāṭiya" was situated between Nārāyan and Rohrī, somewhere near Sind, in the same latitude as Multān.

Gardīzī, p. 66, says that the Sulṭān marched to "Bhāṭiya" by way of Wālishtān[3] (modern Sibī in Balūchistān), and again, on pp. 87–8, he says that the Jāts of "Bhāṭiya" and Multān inhabited the region along the banks of the river Indus between Multān and Manṣūra. This shows that "Bhāṭiya" was also the name given to the country ruled by the Rājā of "Bhāṭiya".

From the foregoing remarks of the writers contemporary with Sulṭān Maḥmūd, it is evident that "Bhāṭiya" could not possibly be Bhera, which is too far to the north of Multān, nor could it be Uchh which does not lie between Nārāyan and Multān, and to reach which the Sulṭān could not have crossed a sandy desert,

1 The references here are given to Sachau's edition of this work in Arabic, and not to his translation into English, because his translation of the passage from p. 100 cited above is misleading. The correct translation is as follows: "From Nārāyan (the original reads Bazāna, but it should be Narāna which, according to al-Bīrūnī, *Qānūnu'l-Mas'ūdī*, f. 90 a, was called Nārāyan by the Muslims) towards the west, Multān is fifty *farsakh*, and Bhātī (or Bhāṭiya) fifteen *farsakh*; and from Bhātī towards the south-west, Aror is fifteen *farsakh*. It (i.e. Aror) is a township between the two arms of the river Sind."

2 For its identification, see Cunningham, *Ancient Geography*, pp. 337–40.

3 This was the usual way from Bust to Multān. See Baihaqī, p. 140.

as it is situated on the Panjnad.[1] Bhatnair seems to suit the brief indications given by the contemporary writers about the locality of "Bhāṭiya"; but firstly, "Bhāṭiya" is not an obvious corruption of Bhatnair; secondly, Bhatnair is not situated in the same latitude as given for "Bhāṭiya" and Multān; and thirdly, the authors of *Malfūẓāt-i-Tīmūrī* and *Ẓafar Nāmah*[2] state that before the capture of Bhatnair by Tīmūr in A.D. 1398 "no hostile army had ever penetrated thither," or, in other words, these authors were not aware of the conquest of Bhatnair by Sulṭān Maḥmūd.

The only place of importance which satisfies the description of "Bhāṭiya" is Bhatinda, which is situated in Lat. 30° 15′ N., that is, nearly the same as that of Multān. It lies between Nārāyan, or Narāyanpūr, and Multān, and to reach it the Sulṭān must have crossed the sandy desert to the east of the Sutlej. The fort of Bhatinda has always been famous for its strength and impregnability.[3] There was also a dense jungle at a distance of about thirty miles from it in the direction of Sirhand.[4] Moreover, the whole stretch of country "lying between 29° 15′ and 30° 15′ N. and 74° 0′. and 75° 45′ E., and comprising the valley of the Ghaggar from Fatehābād in Hissār district to Bhatnair in the state of Bīkaner, together with an undefined portion of the dry country stretching north-west of the Ghaggar towards the old bank of the Sutlej", has always been called "Bhattīāna", that is, the land of the Bhattīs,[5] which was most probably under the

1 In *Ādābu'l-Mulūk*, f. 28 a, "Bhāṭiya" and Uchh are mentioned as two distinct places.

2 E. and D. iii, 422 and 488 respectively.

3 *Gazetteer of Bīkaner* by Captain Powlett, p. 122; and *I.G.I.* viii, 90. The modern fort is built 118 feet above the level ground, and is visible from a long distance. See also Cunningham, *Archaeological Survey of India*, xxiii, 2–5.

4 *Malfūẓāt-i-Tīmūrī* as translated in E. and D. iii, 427.

5 *I.G.I.* viii, 91.

Rājās of Bhatinda.[1] The kingdom of Bhatinda probably extended to the river Indus, as implied by Gardīzī.

Bhatinda was one of the four important forts[2] which were situated at the angles of a nearly square figure with a side about 40 miles long, thus forming a "quadrilateral" in the path of an invader from the north-west. The reduction of Bhatinda was necessary because it guarded the passage into the rich Ganges valley.[3]

The identification of "Bhāṭiya" with Bhatinda is supported by a very interesting derivation of the name Bhatinda given by Cunningham in his *Archaeological Survey of India*, xxiii, 5. He says: "*Bhatti-da-nagara*, or 'the Bhatti's city', was, in all probability, the full form of this name, originally from *Bhatti*, the tribe, and *da*, largely used in the province as the genitive particle in lieu of *sa* or *ka*, of which it is merely a dialectic variation. Of the habit of omitting the final word *nagara* or *pūra* (which merely signifies 'town' or 'city') and retaining the sign of the genitive case, numerous examples exist in which such terminations are *understood*, and the intermediate nasal may or may not be employed; indeed, the word is often pronounced by the people as *Bhatida*, seldom *Bhatinda* and never *Bhātinda*." Moreover, as the people of Bhatinda were known as Bhātīs before the Muslim conquest,[4] their town must have been called Bhātī-dā-nagara, or Bhātīda. In conversation the Muslim conquerors, who were not probably

1 In the time of Sulṭān Maḥmūd, Bhatinda was situated on an affluent of the river Ghaggar, but the surrounding country was barren.

2 The other three forts were Bhatnair, Sirsa and Abohr.

3 Bhatinda was an important fortress on the road connecting Multān with India proper, see *Journal of the Punjab Historical Society*, ii, 109, iii, 35.

4 *I.G.I.* xiii, 38. It is also stated there that those of the Bhātīs who accepted Islam called themselves Bhattīs to distinguish themselves from their Hindū fellow-tribesmen.

acquainted with the derivation of the word Bhātīda, must have dropped the hard *d* at the end and pronounced it as Bhātiya. In writing, the original form Bhātiya (بهاتيه) was changed to Bhāṭiya (بهاطيه), for, when a word is Arabicised, the *t* (ت) in it is usually changed to *ṭ* (ط).[1]

2. *Date of the Expedition to* Bhatinda

'Utbī does not mention the date of this expedition, but it can be ascertained from other circumstances mentioned by him. After his account of the rebellion in Sīstān in Dhu'l-Ḥajja 393 (October 1003), he says, p. 170, that Sulṭān Maḥmūd went to Balkh to make preparations for "a holy war in Hind which shall be mentioned in its proper place". Again, on p. 208, he begins the account of the expedition to "Bhāṭiya" in the following words: "When the Sulṭān had settled the affairs of Sīstān and the action of its beating pulse (i.e. rebellion) had subsided, and the dark clouds (of rebellion) had dispersed, he determined upon invading Bhāṭiya". This undoubtedly signifies that the phrase "a holy war in Hind" refers to the expedition to "Bhāṭiya". Thus 'Utbī makes this expedition subsequent to the year 393 (1003).

Again, according to 'Utbī, p. 169, after the final conquest of Sīstān in Dhu'l-Ḥajja 393 (October 1003), the Sulṭān stayed there for some time to pacify the country. It was therefore probably after the winter that he proceeded to Balkh, as stated above, to make preparations for "a holy war in Hind" which could not have been undertaken before the following winter, i.e. before the end of 394 and the beginning of 395 (September–October 1004).

Gardīzī, pp. 66–7, places this expedition between

1 For example, Jatt (جتّ) is written Zuṭṭ (زطّ) in Ṭabarī.

Rabīʿ ii and D͟hu'l-Qaʿda 393 (February–September 1003), which gives the Sulṭān no time to go to Bal͟kh and make preparations for the expedition, as stated by ʿUtbī. Almost all the later historians, with the exception of Niẓāmu'd-Dīn Aḥmad, place this expedition in the year 395 (1004–5).

APPENDIX K

THE TWO TRILOC<u>H</u>ANPĀLS

RĀJĀ TRILOC<u>H</u>ANPĀL, who prevented the passage of the river Ruhut or Rāmgangā in 410 (1019), was the son of Anandpāl of the Hindū<u>sh</u>āhiyya Dynasty, and not of Rājyapāl of Kanauj, as stated by Sir V. A. Smith, *The Early History of India*, p. 398. Farru<u>kh</u>ī has brought out this point very clearly. He says, f. 1 b:

شنیدهٔ که چه دید است رای ازو و چه دید
شه مخالف بیراه و گمرهش گمراه

Have you heard what treatment the Rāy received from him (Maḥmūd), and what the <u>Sh</u>āh, the rebel, the misguided one who has lost both his wits and his ways?

and on f. 4 b:

شه و نندا و رام و رای و کور از بیم شمشیرش
بدان جایند کاندر گورشان خوشتر مکان باشد
زجنگ شاه و جنگ رای نندا نام کی جو یـد
کسی کز جنگها اورا کمینه جنگ خان باشد

The <u>Sh</u>āh, Nandā, Rām, the Rāy and Kūr, from the fear of his (Maḥmūd's) sword, are in such a fright that they regard the grave as the safest place for themselves.

Why should he (Maḥmūd) seek glory from the fight with the <u>Sh</u>āh or with Rāy Nandā, the least important of whose achievements is the fight with the <u>Kh</u>ān (of Turkistān)?

Again, on ff. 16 a–16 b, Farru<u>kh</u>ī says that after crossing the Ganges,

خبر شنید که پیش پیٔ تو شاه از گنگ
گذشت و پیل پس پشت او قطار قطار

بچاشتگاه ملك با كمركشان سپاه
برفت بر دم او جنگ‌جوی و کینه‌گذار
وزان حصار سوی شاه رو بکرد و برفت

....

بیك شبانروز از پای قلعه سربل
برود راهت شد تازیان بیك هنجار
تروجپال سپه‌را بشب گذاشته بود
به پیل زاب وزان سو گرفته راهگذار
شه سپه‌شکن جنگ‌جوی پیش ملك
میان بیشه گشن اندرون خزید چو مار
درشت بود و چنان نرم شد که روز دگر
بصد شفیع همی خواست از ملك زنهار
چو شاه‌را بزد و مال و پیل ازو بستد

....

ز جنگ شاه سپه‌را بجنگ رای کشید
ز خواب خواست همی کرد رای‌را بیدار
خبر دهنده خبر داد رای‌را که ملك
سوی تو آمده راه گریختن بر دار
هنوز رای تمام این خبر شنیده نبود
که شد ز مملکت خویش یکسره بیزار
چو شهریار زمانه بباری اندر شد
خبر شنید که رفت او ز راه دریا بار

He (Maḥmūd) heard that shortly before him, the Shāh had crossed the Ganges, followed by lines of elephants.
The next morning the *malik* (Maḥmūd) with his army, followed him, intent upon fighting and taking vengeance.

(*After this the Sulṭān takes the fort of Sarbal, and*)

From that fort, he (Maḥmūd) turned his attention to the Shāh,

. . . .

After a day and night's rapid and continuous march from the fort of Sarbal, he reached the river Rāhut.

Tirūjipāl (Trilochanpāl) had crossed over with his army the preceding night, on elephants, and had made preparations to prevent the passage of the river.

The army-routing and fight-seeking Shāh, before the *malik* (Maḥmūd) crept like a snake into the thick jungle.

He (the Shāh) was very aggressive but became so meek (then) that on the following day, he sent a hundred intercessors to demand quarter.

When he (Maḥmūd) defeated the Shāh and captured his riches and elephants,..............................

After the fight with the Shāh, the Sulṭān marched to give battle to the Rāy, as he (Maḥmūd) wanted to rouse him (the Rāy) from his slumber.

The messenger said to the Rāy : The *malik* is advancing on you; take to flight.

And without waiting to hear all the news, the Rāy renounced his kingdom (i.e. fled).

When the ruler of the world (Maḥmūd) entered Bārī, he was told that the Rāy had crossed the river.

The above extracts clearly show (i) that Shāh and Rāy were the titles of two distinct rājās, and (ii) that the Trilochanpāl who tried to prevent the passage of the river Rāhut or Ruhut was called the Shāh, while the other rājā bearing the same name, who fled from Bārī, was known as the Rāy. But as Shāh was the title of the rulers of the Hindūshāhiyya Dynasty, Trilochanpāl the Shāh could not be the ruler of Bārī or Kanauj, who was known as Rāy.

Further, according to al-Bīrūnī, ii, 13, and Ibnu'l-Athīr, ix, 219, Trilochanpāl of the Hindūshāhiyya Dynasty was killed in 412 (1021); while Trilochanpāl, Rāy of Kanauj, lived at least up to A.D. 1027, according to the Jhūsī inscription (*Indian Antiquary*, xviii, 33–5), on which Sir V. A. Smith has chiefly based his conclusions.

APPENDIX L

1. *An extract from* The Syriac Chronicle, *pp.* 211–12

IN A.H. 414 Khwārizmshāh Maḥmūd[1] again invaded India and captured many cities. When he had marched a distance of four months into the land he reached a castle named Kawākīr where lived one of the Indian kings. He attacked it fiercely and then an Indian ambassador in a litter borne by four men came out to him and said: "My lord asks what manner of man you are". Maḥmūd replied: "I am a Muslim, I invite unbelievers to belief in God and persecute idolaters. You Hindūs, either believe in our God, accept our law, and eat beef, or pay tribute—1000 elephants and 1000 *manns* of gold". The ambassador said: "We cannot eat beef. This religion of yours: send us a learned man to teach us your faith and if it is better than ours we will receive it". He sent with him a learned Arab who entered the castle and spoke with them through an interpreter. They said: "We will not change our religion and do not possess the gold you want but have much silver". They agreed to give 300 elephants, much silver, and valuable garments. Maḥmūd said: "I agree. But the king must put on our clothes, tie a sword and belt round his waist and, to ratify the oath, cut off the tip of his finger as is Indian custom". The Arab ambassador said: "When I came into the presence of the Indian king, I found a splendid youth of great beauty, glorious in blackness, on a silver throne, wearing a cloak and trousers of cloth,[2] with a turban on his head. When I saw him I clapped my hands violently and bowed over them as is their custom. I spoke of

1 Obviously a mistake for Sulṭān Maḥmūd of Ghazna.

2 The word in the original is not intelligible but it evidently means some kind of cloth.

the dress he was to wear and entreated him much (to wear it). He said: 'I beg you to excuse me from wearing it and tell your lord that I have put it on'. I replied: 'I cannot deceive my lord'. He only just put it on with the belt and girded on the sword. When he was so dressed I was ashamed to say to him, 'Cut off your finger'. I had only said, 'Swear to us', when he answered: 'Our oath is by images and fire, which is not accepted by you. How shall I swear?' I said: 'You know how to swear'. At once he told a slave to bring him a razor. He took it in his right hand and cut off the tip of his left little finger without changing colour. He sprinkled some drug on it and tied it up. He washed the piece he had cut off, put it with camphor in a bag, and gave it to me with some clothes, silver, and two horses".[1]

2. *An extract from Sibṭ Ibnu'l-Jawzī, f.* 219 *b, which is given as a quotation from aṣ-Ṣābī's* Dhail

He (Maḥmūd) attacked a town and according to other reports the fort which we have already said contained 509,000 souls. He made peace with its master by accepting 500 elephants and 3000 cows. Maḥmūd sent to him a robe of honour, a turban, a belt, a gold caparisoned horse, and a ring with his (Maḥmūd's) name inscribed on it. According to the ceremony which ensured the observance of a compact among the Hindūs, the Sulṭān ordered the small finger of the Rājā to be cut off. Maḥmūd had thus numerous finger-tips of those who had made peace with him. The Rājā put on the dress, took out the knife and cut off his little finger with it without changing colour. He then applied an ointment to the wound to stop bleeding.

1 For pointing out this passage and translating it from the original Syriac into English, the writer's grateful acknowledgments are due to Dr A. S. Tritton, Professor of Arabic in the Muslim University, 'Alīgarh.

APPENDIX M

1. *Authorities on the Expedition to* Somnāth

I HAVE based my account of the expedition to Somnāth on (i) Farrukhī, (ii) Gardīzī, (iii) Ibn Ẓāfir, (iv) Sibṭ Ibnu'l-Jawzī, and (v) Ibnu'l-Athīr. Firishta gives some details which are not improbable, but, as he has considerably diminished the value of his work by incorporating in his account of this expedition most of the extravagant stories connected with the conquest of Somnāth as if they were sober history, I have left him out of consideration.

There are no Hindū sources to correct or supplement the account of the Muslim authors, and though Kāthiāwār can boast of many histories or more properly historical legends, by Jain monks, like the *Dwyāshrāya* of Hemchandra (A.D. 1089–1173), and the *Vichārasrenī* and *Prabandha Chintāmanī* of Mīrutunga, both of which were composed about the beginning of the fourteenth century A.D., none of them contains even the slightest reference to the destruction of the temple of Somnāth.

2. *The Origin and Sanctity of the Idol of* Somnāth

Nothing is known historically about the origin of the idol of Somnāth. According to the Hindū legend, as quoted by al-Bīrūnī, ii, 102–3, the Moon-god committed a sin in expiation of which he was required to raise the *linga* of Mahādeva as an object of worship. He did so, and the *linga* he raised was the stone of Somnāth, for "soma" means the moon, and "nātha" means master, so that the whole word means "the master of the moon". It was erected on the sea-coast, and each time when the moon rose and set, the water of the ocean rose in flood and covered the idol; when the moon reached the meridian of noon and midnight, the water receded in the ebb and the idol became visible again. For this reason, it was believed that the moon was perpetually occupied in serving and bathing the idol.

Muslim writers give a different but an equally fanciful origin of this idol and try to establish connection between Somnāth and Manāt, one of the idols of the Ka'ba. They say that Manāt was hidden by its worshippers and transported to a land "which had from times immemorial been the home of idolatry", namely Kāthiāwār, and set it up there as an object of worship. To account for its sudden appearance, it was given out that it had emerged from the sea. A temple was raised to accommodate it, and it was called "So-Manāt" to perpetuate its old name Manāt in a disguised form. As the Manāt of the Ka'ba most probably had a human figure, the Muslims believed that the idol of Somnāth too had human features.[1]

But whatever the origin of the idol, it cannot be denied that it was of undoubted antiquity. Ibn Khallikān, iii, 333, says that the idol of Somnāth had thirty rings round it, and on enquiry the Sulṭān was told that each ring represented a period of 1000 years for which it had been worshipped.[2] This would place the age of the idol at the evidently exaggerated figure of 30,000 years, but any way it serves to give an idea of its antiquity.[3]

The worship of the *linga* of Mahādeva was not confined to this temple. According to al-Bīrūnī, ii, 104, there were numerous *lingas* in the temples in the south-west of Sind and Cutch, and the reason for the importance of this one in particular was that, the town

1 Farrukhī, f. 19 b; and Gardīzī, p. 86.

2 See also as-Subkī, *Ṭabaqātu'sh-Shāfi'iyya*, iv, 15, and *Bahjatu'l-Ikhwān*, f. 23 a.

3 The discovery of *linga*-shaped stones at the prehistoric site of Mohen-jo-daro in Sind shows that *linga* worship was probably common in western India in very ancient times.

of Somnāth being a port of call for ships sailing between Africa and China, its fame was carried to distant countries by the sailors who probably looked upon it as their patron god. In the time of Sulṭān Maḥmūd its fame had considerably increased for another reason. The devotees of this idol, probably thinking that Somnāth was too far out of the way and was too well protected by the desert on one side and the sea on the other, had boasted that the only reason why the Sulṭān had been able to demolish other idols of India was that Somnāth was displeased with them. This naturally increased the sanctity of the idol in the eyes of the pious Hindūs who could not find any other reason for the desecration of their cherished idols at the hands of this invader from the north. The consequence was that thousands of pilgrims from all parts of India came to swell the crowds that already assembled there, especially at the time of lunar eclipse.[1]

As stated by Muslim writers, the Hindūs believed that the idol possessed divine powers, that it gave life and death, that after death spirits assembled before it and were re-allotted to different bodies, that it apportioned to human beings pleasure and pain, happiness and sorrow, and that it could cure all forms of disease. The idol reckoned among its devotees numerous rājās who either came personally, or sent their deputies to attend to its worship on their behalf.[2]

The temple of Somnāth was very rich. It is said that it was endowed with 10,000 villages, the revenue of which was spent on its upkeep, that there were 1000 Brahmins to perform the elaborate ritual and to admit worshippers to the sanctuary, 300 musicians and dancers to sing and dance at the gates of the temple, 300 servants to look after the comfort of the pilgrims, and a large staff of couriers whose daily duty was to bring

1 Farrukhī, f. 20 a.
2 Ibn Ẓāfir, f. 150 b; and Sibṭ Ibnu'l-Jawzī, f. 214 a.

fresh Ganges water with which the idol was washed, and fresh Kashmīr flowers with which it was garlanded. In addition to the revenue from these villages, the rich offerings of its devotees had filled the coffers of the temple with gold and precious stones of incalculable value.[1]

3. *The Original Temple*

The original temple was a big edifice, spacious enough to accommodate a part at least of the staff attached to its service. It was situated on the sea-shore within the high-tide mark, so that its walls were washed by the waves.[2] Its foundation was laid on large blocks of stone,[3] and the roof was raised on 56 columns of teak which had been imported from Africa.[4] The temple had a pyramidal roof thirteen storeys high,[5] the top of which was surmounted by fourteen spherical knobs of gold which glittered in the sun and were visible from a long distance.[6] The floor was made of planks of teak, and the interstices were filled with lead.[7]

The idol lodged in this temple was the phallic representation of the *linga* of Mahādeva. It was seven cubits in height of which two were hidden in the basement, and about three cubits in girth. It had a covering of rich material with figures of animals embroidered on it,[8] and a crown set with precious stones was hung above it from the ceiling.[9] There were minor idols of gold and silver under its raised pedestal and along the ceiling, to signify that they were attendant on it.[10] The

1 Ibn Jawzī, f. 175 a; Ibn Ẓāfir, f. 150 b; al-Bīrūnī, ii, 103; Ibnu'l-Athīr, ix, 241; and Sibṭ Ibnu'l-Jawzī, f. 215 a.

2 Al-Bīrūnī, ii, p. 105; and Ibn Ẓāfir, f. 150 b.

3 Ibn Ẓāfir, 150 b; Sibṭ Ibnu'l-Jawzī, f. 215 b.

4 Ibn Ẓāfir, 150 b; Ibnu'l-Athīr, ix, 241; Sibṭ Ibnu'l-Jawzī, f. 215 b.

5 Ibn Ẓāfir, 150 b.

6 Ibn Ẓāfir, 151 a; Sibṭ Ibnu'l-Jawzī, f. 215 b.

7 Ibn Ẓāfir, 150 b.

8 Al-Bīrūnī, ii, 105; Ibn Ẓāfir, f. 151 a; and Ibnu'l-Athīr, ix, 241.

9 Farrukhī, f. 19 b; and Ibn Ẓāfir, f. 151 a.

10 Ibn Ẓāfir, f. 151 a.

idol-chamber was illuminated by exquisitely jewelled chandeliers,[1] and draped curtains of great value were hung over the doorway. All along the passage leading to this chamber there were standing posts for ushers who admitted the worshippers to the sanctuary.[2] In front of this chamber was suspended, from a massive chain of gold weighing 200 *manns*,[3] a bell which was rung at specified times of worship. By the side of the chamber there was a repository in which jewels and idols of gold and silver were stored.[4]

4. *The Site of the Original Temple*

From the description given above it is evident that the ancient temple could not be identified with the one the ruins of which are shown to-day,[5] nor could it have stood on the same site. The question then arises: Where did the original temple stand? Al-Bīrūnī, ii, 105, says that it was situated three miles to the west of the mouth of the river Saraswatī. With this clue in mind, I searched for the site of the original temple during my visit to Somnāth Pātan, and about 200 yards to the west of the temple of Bhidiā, about three miles from the mouth of the river Saraswatī, I found the remains of large blocks of stone joined together with a whitish cement, partly buried in sand and partly washed over by the sea at high-tide. I believe that

1 Ibnu'l-Athīr, ix, 241.

2 Sibṭ Ibnu'l-Jawzī, f. 215 b.

3 A *mann* was equal to 2 *raṭls* or about 2 lb. See *JASB.* (1892), p. 192.

4 Sibṭ Ibnu'l-Jawzī, f. 215 b. Ibnu'l-Athīr, ix, 241, says that this repository was under the idol-chamber.

5 The present ruins measure 90 feet by 68 feet, and stand about 60 feet away from the sea, and about 40 feet above its level. They are the ruins of a one-storey building, with one dome in the centre and two smaller ones on its sides. This temple was constructed in A.D. 1169; see *Progress Report of the Archaeological Survey of Western India* (1898–9), p. 9; and J. Burgess, *List of Antiquarian Remains in the Bombay Presidency* (1885), p. 182.

this was the place where stood the temple which Sulṭān Maḥmūd captured and burnt. Midway between this site and the temple of Bhidiā, a *linga* has been placed in the sea in ancient times, probably to commemorate the original site.

The whole sea coast around this site is littered with ruins. Every now and then the sea washes away the sand and exposes some of them to view. When I was at Somnāth, the ruins of what looked like a small cell were thus uncovered close to Verāwal. I am sure that if this site were excavated, some additional details regarding the size and plan of the ancient temple might be brought to light.[1]

5. *The Date of the Expedition*

There is very little disagreement among the chief authorities with regard to the date of this expedition. Al-Bīrūnī, Gardīzī, Ibn Ẓāfir, and Ibnu'l-Athīr place it in the year 416 (1025); but some later Arab chroniclers, like adh-Dhahabī and al-Yāfi'ī, have erroneously mentioned it among the events of the year 418 (1027); while a little vagueness of Firishta and a careless mistake of Elliot and Dowson in translating Ibnu'l-Athīr's account of this expedition have misled modern writers like Elphinstone, Colonel Malleson, J. Burgess, and Sir W. Haig, to ascribe it to the years 414 (1023) or 415 (1024).

1 Professor M. Ḥabīb, *Sultan Mahmud of Ghaznin*, p. 51, suggests that Somnāth was situated at the mouth of another river also named Saraswatī which falls into the Rann of Cutch. He takes the Sulṭān from Anhalwār (which was situated on this river) straight down the river Saraswatī to Somnāth. This is entirely unauthorised, see *infra*, pp. 215–18, where the route of the Sulṭān has been outlined.

6. *The Route of the Sulṭān*

Gardīzī, Ibn Ẓāfir, Sibṭ Ibnu'l-Jawzī and Ibnu'l-Athīr take the Sulṭān directly from Multān to Anhalwāra, without naming any of the intermediary stages. *Ta'rīkh-i-Firishta*, written in the beginning of the eleventh century A.H., mentions Ajmer as one such place, and has been followed by almost all the modern writers. It has, however, been shown in recent years that Ajmer was founded in A.D. 1100,[1] that is, about 75 years after the Sulṭān's expedition to Somnāth. Apart from this, it is very unlikely that the Sulṭān passed by Ajmer, because, firstly, it would have prolonged his march by at least 100 miles without reducing the length of the journey across the desert; secondly, it would have necessitated penetration, without any particular reason, into the mountains that protect Ajmer on the north; and thirdly, it would have made the Sulṭān run the unnecessary risk of encountering numerous Rājpūt chieftains who held sway on the northern slopes of the Arāvallī hills.[2] A nearer approach to the truth is made, perhaps accidentally, in *Ta'rīkh-i-Alfī*, f. 383 a, where Jaisalmīr is substituted for Ajmer, but Jaisalmīr too was not founded until A.D. 1156, that is, about 130 years after the destruction of the temple of Somnāth.[3]

I have been able to determine the route which the Sulṭān followed by references to a *qaṣīda* of Farrukhī,

1 *Indian Antiquary*, xxvi, 162. Sir W. Haig, p. 23, to overcome this objection, has substituted for Ajmer the town of Sāmbhar, the Chauhān capital.

2 Tod, i, 292, says, on the alleged authority of Firishta, that Nadol, a town in Rājpūtāna, was taken by Maḥmūd, but this fact is not mentioned in any edition of Firishta.

3 *I.G.I.* xiv, 9.

who accompanied the Sulṭān on this expedition.[1] He says, f. 19 a:

بدان ره اندر چندان حصارهای بزرگ
خراب کرد و بکند اصل هر یك از بن و بر
نخست لدروه کز روی برج و بارهٔ او
چو کوه کوه فرو ریخت آهن و مرمر
حصار او قوی و بارهٔ حصار قوی
حصاریان همه بر سان شیر شرزهٔ نر
مبارزانی همدست و لشکری همپشت
درنگ‌پیشه بغزو شتاب کاریگر
چو چیکودر که صندوقهای گوهر یافت
بکوه‌پایهٔ آن شهریار شیرشکر
چگونه کوهی چونانکه از بلندی او
ستارگان‌را گوی فرود اوست مقر
چو نهرواله که اندر دیار هند بهیم
به نهرواله همیکرد بر شهان مفخر
دویست پیل و کما بیش صد هزار سوار
نود هزار پیاده مبارز و صفدر
همیشه رای بهیم اندرو مقیم نعیم
نشسته ایمن و دل پر نشاط و تازه و تر
چو مندهیر که. در مندهیر حوضی بود
چنانکه خیره شدی اندرو دو چشم فکر
چگونه حوضی چونانکه هرچه اندیشم
نمیتوانم گفتن صفاتش اندر خور
فراخ‌پهنا حوضی بصد هزار عمل
هزار بتکدهٔ خرد کرده حوض اندر

1 In *Ta'rīkh-i-Fakhru'd-Dīn Mubārakshāh*, p. 52, it is stated that Sulṭān Maḥmūd bestowed an elephant load of gold on Farrukhī for this *qaṣīda*.

دگر چو دیولواره که همچو دیو سفید
پدید بود سر افراشته میان گذر
یکی حصار قوی بر کران شهر و درو
ز بت‌پرستان گرد آمده یکی محشر
بکشت مردم و بت خانها بکند و بسوخت
چنانکه بتکدهٔ وارنی و تانیسر

On the way (to Somnāth) the Sulṭān captured many forts and towns, and rased them to the ground.

The first such place was Ludrava from whose towers and fortifications, mountains of steel and stone rolled down.

The citadel and fortifications were strong, and the garrison were like roaring lions.

The champions were equal in valour and the soldiers backed each other up; the army was slow to move but swift in action.

(The next place) was C͟hīkūdar (?) hill at the foot of which the lion-vanquishing Sulṭān obtained coffers of jewels.

This hill was so high that, you would say, the passage of the stars was below it.

(The next place) was Nahrwāla, on the possession of which Bhīm prided himself over other princes of India.

He had an army of 200 elephants, and nearly 100,000 horse and 90,000 foot.

Rāy Bhīm resided in luxury in this fort and enjoyed his life.

(The next place) was Mundher, where there was a tank which dazzled the eyes of thought.

The more I think of this tank, the less capable I feel of praising it adequately.

The tank was of wide expanse and accommodated 1000 small idol-temples.

(The next place) was Dewalwāra which like the bright day, was visible to the traveller on the road.

There was a strong fort on one side of the town, and in it had assembled a large number of idolaters.

(The Sulṭān) killed the people, overturned their idol-temples, and burnt them like the idol-temples of Wārnī (?) and Tānīsar.

Farrukhī thus mentions five places, namely, Ludrava, Chīkūdar, Nahrwāla, Mundher and Dewalwāra which the Sulṭān passed between Multān and Somnāth. Ludrava, or Lodorva as it is written on modern maps, is situated about ten miles west by north of the town of Jaisalmīr, and, at the time of the invasion of Sulṭān Maḥmūd, was the capital of the Bhāṭī Jādons. It is said to have been an immense city with twelve gates.[1] Chīkūdar cannot be properly deciphered as the text of Farrukhī is very corrupt, but it probably stands for the Chiklodar Mātā hill which is about seventeen miles north of Pālanpūr.[2] Nahrwāla was the name of modern Pātan,[3] in the Aḥmadābād District of Bombay. Mundher is situated about eighteen miles south of Pātan, and, from the extent of its ruins, "seems at one time to have been of considerable note". It has "a large tank or *talāv*, that has, at one time, been surrounded by steps, and also perhaps with shrines".[4] Dewalwāra is modern Delvāda, which is situated between Unā and the island of Diu, at a distance of about forty miles east of Somnāth.[5]

The Sulṭān thus marched from Multān to Lodorva, probably by way of Uchh or Bahāwalpūr, and thence along the low ridge that traverses the Jaisalmīr state and Mallānī,[6] to Pātan. From Pātan he proceeded to Mundher, and then straight across the Kāthiāwār peninsula to Delvāda and Somnāth.[7]

1 *Gazetteer of Marwar, Mallani and Jeysulmere* by C. K. M. Walter, pp. 84, 96; and *I.G.I.* (*Provincial Series*), *Rajputana*, pp. 209–10.

2 *Bombay Gazetteer*, v, 282

3 *I.G.I.* xx, 24.

4 J. Burgess, *Archaeological Survey of Western India*, ix, 71.

5 Ibnu'l-Athīr says that it was two days' march from Somnāth.

6 Briggs, Firishta, i, 79, quotes a tradition to the effect that the Sulṭān conquered a fort named Chotan which is about fifty miles east of 'Umarkot. See also the *Gazetteer of Marwar, etc.*, by C. K. M. Walter, p. 56.

7 This clearly shows that Professor Ḥabīb's theory that Somnāth was close to Nahrwāla or Pātan, is unfounded.

7. *Stories connected with the Expedition*

The destruction of the temple of Somnāth was looked upon as the crowning glory of Islam over idolatry, and Sulṭān Maḥmūd as the champion of the Faith, received the applause of all the Muslim world. Poets vied with each other in extolling the real or supposed virtues of the idol-breaker, and the prose-writers of later generations paid their tribute of praise to him by making him the hero of numerous ingenious stories. Most of these stories, by a natural process of assimilation and adaptation, were incorporated in works of history and handed down as well-authenticated facts. I propose therefore to take some of them, and attempt to ascertain the amount of historical truth, if any, which they contain.

(1) The best known of these stories is the one about Dābishlīm. It is first mentioned in the *Waṣāyā-i-Niẓāmu'l-Mulk*, a work of the ninth century A.H. Briefly stated it is as follows:

After the conquest of Somnāth, the Sulṭān was so charmed with the climate that he resolved to settle there, but his noblemen induced him to return to Ghazna and leave a deputy in Kāthiāwār. The names of two candidates were suggested to him, one was Dābishlīm the Ascetic, and the other, also named Dābishlīm, was the Rājā of a neighbouring state. The Sulṭān appointed the Ascetic as his deputy and, at his request, undertook an expedition against the other Dābishlīm. On this occasion the Sulṭān is made to say, "As I left my country with the intention of carrying on a holy war and have done so for three years, I may as well remain another six months to settle this affair". The Sulṭān then marched against the other Dābishlīm, took him prisoner and, as the Ascetic was afraid of keeping him in custody, carried him to Ghazna. After some time, the Ascetic sent his officers to fetch the captive Dābishlīm. When he was due to arrive, the

Ascetic went some distance out of his capital to meet him according to the custom of the country, but as the captive was a little late in arriving, the Ascetic went to sleep under the shade of a tree, covering his face with a red handkerchief. A bird of prey, mistaking the red handkerchief for a piece of flesh, swooped down upon it and tore away, along with the handkerchief, the eyes of the sleeping monarch. When the captive arrived his rival had become unfit to rule as he had lost his eyesight. The people therefore greeted the captive as their king, and the Ascetic was consigned to the cell which he had prepared for the other.[1]

This story implies that (i) the Sulṭān stayed for three years and a half in Kāthiāwār, (ii) that he fought against a Rājā named Dābishlīm, and (iii) that he appointed a deputy at Somnāth. The first inference is contradicted by the contemporary authorities like Baihaqī and Gardīzī, who state that the Sulṭān was in Transoxiana or Ghazna during the years immediately preceding and following the expedition to Somnāth,[2] while Ibnu'l-Athīr says that the Sulṭān had returned to Ghazna within four months of the fall of Somnāth.[3] The second and third inferences, besides being very unlikely under the circumstances, are not supported by any work written before the middle of the ninth century A.H. which is the probable date of the composition of the *Waṣāyā-i-Niẓāmu'l-Mulk*. Gardīzī, p. 86, in fact, suggests, on the contrary, that the Hindū governor of Somnāth, who had fled at the approach of the Sulṭān, returned after the departure of the Muslim army. Thus from the historical point of view this story is absolutely of no value. Sir E. C. Bayley, however, in his translation of *Mir'āt-i-Aḥmadī*, p. 33, has tried to show that there is nothing improbable in this story,

1 The complete story is given in *Rawḍah*, pp. 741–2; and Firishta, pp. 34–5.

2 See pp. 55–6, and 80.

3 See p. 120.

but obviously he had not considered it in the light of historical evidence.

(2) The next important story comes from the *Maṇṭiqu'ṭ-Ṭair* of Sh͟aik͟h Farīdu'd-Dīn 'Aṭṭār, the famous mystic poet of the seventh century A.H. In this story the Sulṭān is made to show his preference for the title of idol-breaker to that of idol-seller. It is said that when the Sulṭān captured Somnāth and wanted to break the idol, the Brahmins offered to redeem it with its weight in gold, but the Sulṭān refused to accept the offer and ordered the idol to be broken. The officers of the Sulṭān, however, pointed out to him the advantages of accepting the offer, but he replied, "I am afraid that on the Day of Judgment when all the idolaters are brought into the presence of God, He would say, 'Bring Ād͟har and Maḥmūd together: one was idol-maker, the other idol-seller'." The Sulṭan then ordered a fire to be lighted round it. The idol burst, and 20 *manns* of precious stones poured out from its inside. The Sulṭān said, "This (fire) is what Lāt (by which name 'Aṭṭār calls Somnāth) deserves; and that (the precious stones) is my guerdon from my God".

This story implies that the idol was hollow, which is incorrect. Al-Bīrūnī, ii, 103–4, gives minute rules which had to be observed with regard to the construction of such idols, but he does not mention that they were ever hollow. Further, this unexpected find of precious stones is not mentioned by the early authorities in which the Sulṭān's letter of victory to the Caliph is quoted. If this had actually happened, Farruk͟hī, of all others, could not have neglected to utilise this excellent theme in the *qaṣīda* in which he gives a lengthy account of this expedition.

(3) Another story, which is apparently a fabrication of inferior quality, is given in the *Futūḥu's-Salāṭīn*, ff. 32 b–35 b, a work of the eighth century A.H. It is stated that shortly after the birth of Maḥmūd, the

astrologers of India divined that a prince had been born at Ghazna who would demolish the temple of Somnāth. They therefore persuaded Rājā Jaipāl to send an embassy to Maḥmūd while he was still a boy, offering to pay him a large sum of money if he promised to return the idol to the Hindūs whenever he should capture it. When Maḥmūd captured Somnāth the Brahmins reminded him of his promise and demanded the idol in compliance with it. Maḥmūd did not like either to return the idol or to break his promise. He therefore ordered the idol to be reduced to lime by burning and when, on the following day, the Brahmins repeated their demand, he ordered them to be served with betel-leaves which had been smeared with the lime of the idol. When the Brahmins had finished the chewing of the betel-leaves they again repeated their demand, on which the Sulṭān told them that they had their idol in their mouths.

Soon after this, a Brahmin made an idol similar to the one which the Sulṭān had destroyed and buried it at a distance from the town. He then trained a calf to run to that spot and scratch it with its hoofs. One morning he called all the people together and said to them that the idol of Somnāth had appeared to him in a dream and told him that it was hidden at a certain spot in the neighbourhood, and that if he (the Brahmin) would let his calf loose, it would run to the spot and scratch it with its hoofs. This was done, and, on digging, the idol was discovered. It was washed with rose-water and re-instated in the temple.

(4) In addition to these stories there is a local tradition in which the name of Sulṭān Maḥmūd has been confused with some later Muslim sovereign of Kāthiāwār, most probably Sulṭān Maḥmūd Bīgarha (1459–1511 A.D.). This tradition was versified by Shaikh Dīn in 1216 (1801) and translated into English by Major J. W. Watson, in the *Indian Antiquary*, viii,

153–61. Divested of some of its supernatural element, it runs as follows:

Some Muslims used to live at Somnāth before it was captured by Sulṭān Maḥmūd, but they were sorely oppressed by the Rājā named Kunwar Rāy, by whose orders a Muslim was slain every day in front of the idol of Somnāth. The Prophet Muḥammad appeared to Ḥājjī Muḥammad of Mecca in a dream and commanded him to go to Somnāth and save the Muslims. The Ḥājjī came, and, by means of his supernatural powers, brought himself into the notice of the Rājā. One day the Ḥājjī found an old woman in great distress because her son had to be slain next morning in front of the idol. The Ḥājjī was moved to pity and offered to go in place of her son. When the Rājā learnt this, he became exceedingly angry, but as he knew that he could not injure the Ḥājjī openly, he waited for an opportunity to take him unawares. One day the Ḥajjī fell into a trance, while the Rājā was showing him round the temple of Somnāth. The Rājā whispered a command to his soldiers to slay him, but when they tried to advance towards him, they found themselves fixed to the spot.

The Ḥājjī now invited Sulṭān Maḥmūd of Ghazna to come with his army and stop this iniquity. The Sulṭān came and on his way thither he attacked Jaipāl, Rājā of Mangrol, who was a brother-in-law of the Rājā of Somnāth, and forced him to offer submission. He then marched to Somnāth and defeated Kunwar Rāy. The Rājā sued for peace but the Sulṭān would not listen to him till he consented to embrace Islam. The Rājā refused to do so and decided to fight to the last. About this time the Ḥājjī died, offended with the Sulṭān as he had not visited him on his death-bed.

After fighting for some time, the Rājā took refuge in the fort. A sharp fire was kept up on both sides. The siege lasted for twelve years till the patience of the Sulṭān was exhausted. His wazīr then advised him to go to the tomb of the Ḥājjī in order to appease his anger, and to invoke his assistance in reducing the fort. The Sulṭān did so, and according to the instructions of the Ḥājjī, he adopted the following artifice. One morning, leaving everything behind, including his batteries, the Sulṭān withdrew to a place five miles away. The Rājā mistook it for a flight and was put off his guard. The Sulṭān returned at night and with the assistance of two of his troopers whom the Ḥājjī had specially blessed, took the fort of Somnāth in the year 470 (1077–78). During the course of this long struggle the Sulṭān is said to have lost 125,000 men.

Rājā Kunwar Rāy then tried to save the idol and offered to pay a huge sum of money if it was spared. The Sulṭān ordered the idol to be reduced to powder, and gave it to the Rājā and his courtiers in betel-leaves, as stated in the last story. He then appointed an officer named Mithā K͟hān as his deputy at Somnāth and returned to G͟hazna. After this Mithā K͟hān demolished the temple and set fire to it.

The story needs no comment, but it is surprising that Major Watson, the translator of the ballad, should have given to it the credit of being an "account of the destruction of Somanāth" differing "from any given in the Persian histories of the siege", in spite of its obvious incongruities and anachronisms in allowing the siege to continue for twelve years and making the combatants keep up a brisk fire on each other.

APPENDIX N

CHRONOLOGY OF THE LIFE AND TIMES OF SULṬĀN MAḤMŪD AND HIS PREDECESSORS

APPENDIX N

CHRONOLOGY OF THE LIFE AND TIMES OF SULṬĀN MAḤMŪD AND HIS PREDECESSORS

DATE		EVENT
A.H.	A.D.	
204	819–20	Nūḥ, Aḥmad, Yaḥyā, and Ilyās, sons of Asad b. Sāmān, appointed governors of Samarqand, Farghāna, Shāsh and Ushrūsana, and Herāt respectively
205	821	Ṭāhir b. Ḥusain appointed governor of Khurāsān
227	842	Death of Nūḥ b. Asad
237	851–2	Ya'qūb b. Laith got government of Bust
241	855–6	Death of Yaḥyā b. Asad
242	856–7	Death of Ilyās b. Asad
249	863–4	Death of Aḥmad b. Asad
253	867	Ya'qūb conquered Herāt, Balkh and Bāmiyān
259	872–3	Ya'qūb defeated Muḥammad the Ṭāhirid
260	873–4	Ya'qūb conquered Ṭabaristān
		Naṣr b. Aḥmad conquered Bukhārā and gave it to his brother Ismā'īl
14 Shawwāl, 265	9. vi. 879	Death of Ya'qūb
(circa) 267	880–1	Birth of Alptigīn
275	888–9	Naṣr b. Aḥmad attacked Bukhārā
279	892–3	Death of Naṣr b. Aḥmad

285	898	Aḥmad b. Farīghūn did homage to Ismā'īl b. Aḥmad
15 Rabī' i, 287	20. iii. 900	Ismā'īl b. Aḥmad defeated 'Amr b. Laith at Bukhārā
	(circa) 903	Gopālvarman deposed Sāmantdeva, and raised Kamaluka, son of Lalliya, to the throne
293	905–6	Revolt of Subkarī in Sīstān
14 Ṣafar, 295	24. xi. 907	Death of Ismā'īl b. Aḥmad
Rajab, 298	iii. 911	Aḥmad b. Ismā'īl defeated Mu'addal b. Laith, ruler of Sīstān
Dhu'l-Ḥ. 300	vii. 913	Aḥmad b. Ismā'īl defeated 'Amr b. Laith, ruler of Sīstān
23 Jumādī ii, 301	24. i. 914	Death of Aḥmad b. Ismā'īl
309	921–22	Aḥmad b. Muḥammad, the Ṣaffārid, appointed governor of Sīstān
315	927–8	Asfār b. Shīrawaih defeated Mākān b. Kākī and took Raiy
316	928–9	Mardāwīj b. Ziyār put Asfār to death
319	931	Mardāwīj appointed 'Alī b. Buwaih governor of Karaj
323	934–5	Death of Mardāwīj
326	937–38	Birth of Khalaf
(circa) 331	942–3	Birth of Subuktigīn
27 Rajab, 331	6. iv. 943	Death of Naṣr b. Aḥmad
334	945–6	Mu'izzu'd-D. took Baghdād
Jumādī ii, 338	xii. 949	Death of 'Imādu'd-D., and accession of Fannākhusraw, son of Ruknu'd-D.
19 Rabī'ii, 343	22. viii. 954	Death of Nūḥ b. Naṣr
Ramaḍān, 345	xii. 956	Alptigīn put Bakr b. Malik to death
(circa) 348	959	Alptigīn purchased Subuktigīn
	(circa) 960	Death of Bhīm, probably son of Kamaluka, and accession of Jaipāl
20 Dhu'l-Ḥ. 349	10. ii. 961	Alptigīn took charge of Nīshāpūr
11 Shawwāl, 350	23. xi. 961	Death of 'Abdu'l-Malik b. Nūḥ
Dhu'l-Ḥ. 350	xii. 961	Alptigīn advanced on Bukhārā
15 Rabī' i, 351	23. iv. 962	Alptigīn defeated Ash'ath b. Muḥammad, general of Manṣūr b. Nūḥ

DATE		EVENT
A.H.	A.D.	
13 Dhu'l-Ḥ. 351	12. i. 963	Alptigīn took Ghazna
352	963	Alptigīn defeated Abū Ja'far, general of Manṣūr b. Nūḥ
20 Sha'bān, 352	13. ix. 963	Death of Alptigīn, and accession of his son Abū Isḥāq Ibrāhīm
(circa) 353	964	Death of Aḥmad b. Muḥammad and accession of his son Khalaf
27 Shawwāl, 354	26. ix. 965	Abū Ibrāhīm Isḥāq defeated Abū 'Alī Lawīk
354	965	Ṭāhir b. Ḥusain usurped Sīstān during the absence of Khalaf
25 Dhu'l-Q. 355	12. xi. 966	Death of Abū Isḥāq Ibrāhīm, and accession of Bilkātigīn
Rabī' ii, 356	iii. 967	Death of Mu'izzu'd-D., and accession of 'Izzu'd-D. Bakhtiyār
Dhu'l-Ḥ. 356	xi. 967	Death of Washmgīr b. Ziyār, and accession of his son Bihistūn
10 Muḥarram, 361	1. xi. 971	Birth of Maḥmūd
364	974–5	Death of Bilkātigīn, and accession of Pirītigīn
11 Shawwāl, 365	12. vi. 976	Death of Manṣūr b. Nūḥ, and accession of his son Nūḥ
Muḥarram, 366	ix. 976	Death of Ruknu'd-D., and division of his kingdom among his three sons
Sha'bān, 366	iv. 977	Deposition of Pirītigīn
27 Sha'bān, 366	20. iv. 977	Elevation of Subuktigīn to the throne of Ghazna
Rajab, 367	ii. 978	Death of Bihistūn, and accession of his brother Qābūs
Shawwāl, 367	v. 978	'Izzu'd-D. beheaded
		'Aḍudu'd-D. conquered 'Irāq
		Subuktigīn conquered Bust and Quṣdār
(circa) 369	979–80	Death of Ḥasanawaih b. Ḥusain
		Nūḥ b. Manṣūr sent an expedition to Ghūr
370	980–1	Fakhru'd-D. forced to leave Hamadān

Jumādī i, 371	xi. 981	Mu'ayyidu'd-D. defeated Qābūs
		Flight of Fakhru'd-D. to Khurāsān
		Khalaf evacuated the fort of Ūk
Ramaḍān, 372	ii–iii. 983	Death of 'Aḍudu'd-D.
Sha'bān, 373	i. 984	Death of Mu'ayyidu'd-D.
		Return of Fakhru'd-D. to Jurjān
375	985–6	Settlement of the Seljuks at Nūr
(circa) 376	986–7	Subuktigīn defeated Jaipāl who probably left Sukhpāl as a hostage
		Khalaf occupied Bust but evacuated it shortly afterwards
		Sharafu'd-D. defeated Ṣamṣāmu'd-D.
Rabī' ii, 379	vii. 989	Birth of Majdu'd-D.
Jumādī ii, 379	ix. 989	Death of Sharafu'd-D., and accession of Bahā'u'd-D.
		Ṣamṣāmu'd-D. released
380	990–1	Subuktigīn confined Maḥmūd in the fort of Ghazna
381	991	Deposition of aṭ-Ṭā'ī
		Rājā Bharat of Lahore invaded the kingdom of Jaipāl
Muḥarram, 382	iii. 992	Defeat of 'Amr b. Khalaf near Sīrjān
Rabī' i, 382	v–vi. 992	Bughrā Khān occupied Bukhārā
Jumādī i, 382	vii. 992	Bughrā Khān evacuated Bukhārā
15 Jumādī ii, 382	18. viii. 992	Nūḥ occupied Bukhārā
383	993–4	Execution of sons of 'Izzu'd-D.
15 Ramaḍān, 384	23. x. 994	Subuktigīn and Maḥmūd defeated Abū 'Alī Sīmjūrī
		Nūḥ b. Manṣūr granted Balkh and the title of *Nāṣiru'd-Dīn wa'd-Dawlah* to Subuktigīn, and the command of the troops of Khurāsān and the title of *Saifu'd-Dawlah* to Maḥmūd
Rabī' i, 385	iv. 995	Maḥmūd forced by Abū 'Alī Sīmjūrī and Fā'iq to evacuate Nīshāpūr
20 Jumādī ii, 385	22. vii. 995	Subuktigīn and Maḥmūd defeated Abū 'Alī and Fā'iq

DATE		EVENT
A.H.	A.D.	
385	995	Abu'l-'Abbās Faḍl b. Aḥmad appointed wazīr of Maḥmūd
		Ma'mūn conquered Khwārizm
		Sukhpāl taken prisoner by Abū 'Alī Sīmjūrī and converted to Islam
386	996	Khalaf invited Īlak Khān to attack Ghazna
		Abū 'Alī Sīmjūrī taken prisoner
386	996	Īlak Khān advanced on Bukhārā
387	997	Death of Abū 'Alī Sīmjūrī
		Death of Abū 'Alī Ma'mūn b. Muḥammad, ruler of Jurjāniyyah and Khwārizm, and accession of his son Abu'l-Ḥasan 'Alī
13 Rajab, 387	22. vii. 997	Death of Nūḥ b. Manṣūr, and accession of his son Abu'l-Ḥārith Manṣūr
Sha'bān, 387	viii. 997	Death of Subuktigīn, and accession of his son Ismā'īl
		Death of Fakhru'd-D., and accession of his son Majdu'd-D.
Rabī' i, 388	iii. 998	Maḥmūd captured the fort of Ghazna, took Ismā'īl prisoner, and ascended the throne
388	998	Khalaf occupied Fūshanj, but forced to evacuate it
		Death of Bughrājuq, uncle of Maḥmūd
Sha'bān, 388	viii. 998	Qābūs took Jurjān
Dhu'l-Ḥ. 388	xii. 998	Death of Ṣamṣāmu'd-D.
12 Ṣafar, 389	2. ii. 999	Deposition of Abu'l-Ḥārith Manṣūr b. Nūḥ, and accession of his brother Abu'l-Fawāris 'Abdu'l-Malik
27 Jumādī i, 389	16. v. 999	Maḥmūd defeated 'Abdu'l-Malik at Marv, and occupied Khurāsān
		Maḥmūd recognised overlord of Gharshistān
		Ismā'īl sent to Jūzjānān

Sha'bān, 389	vii–viii. 999	Death of Fā'iq
10 Dhu'l-Q. 389	23. x. 999	Īlak Khān conquered Bukhārā, and took 'Abdu'l-Malik prisoner
Dhu'l-Ḥ. 389	xi. 999	The Caliph al-Qādir Bi'llāh bestowed on Maḥmūd the title of *Yamīnu'd-Dawlah wa Amīnu'l-Millah*
		Maḥmūd resolved to go on a holy war to India every year
389	999	Anandpāl, son of Jaipāl, defeated Chandardat, Rājā of Lahore, and annexed his kingdom
Muḥarram, 390	xii. 999	Maḥmūd sent his representatives to Īlak Khān
Muḥarram, 390	xii. 999	Investment of the fort of Iṣpahbud, and submission of Khalaf
390	ix. 1000	Maḥmūd captured some forts near Lamaghān
28 Rabī' i, 391	25. ii. 1001	Naṣr defeated by Muntaṣir near Nīshāpūr
Shawwāl, 391	ix. 1001	Maḥmūd left Ghazna for Hind
		Naṣr evacuated Nīshāpūr
391	1001	Wāthiqī captured and imprisoned by Maḥmūd
8 Muḥarram, 392	27. x. 1001	Jaipāl defeated and taken prisoner. Waihand annexed
	iv. 1002	Return of Maḥmūd to Ghazna
Muḥarram, 393	xi. 1002	Maḥmūd left Ghazna for Sīstān
		Khalaf taken prisoner and sent to Jūzjānān
		Sīstān placed under the Ḥājib Qinjī
		Revolt in Sīstān
	1002–3	Death of Jaipāl
Dhu'l-Q. 393	ix. 1003	Maḥmūd left Ghazna for Sīstān
15 Dhu'l-Ḥ. 393	15. x. 1003	Maḥmūd defeated the rebels of Sīstān
		Sīstān placed in charge of Naṣr
(circa) 393	1002–3	Death of Jaipāl, and accession of his son Anandpāl
Sha'bān, 394	vi. 1004	Īlak Khān defeated Muntaṣir
395	x. 1004	Maḥmūd left Ghazna for Bhatinda
		Defeat and death of Bijī Rāy, Rājā of Bhatinda

DATE		EVENT
A.H.	A.D.	
Rabīʿ i, 395	xii. 1004	Death of Muntaṣir
395	v–vi. 1005	Maḥmūd returned to Ghazna
396	iii–iv. 1006	Defeat of Anandpāl on the banks of the Indus
396	1006	Fall of Multān and flight of Dā'ūd
		Sukhpāl appointed governor of Multān
396	1006	Īlak Khān's invasion of Khurāsān
396	vii–viii. 1006	Arslān Jādhib drove Subāshītigīn out of Khurāsān
397	ix–x. 1006	Īlak Khān's troops driven out of Khurāsān
397	1006–7	Khalaf sent to Gardīz
		Majdu'd-D. taken prisoner by his mother
22 Rabīʿ ii, 398	5. i. 1008	Īlak Khān again invaded Khurāsān, but defeated on the plain of Katar
398	xii. 1007	Rebellion of Sukhpāl
Rabīʿ ii, 398	i. 1008	Maḥmūd received news of Sukhpāl's rebellion
		Sukhpāl defeated and taken prisoner
399	1008	Anandpāl marched on Ghazna
29 Rabīʿ ii, 399	31. xii. 1008	Maḥmūd left Ghazna to meet Anandpāl
		Anandpāl defeated near Waihand
399	1009	Fall of Nagarkot
Rajab, 399	iii. 1009	Death of Khalaf
399	vi. 1009	Maḥmūd returned to Ghazna
(circa) 399	1008–9	Death of Abu'l-Ḥasan ʿAlī b. Ma'mūn, and accession of his brother Abu'l-ʿAbbās Ma'mūn
400	viii–ix. 1009	Spoils from Nagarkot displayed in Ghazna

400	viii. 1009	Ṭughān Khān's ambassador arrived in Ghazna
400	x. 1009	Maḥmūd left Ghazna for Narāyanpūr
401	x. 1010	Maḥmūd left Ghazna for Multān
		Dā'ūd taken prisoner and sent to Ghūrak
(circa) 401	x. 1010	Īlak Khān invaded the kingdom of Ṭughān Khān, but forced to return
401	iii. 1011	Īlak Khān again invaded the kingdom of Ṭughān Khān
401	vi. 1011	Maḥmūd attacked Ghūr, and took Ibn Sūrī prisoner
		Death of Ibn Sūrī
401	1010–11	Famine in Khurāsān
		Rebellion of the ruler of Quṣdār
		Death of Abū Naṣr Muḥammad, ruler of Jūzjānān, and appointment of Muḥammad b. Maḥmūd as governor
(circa) 401	1010–11	Death of Anandpāl
Jumādī i, 402	xii. 1011	Attack on Quṣdār and submission of its ruler
402	1012	Deposition of Qābūs
403	viii. 1012	Gharshistān conquered and annexed
Jumādī ii, 403	xii. 1012	Death of Bahā'u'd-D., and accession of his son Sulṭānu'd-D.
403	1012–13	Death of Qābūs
		Death of Īlak Khān
		Al-Ḥākim sent a letter to Maḥmūd
404	xi. 1013	Maḥmūd left Ghazna for Nandana but forced to return
404	1013	Faḍl b. Aḥmad dismissed
	iii. 1014	Maḥmūd again left Ghazna for Nandana
		Defeat of Bhīmpāl and fall of Nandana
		Defeat of Trilochanpāl and Tunga above Jhelum
		Death of Faḍl b. Aḥmad
405	vii–viii. 1014	Maḥmūd returned to Ghazna

DATE		EVENT
A.H.	A.D.	
405	1014	Abu'l-Qāsim Aḥmad b. Ḥasan al-Maimandī appointed wazīr
405	x. 1014	Maḥmūd left Ghazna for Thānesar
		Defeat of Rājā Rām
		Fall of Thānesar
405	iii. 1015	Maḥmūd returned to Ghazna
405	v. 1015	Maḥmūd attacked Khwābīn
405	1014–15	Death of Badr b. Ḥasanawaih
406	1015–16	Maḥmūd advanced to Balkh
		Mas'ūd nominated heir-apparent
		First invasion of Kashmīr and investment of Lohkot
		Death of Abū Naṣr Muḥammad, the Shār
406	iii. 1016	Maḥmūd returned to Ghazna
15 Shawwāl, 407	17. iii. 1017	Assassination of Abu'l-'Abbās Ma'mūn
407	1016–17	Qawāmu'd-D. came to Ghazna to implore assistance of Maḥmūd
5 Ṣafar, 408	3. vii. 1017	Maḥmūd defeated the army of Khwārizm, and annexed the country
408	1017	Khwārizm placed under Altūntāsh
		Death of Ṭughān Khān
		Mas'ūd appointed governor of Herāt
409	1018	Maḥmūd ordered the construction of a mosque in Ghazna
13 Jumādī i, 409	27. ix. 1018	Maḥmūd left Ghazna for Kanauj, and appointed his son Muḥammad as his deputy
20 Rajab, 409	2. xii. 1018	Maḥmūd crossed the Jumna
8 Sha'bān, 409	20. xii. 1018	Maḥmūd took Kanauj

25 Sha'bān, 409	6. i. 1019	Defeat of Rājā of Sharwa
Dhu'l-Ḥ., 409	iv. 1019	Maḥmūd marched against the Afghāns
409	1019	Alliance between Trilochanpāl and Ganda
		Rājyapāl of Kanauj defeated by Ganda and slain
410	x. 1019	Maḥmūd left Ghazna to punish Ganda and the new Rājā of Kanauj
14 Sha'bān, 410	15. xii. 1019	Maḥmūd defeated Trilochanpāl
410	1019	Maḥmūd took Bārī
	1019–20	Flight of Ganda at the approach of Maḥmūd
411	v–vi. 1020	Maḥmūd left Ghazna for the valleys of the rivers Nūr and Qīrāt
10 Jumādī i, 411	1. ix. 1020	Mas'ūd marched to Tab in Ghūr
411	1020	Submission of the ruler of Tab
Dhu'l-Ḥ. 411	iii–iv. 1021	Musharrafu'd-D. took 'Irāq
412	1021	Death of Naṣr
412	ix–x. 1021	Second unsuccessful invasion of Kashmīr and siege of Lohkot
412	1021–2	Mas'ūd sent as a prisoner to Multān
		Trilochanpāl, son of Anandpāl, killed
412	iii–iv. 1022	Maḥmūd returned to Ghazna
413	1022–3	Submission of the Rājā of Gwālior
		Submission of Ganda, Rājā of Kālinjar
	iii–iv. 1023	Maḥmūd returned to Ghazna
414	1023	Maḥmūd reviewed his army in the plain of Shābahār
(circa) 414	1023	Death of Arslān Khān
414	1023	Ḥasanak went on a pilgrimage to Mecca
415	ix. 1024	Maḥmūd went to Balkh
Shawwāl, 415	xii. 1024	Death of Sulṭānu'd-D. and accession of his son Abū Kālinjār
27 Ṣafar, 416	29. iv. 1025	Meeting of Maḥmūd and Qadir Khān
416	1025	Isrā'īl b. Seljuk taken prisoner and sent to the fort of Kālanjar
		The Seljuks permitted to settle in Khurāsān

DATE		EVENT
A.H.	A.D.	
Rabīʿ i, 416	v. 1025	Death of Musharrafu'd-D. and accession of his son Jalālu'd-D.
416	1025	Dismissal of Aḥmad b. Ḥasan al-Maimandī
		Appointment of Ḥasanak as wazīr
22 Shaʿbān, 416	18. x. 1025	Maḥmūd left Ghazna for Somnāth
15 Ramaḍān, 416	9. xi. 1025	Arrival at Multān
2 Shawwāl, 416	26. xi. 1025	Departure from Multān
Shawwāl, 416	xii. 1025	Maḥmūd took Lodorva
Dhu'l-Q. 416	xii. 1025	Arrival at Anhalwāra, and flight of Rājā Bhīm
14 Dhu'l-Q. 416	6. i. 1026	Arrival at Somnāth
16 Dhu'l-Q. 416	8. i. 1026	Fall of Somnāth
Dhu'l-Ḥ. 416	i. 1026	Maḥmūd took the fort of Kanthkot
		Maḥmūd defeated Khafīf, ruler of Manṣūra
416	1025–6	Death of Maʿdān, accession of his son ʿĪsā, and flight of Abu'l-Muʿaskar to Ghazna
10 Ṣafar, 417	2. iv. 1026	Maḥmūd arrived in Ghazna
417	1026	Maḥmūd received embassies from Qatā Khān and Īghur Khān
		Maḥmūd sent Abū Bakr Ḥaṣīrī to help Qadir Khān
Shawwāl, 417	xi–xii. 1026	The Caliph granted to Maḥmūd the title of *Kahfu'd-Dawlah wa'l-Islām*, and other titles to his sons and brother
		Death of Bhīmpāl
418	iii. 1027	Maḥmūd left Ghazna to punish the Jāts
418	vi–vii. 1027	Maḥmūd returned to Ghazna
418	xii. 1027	Complaints of the people of Nasā and Abīward against the Seljuks
419	1028	Death of Sayyida, mother of Majdu'd-D.

419	1028	Maḥmūd marched against the Seljuks
Dhu'l-Q. 419	xi–xii. 1028	Death of Qawāmu'd-D. Conquest of Kirmān by Abū Kālinjār
Rabī' ii, 420	v. 1029	Arrival of Maḥmūd's army at Raiy
9 Jumādī i, 420	26. v. 1029	Majdu'd-D. taken prisoner, and the town of Raiy captured
		Mas'ūd placed in charge of Raiy
		Rebellion of Mīnūchihr
1 Ramaḍān, 420	13. ix. 1029	Mas'ūd defeated the Sālār
420	1029	Rebellion of 'Īsā b. Ma'dān
		Death of Mīnūchihr
421	i. 1030	Mas'ūd conquered Iṣfahān
15 Rabī' ii, 421	22. iv. 1030	Maḥmūd arrived in Ghazna from Balkh
23 Rabī' ii, 421	30. iv. 1030	Death of Maḥmūd
20 Jumādī i, 421	26. v. 1030	Mas'ūd received news of the death of Maḥmūd
421	1030	Assassination of Abū 'Alī b. Ibn Sūrī
422	1031	Mas'ūd appointed Aḥmad b. Ḥasan al-Maimandī wazīr
		Ḥasanak executed
423	1032	Death of Qadir Khān
Muḥarram, 424	xii. 1032	Death of Aḥmad b. Ḥasan al-Maimandī
11 Jumādī i, 432	17. i. 1041	Death of Sulṭān Mas'ūd
435	1043–44	Sukhpāl attacked Lahore but defeated and slain
Sha'bān, 435	iii. 1044	Death of Jalālu'd-D., and conquest of 'Irāq by Abū Kālinjār
Jumādī i, 440	x. 1048	Death of Abū Kālinjār, and accession of his son al-Maliku'r-Raḥīm
Ramaḍān, 447	xii. 1055	Ṭughrilbek defeated al-Maliku'r-Raḥīm and took him prisoner

APPENDIX O

BIBLIOGRAPHY AND ABBREVIATIONS

Only works cited in the text are here included. When a work is cited in the text by the name of its author, it is the one given first against the name of that author in this Bibliography.

'Abdu'l-Malik b. 'Abdu'llāh. *Mughīthu'l-Khalq fī Bayān Taqdīmi'l-Aḥaqq* (Brit. Mus. Or. 3854).

Abu'l-Fidā. *Al-Mukhtaṣar fī Akhbāri'l-Bashar* (Cairo ed.).

Ādābu'l-Mulūk. See under Fakhr-i-Mudīr.

Aḥmad Thatawī. *Ta'rīkh-i-Alfī* (Brit. Mus. Add. 16,681). (See p. 13.)

Aḥsanu't-Taqāsīm. See under Maqdisī.

Akhbāru'd-Duwali'l-Munqaṭi'a. See under Ibn Ẓāfir.

Alfī; *Ta'rīkh-i-Alfī*. See under Aḥmad Thatawī.

Arba' Rasā'il. See under ath-Tha'ālibī.

Archaeological Survey of India (*Annual Reports*).

Asia Major, a journal dealing with the Language, Arts, and Civilisation of the Far East and Central Asia.

Āthāru'l-Bāqiya. See under al-Bīrūnī.

Āthāru'l-Wuzarā. See under al-Faḍlī.

'Aṭṭār, Farīdu'd-Dīn. *Tadhkiratu'l-Awliyā*, ed. R. A. Nicholson.

—— *Kulliyyāt*.

—— *Manṭiqu'ṭ-Ṭair*.

'Awfī. *Jawāmi'u'l-Ḥikāyāt* (Brit. Mus. Or. 236). (See p. 9.)

—— *Lubābu'l-Albāb*, ed. E. G. Browne. (See p. 9.)

'Azīzu'llāh. *Zubdatu't-Tawārīkh* (Ḥabībganj Library, Bhīkampūr, 'Alīgarh).

Bābur. *Memoirs*, translated by A. S. Beveridge (1922).

Bahār-i-'Ajam, a dictionary of the Persian Language.

Bahjatu'l-Ikhwān fī Dhikri'l-Wazīr Sulaimān (Brit. Mus. Add. 7336).

Baiḍāwī, Abū Sa'īd 'Abdu'llāh b. Abu'l-Ḥasan 'Alī. *Niẓāmu't-Tawārīkh*.

al-Baihaqī, Abu'l-Faḍl Muḥammad b. Ḥusain. *Ta'rīkh-i-Mas'ūdī*, ed. Morley. (See pp. 6–7.)

Bākharzī, Abu'l-Ḥasan 'Alī. *Dumyatu'l-Qaṣr* (Bod. Arab. Sale, 24).

Banākathī, Abū Sulaimān Dā'ūd b. Abu'l-Faḍl Muḥammad. *Rawḍatu'l-Albāb fī Tawārīkhi'l-Akhbār wa'l-Ansāb* (King's College, Cambridge, MS).

Bar Hebraeus, alias Gregory Abu'l-Faraj b. Hārūn. *The Syriac Chronicle* (Paris, 1890).

Barthold, W. *Turkestan* (G.M.S.).

—— *Ibid.* (Russian ed.), vol. i, *Texts*.

—— Articles in the *Encyclopaedia of Islam*.

Bayley, Sir E. C. Article in *The Numismatic Chronicle* (1882).
Bird, J. English translation of *Mir'āt-i-Aḥmadī* under the title of *History of Gujrat*.
al-Bīrūnī. *India*. English translation of *Taḥqīq mā li'l-Hind*, by E. C. Sachau (see p. 6). Trübner's Oriental Series, 1888.
—— Original Arabic Text of the above, edited by E. C. Sachau.
—— *Qānūnu'l-Mas'ūdī* (Berlin MS).
—— *The Chronology of Ancient Nations*, English translation of *Āthāru'l-Bāqiya*, by E. C. Sachau.
—— *Ghurratu'z-Zījāt*, being a translation into Arabic of the Sanskrit *Karanatilaka* of Vijayānanda, son of Jayānanda, of Benares. (Pīr Muḥammad Shāh's Dargāh Library, Aḥmadābād.)
Bombay Gazetteer, The (1896).
Bretschneider, E. *Medieval Researches from Eastern Asiatic Sources*.
Briggs, J. English translation of *Ta'rīkh-i-Firishta* (Calcutta ed.).
Brockelmann, C. *Geschichte der Arabischen Litteratur*.
Browne, E. G. *A Literary History of Persia*.
Burgess, J. *Archaeological Survey of Western India*.
—— *Progress Report of the Archaeological Survey of Western India*.
—— *Lists of the Antiquarian Remains in the Bombay Presidency*.
—— Translation into English of *Ta'rīkh-i-Sorath*.

Cambridge History of India, The. See under Haig.
Chahār Maqāla. See under Niẓāmī al-'Arūḍī.
Cunningham, Sir A. *The Ancient Geography of India* (1871).
—— *Coins of Mediaeval India*.
—— *Archaeological Survey of India*.
Curzon, Lord. *Persia and the Persian Question*.

Dawlat Shāh. *Tadhkiratu'sh-Shu'arā*, ed. E. G. Browne.
adh-Dhahabī, Shamsu'd-Dīn Abū 'Abdu'llāh Muḥammad b. Aḥmad b. 'Uthmān. *Ta'rīkh Duwalu'l-Islām* (Berlin MS, Fol. 3308).
Dhail; *Dhail Tajāribu'l-Umam* by Hilāl b. Muḥassin aṣ-Ṣābī. See under *Tajārib* (see also p. 3).
Dhakā'u'llāh Khān. *Ta'rīkh-i-Hindūstān* (Institute Press, 'Alīgarh, 1915).
Dīwān Lughātu't-Turk. See under Kāshgharī.
Dīwān-i-Farrukhī. See under Farrukhī.
Dīwān-i-'Unṣurī. See under 'Unṣurī.
Dumyatu'l-Qaṣr. See under Bākharzī.

E. and D. See under Elliot and Dowson.
Elliot and Dowson. *History of India as told by its own Historians*.
Elphinstone, M. *History of India* (ed. E. B. Cowell, 1889).
Encyclopaedia of Islam, ed. M. Th. Houtsma and others (proceeding).
Epigraphia Indica, a collection of Indian Inscriptions.

Ethé, H. *Catalogue of Persian MSS in the Library of the India Office.*
—— *Catalogue of the Persian MSS in the Bodleian Library.*

al-Faḍlī. *Āthāru'l-Wuzarā* (Ind. Office MS 1569). (See pp. 11–12.)
Fakhr-i-Mudīr. *Ādābu'l-Mulūk wa Kifāyatu'l-Mamlūk* (Ind. Office MS 647). (See p. 9.)
—— *Ta'rīkh-i-Fakhru'd-Dīn Mubārakshāh* (James G. Forlong Fund), ed. Sir E. Denison Ross.
Farrukhī. *Dīwān* (India Office MS 1841). (See p. 7.)
Fārs Nāmah. See under Ibn Balkhī.
Faṣīḥī. *Mujmal-i-Faṣīḥī* (Gibb Memorial Trust Fund MS). (See p. 12.)
Fatḥu'l-Wahbī. See under al-Manīnī.
Fergusson, J. *A History of Indian and Eastern Architecture* (1910).
Firdawsī, Abu'l-Qāsim. *Shāhnāmah.*
Firishta. *Ta'rīkh-i-Firishta* (Newalkishore Press, 1874). (See p. 13.)
Führer, A. *Archaeological Survey of India.* N.W. Provinces and Oudh.
Futūḥu's-Salāṭīn (Ind. Office MS 3089).

Gardīzī. *Zainu'l-Akhbār*, ed. M. Nāẓim. (See pp. 5–6.)
Ghaffārī, Qāḍī Aḥmad. *Jahān Ārā* (Brit. Mus. Or. 141).
—— *Zīnatu'l-Majālis* (Brit. Mus. Or. 239).
Gulshan-i-Ibrāhīmī, another name of *Ta'rīkh-i-Firishta.*
Ghurratu'z-Zījāt. See under al-Bīrūnī.
Gūrgānī, Muḥammad Ḥaidar b. Muḥammad Ḥusain. *Ta'rīkh-i-Rashīdī*, English translation by Sir E. Denison Ross.
Guzīda; *Ta'rīkh-i-Guzīda.* See under Mustawfī.

Ḥabīb, Professor M. *Sultan Mahmud of Ghaznin.*
Ḥabību's-Siyar. See under Khwānd-Amīr.
Ḥadīqah. See under Sanā'ī.
Ḥāfiẓ Abrū. *Zubdatu't-Tawārīkh* (Brit. Mus. Or. 1577).
Haft Iqlīm. See under Rāzī.
Haig, Sir Wolseley. *The Cambridge History of India*, vol. iii.
Ḥājjī Khalīfa; Haji Khalfa. *Kashfu'z-Ẓunūn*, ed. Flügel.
Ḥikāyātu's-Salāṭīn (Lytton Library, 'Alīgarh, MS).
Howorth, Sir Henry H. Article in *JRAS.* 1898.
Huart, C. *History of Arabic Literature.*

Ibnu'l-Athīr. *al-Kāmil fi't-Ta'rīkh*, ed. Tornberg. (See p. 9.)
Ibn Balkhī. *Fārs Nāmah* (G.M.S.).
Ibn Funduq. *Ta'rīkh-i-Baihaq* (Brit. Mus. Or. 3587).
Ibn Ḥawqal. *Kitābu'l-Masālik wa'l-Mamālik*, ed. de Goeje.
Ibn Isfandiyār. *Ta'rīkh-i-Ṭabaristān*, translation by E. G. Browne (G.M.S.).

Ibn Jawzī. *al-Muntaẓam fī Tawārīkhi'l-Mulūk wa'l-Umam* (Berlin MS 9436 WE. 8). (See p. 8.)

Ibn Khaldūn. *Kitābu'l-'Ibar*, ed. Būlāq. (See p. 11.)

Ibn Khallikān. *Wafayātu'l-A'yān*, English translation by De Slane.

Ibn Qutaiba. *'Uyūnu'l-Akhbār*, ed. Brockelmann.

Ibn Ẓāfir. *Akhbāru'd-Duwali'l-Munqaṭi'a* (Brit. Mus. Or. 3685). (See p. 8.)

I.G.I. *The Imperial Gazetteer of India* (1907).

Indian Antiquary, The, a journal of Oriental Research.

Irshād; *Irshādu'l-Arīb*. See under Yāqūt.

Iṣfahānī, Faḍl b. Rūzbahān. *Sulūku'l-Mulūk* (Brit. Mus. Or. 253).

Iṣṭakhrī. *Masālik wa'l-Mamālik*, ed. de Goeje.

Jahān Ārā. See under Ghaffārī.

Jahān Nāmah. See under Muḥammad b. Najīb.

Jāmi'u't-Tawārīkh. See under Rashīdu'd-Dīn.

Jannātu'l-Firdaws. See under Muḥammad, Mīrzā.

JASB. *Journal of the Asiatic Society of Bengal*.

Jawāmi'u'l-Ḥikāyāt. See under 'Awfī.

Journal of the Punjab Historical Society.

JRAS. *Journal of the Royal Asiatic Society of London*.

Jurbādhqānī. *Tarjuma-i-Ta'rīkh-i-Yamīnī*, being a translation into Persian of 'Utbī's *Kitābu'l-Yamīnī*, ed. Ṭeherān, A.H. 1272. (See p. 5, note.)

Juwainī, 'Alā'u'd-Dīn 'Aṭā Malik b. Muḥammad. *Ta'rīkh-i-Jahān-Gushā* (G.M.S.).

Jūzjānī. *Ṭabaqāt-i-Nāṣirī*, English translation by Major H. G. Raverty. (See p. 10.)

Kalhana. *Rājataranginī*, English translation by Sir Aurel Stein. (See p. 8.)

Al-Kāmil fi't-Ta'rīkh. See under Ibnu'l-Athīr.

Kashfu'ẓ-Ẓunūn. See under Ḥājjī Khalīfa.

Kāshgharī, Maḥmūd b. Ḥusain b. Muḥammad. *Dīwān Lughātu't-Turk*.

Kāvah, a monthly Persian journal published in Berlin (A.H. 1338).

Khwānd-Amīr. *Ḥabību's-Siyar*. (See p. 13.)

—— *Khulāṣatu't-Tawārīkh* (Brit. Mus. Or. 1292). (See p. 12.)

Khulāṣatu't-Tawārīkh. See under Khwānd-Amīr and Sujān Rāy.

Kitāb fī Ghurar. See under ath-Tha'ālibī.

Kitāb Mu'īdu'n-Ni'am. See under as-Subkī.

Kitābu'l-Ansāb. See under as-Sam'ānī.

Kitābu'l-'Ibar. See under Ibn Khaldūn.

Kitābu'l-Masālik wa'l-Mamālik. See under Ibn Ḥawqal.

Kitābu'l-Yamīnī. See under al-'Utbī.

Kulliyyāt-i-'Aṭṭār. See under 'Aṭṭār.

Lane-Poole, S. *The Mohammadan Dynasties*.
—— *Catalogue of Oriental Coins in the British Museum*.
—— *Additions to the Oriental Collection of Coins in the British Museum*.
Lubāb; *Lubābu'l-Albāb*. See under 'Awfī.

al-Ma'arrī, Abu'l-'Alā. *Risālatu'l-Ghufrān* (Amīn Hindiyya Press).
Majma'u'l-Ansāb. See under Muḥammad b. 'Alī.
Majmū'a-i-Sulṭānī (Ind. Office MS 508).
Malfūẓāt-i-Tīmūrī (E. and D. iii).
Malleson, G. B. *A History of A'ghanistan*.
al-Manīnī. *Fatḥu'l-Wahbī* (Cairo ed.). (See p. 5, note.)
Manṭiqu'ṭ-Ṭair. See under 'Aṭṭār.
Maqdisī. *Aḥsanu't-Taqāsīm*, ed. de Goeje.
Masālik wa'l-Mamālik. See under Iṣṭakhrī.
Mas'ūdī, Abu'l-Ḥasan 'Alī b. Ḥusain. *Murūju'dh-Dhahab*, English translation by A. Sprenger.
Minhāju's-Salāṭīn (Ind. Office MS 1623).
Mir'āt-i-Aḥmadī. See under Bird.
Mir'āt-i-Mas'ūdī by 'Abdu'r-Raḥmān Chishtī.
Mir'ātu'z-Zamān. See under Sibṭ Ibnu'l-Jawzī.
Mīr-Khwānd. *Rawḍatu'ṣ-Ṣafā* (Newalkishore Press, 1883). (See p. 12.)
Mughīthu'l-Khalq. See under 'Abdu'l-Malik.
Muḥammad b. 'Alī. *Majma'u'l-Ansāb* (Bibl. Nat., Supplément persan, 1278).
Muḥammad b. Najīb. *Jahān Nāmah* (Bibl. Nat., ancien fonds, persan, 384).
Muḥammad, Mīrzā. *Jannātu'l-Firdaws* (Brit. Mus. Or. 144).
Muir, Sir William. *The Caliphate; its rise, decline and fall* (1892).
Mujmal. See under *Mujmalu't-Tawārīkh*.
Mu'jamu'l-Buldān. See under Yāqūt.
Mujmal-i-Faṣīḥī. See under Faṣīḥī.
Mujmalu't-Tawārīkh (Bibl. Nat., ancien fonds, persan, 62). (See p. 8.)
Al-Mukhtaṣar fī Akhbāri'l-Bashar. See under Abu'l-Fidā.
Al-Muntaẓam. See under Ibn Jawzī.
Muqaddasī, Maqdisī's *Aḥsanu't-Taqāsīm*, translation into English by G. S. A. Ranking.
Murūju'dh-Dhahab. See under Mas'ūdī.
Mustawfī. *Ta'rīkh-i-Guzīda* (G.M.S.). (See p. 10.)
—— *Nuzhatu'l-Qulūb* (G.M.S.).
—— *Ẓafar Nāmah* (Brit. Mus. Or. 2833).

Narshakhī, Abū Bakr Muḥammad b. Ja'far. *Ta'rīkh-i-Bukhārā*, ed. Schefer.
Nāẓim, M. Articles in the *Encyclopaedia of Islam*.

Nāẓim, M. Articles in *JRAS.* (1927).
Niẓāmī al-'Arūḍī. *Chahār Maqāla*, ed. Mīrzā Muḥammad (G.M.S.). (See p. 8.)
Niẓāmu'd-Dīn Aḥmad. *Ṭabaqāt-i-Akbarī.* (See p. 13.)
Niẓāmu'l-Mulk. *Siyāsat Nāmah*, ed. Schefer. (See p. 7.)
Niẓāmu't-Tawārīkh. See under Baiḍāwī.
Numismatic Chronicle, The.
An-Nuwairī, Aḥmad b. 'Abdu'l-Wahhāb b. Muḥammad. History of unknown title (Berlin MS 9806 WE. 2).
Nuzhatu'l-Qulūb. See under Mustawfī.

Plutarch. *Lives* (Langhorne's translation).
Powlett, Captain P. W. *Gazetteer of Bīkaner State* (1874).
PRGS. Proceedings of the Royal Geographical Society of London.

Qābūs Nāmah. See under 'Unṣuru'l-Ma'ālī.
al-Qalqashandī, Abu'l-'Abbās Aḥmad b. 'Alī. *Ṣubḥu'l-A'shā fī Ṣinā'ati'l-Inshā*, ed. Būlāq.
Qānūnu'l-Mas'ūdī. See under al-Bīrūnī.
al-Qifṭī, Jamālu'd-Dīn Abu'l-Ḥasan 'Alī b. Yūsuf. *Ta'rīkhu'l-Ḥukamā*, ed. J. Lippert.

Rabino, H. L. *Māzandarān and Astarābād* (G.M.S.).
Rabī'u'l-Abrār. See under al-Zamakhsharī.
Rāḥatu'ṣ-Ṣudūr. See under Rāwandī.
Rājatarangini. See under Kalhana.
Ranchodjī Amarjī. *Ta'rīkh-i-Sorath*, English translation by J. Burgess.
Rashīdu'd-Dīn. *Jāmi'u't-Tawārīkh* (Brit. Mus. Add. 7628). (See p. 10.)
Raverty, Major H. G. Translation of *Ṭabaqāt-i-Nāṣirī.*
—— *Notes on Afghanistan.*
—— *The Mihrān of Sind* in *JASB.* 1892.
Rāwandī, Muḥammad b. 'Alī b. Sulaimān. *Rāḥatu'ṣ-Ṣudūr* (G.M.S.).
Rawḍah; *Rawḍatu'ṣ-Ṣafā.* See under Mīr-Khwānd.
Rawḍatu'l-Albāb. See under Banākathī.
Rawḍatu'ṣ-Ṣafā. See under Mīr-Khwānd.
Rāzī, Amīn Aḥmad. *Haft Iqlīm* (Brit. Mus. Add. 24,092).
Reynolds, Rev. J. English translation of *Kitābu'l-Yamīnī* from the Persian version of Jurbādhqānī (Oriental Transl. Fund).
Risālatu'l-Ghufrān. See under al-Ma'arrī.
Ross, Sir E. Denison. *The Heart of Central Asia.*
—— English translation of *Ta'rīkh-i-Rashīdī* of Gūrgānī.
—— Article in *Asia Major*, vol. ii.

Aṣ-Ṣābī. *Dhail Tajāribu'l-Umam.* See under *Tajāribu'l-Umam.*
Sachau, E. C. English translation of *Taḥqīq mā li'l-Hind.* See under al-Bīrūnī.

Aṣ-Ṣābī. English translation of *Āthāru'l-Bāqiya*. See under al-Bīrūnī.

Ṣādiq, Muḥammad. *Ṣubḥ-i-Ṣādiq* (Bānkīpūr MS 471).

as-Sam'ānī, 'Abdu'l-Karīm b. Muḥammad. *Kitābu'l-Ansāb* (G.M.S.).

Sanā'ī, Ḥakīm. *Ḥadīqah*.

Shāhnāmah. See under Firdawsī.

Sibṭ Ibnu'l-Jawzī. *Mir'ātu'z-Zamān* (Brit. Mus. Or. 4619). (See pp. 9–10.)

Siyāsat Nāmah. See under Niẓāmu'l-Mulk.

Smith, Sir Vincent. *The Early History of India* (1924).

—— Articles in *JRAS*.

Stein, Sir Aurel. English translation of *Rājataranginī*. See under Kalhana.

—— *Serindia*.

—— *Ruins of Desert Cathay*.

Strange, G. Le. *The Lands of the Eastern Caliphate*.

Ṣubḥ-i-Ṣādiq. See under Ṣādiq.

Ṣubḥu'l-A'shā. See under al-Qalqashandī.

as-Subkī, Tāju'd-Dīn Abū Naṣr 'Abdu'l-Wahhāb. *Ṭabaqātu'sh-Shāfi'iyyati'l-Kubrā*, ed. Cairo.

—— *Kitāb Mu'īdu'n-Ni'am wa Mubīdu'n-Niqam*, ed. Myhrman.

Sujān Rāy. *Khulāṣatu't-Tawārīkh*.

Sulūku'l-Mulūk. See under Iṣfahānī.

Sykes, Sir Percy. *A History of Persia*.

Syria, a quarterly review of Oriental Art and Archaeology (Paris).

Syriac Chronicle, The. See under Bar Hebraeus.

Ṭabaqāt-i-Akbarī. See under Niẓāmu'd-Dīn.

Ṭabaqāt-i-Nāṣirī. See under Jūzjānī.

Ṭabaqātu'sh-Shāfi'iyya. See under as-Subkī.

Ṭabarī, Abū Ja'far Muḥammad b. Jarīr. *Ta'rīkhu'r-Rusul wa'l-Mulūk*, ed. de Goeje and others.

Ṭab. Nāṣ.; *Ṭabaqāt-i-Nāṣirī*. See under Jūzjānī.

Tadhkiratu'l-Awliyā. See under 'Aṭṭār.

Tadhkiratu'sh-Shu'arā. See under Dawlat Shāh.

Taḥqīq mā li'l-Hind. See under al-Bīrūnī.

Tajārib. See under *Tajāribu'l-Umam*.

Tajāribu'l-Umam and its continuation by Abū Shujā' ar-Rūdhrāwarī, and Hilāl b. Muḥassin aṣ-Ṣābī, ed. D. S. Margoliouth and H. F. Amedroz

Tāju'l-'Arūs, a dictionary of the Arabic language.

Ta'rīkh Duwali'l-Islām. See under adh-Dhahabī.

Ta'rīkh-i-Alfī. See under Aḥmad Thatawī.

Ta'rīkh-i-Baihaq. See under Ibn Funduq.

Ta'rīkh-i-Bukhārā. See under Narshakhī.

Ta'rīkh-i-Fakhru'd-Dīn Mubārakshāh. See under Fakhr-i-Mudīr.

Ta'rīkh-i-Firishta. See under Firishta.
Ta'rīkh-i-Guzīda. See under Mustawfī.
Ta'rīkh-i-Hindūstān. See under Dhakā'u'llāh.
Ta'rīkh-i-Jahān-Gushā. See under Juwainī.
Ta'rīkh-i-Mas'ūdī. See under Baihaqī.
Ta'rīkh-i-Rashīdī. See under Gūrgānī.
Ta'rīkh-ī-Sīstān, published in *Kāvah*, vol. II, No. 2.
Ta'rīkh-i-Sorath. See under Ranchodjī.
Ta'rīkh-i-Ṭabaristān. See under Ibn Isfandiyār.
Ta'rīkh-i-Ṭabaristān wa Rūyān. See under Ẓahīru'd-Dīn.
Tarjuma-i-Faḍā'il-i-Balkh. See under al-Wā'iẓ.
Ta'rīkhu'l-Ḥukamā. See under al-Qifṭī.
Ta'rīkhu'l-Yamīnī, another name of *Kitābu'l-Yamīnī.*
Ta'rīkhu'r-Rusul wa'l-Mulūk. See under Ṭabarī.
Tarjuma-i-Ta'rīkh-i-Yamīnī. See under Jurbādhqānī.
ath-Tha'ālibī, 'Abdu'l-Malik b. Muḥammad. *Yatīmatu'd-Dahr*, ed. Damascus.
—— *Arba' Rasā'il.*
—— *Kitāb fī Ghurar-i-Mulūki'l-Furs*, ed. Zotenberg.
Thomas, E. *The Coins of the Kings of Ghazni* in *JRAS.* xvii.
Tod, Lieut.-Col. J. *Annals and Antiquities of Rajasthan*, ed. W. Crooke.

'Unṣurī. *Dīwān*, ed. Ṭeherān. (It is not paginated.)
'Unṣuru'l-Ma'ālī Kaikā'ūs b. Iskandar b. Qābūs. *Qābūs Nāmah*, ed. Bombay.
U.P. District Gazetteers.
Urdū, a quarterly journal of the Anjuman-i-Taraqqī-i-Urdū, Aurangābād, Deccan.
al-'Utbī. *Kitābu'l-Yamīnī*, or *Ta'rīkh-i-Yamīnī*, Lahore ed., A.H. 1300. (See pp. 4–5.)
'Uyūnu'l Akhbār. See under Ibn Qutaiba.

Vigne, G. T. *A Personal Narrative of a Visit to Ghuzni, Kabul and Afghanistan.*

Wafayātu'l-A'yān. See under Ibn Khallikān.
al-Wā'iẓ, Abū Bakr 'Abdu'llāh b. 'Umar. *Tarjuma-i-Faḍā'il-i-Balkh* (Bibl. Nat., ancien fonds, persan, 115).
Walters, C. K. M. *Gazetteer of Marwar, Mallani and Jeysulmere.*

Waṣāyā-i-Niẓāmu'l-Mulk.
Watson, Major J. W. Article in *The Indian Antiquary*, vol. viii.

Yāqūt, Abū 'Abdu'llāh. *Mu'jamu'l-Buldān*, ed. Wüstenfeld.
—— *Irshādu'l-Arīb*, ed. D. S. Margoliouth.
Yatīma; *Yatīmatu'd-Dahr.* See under ath-Tha'ālibī.

Ẓafar Nāmah. See under Mustawfī.
Ẓahīru'd-Dīn. *Ta'rīkh-i-Ṭabaristān wa Rūyān*, ed. B. Dorn.
Zainu'l-Akhbār. See under Gardīzī.
al-Zamakhsharī, Abu'l-Qāsim Muḥammad b. 'Umar. *Rabī'u'l-Abrār* (Brit. Mus. Or. 3183).
Zambaur, E. de. *Manuel de généalogie et de chronologie pour l'histoire de l'Islam*.
Zīnatu'l-Majālis. See under Ghaffārī.
Zubdatu't-Tawārīkh. See under 'Azīzu'llāh and Ḥāfiẓ Abrū.

INDEX

For EU product safety concerns, contact us at Calle de José Abascal, 56–1°,
28003 Madrid, Spain or eugpsr@cambridge.org.

www.ingramcontent.com/pod-product-compliance
Ingram Content Group UK Ltd.
Pitfield, Milton Keynes, MK11 3LW, UK
UKHW010346140625
459647UK00010B/870

* 9 7 8 1 1 0 7 4 5 6 5 9 4 *